I0800166

BLACK AMERICA SERIES

PORTSMOUTH
VIRGINIA

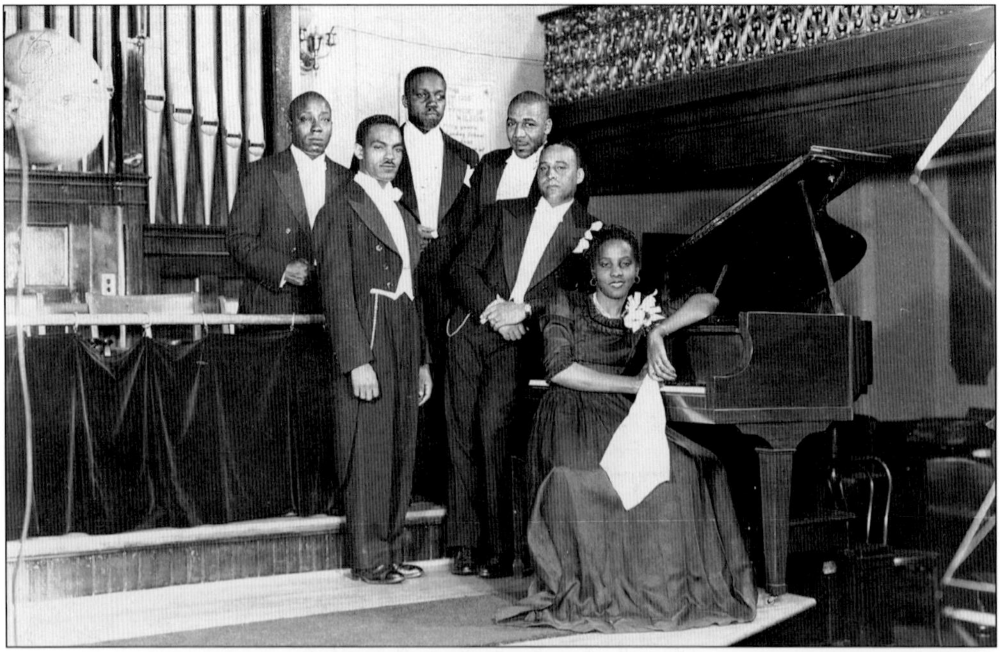

(front cover) This 1950s photograph is of a popular local quartet, the Lawson Harmony Singers. Even though most of the quartets had more than four members these groups took that designation because of the local music tradition. This group, popularly known as the Lawson Harmony Boys, was in tremendous demand by churches and social organizations. The group even performed on radio. Pictured from left to right are W. Samuel Pierce (second tenor), James Hargrave (baritone), Rufus Wright (first tenor), William Harding (bass), Walter Scott (first tenor), and Mrs. Margaret Blacken (accompanist). W. Maurice Daughtry was the business manager. (Courtesy Lee Rodgers Collection, Portsmouth Public Library.)

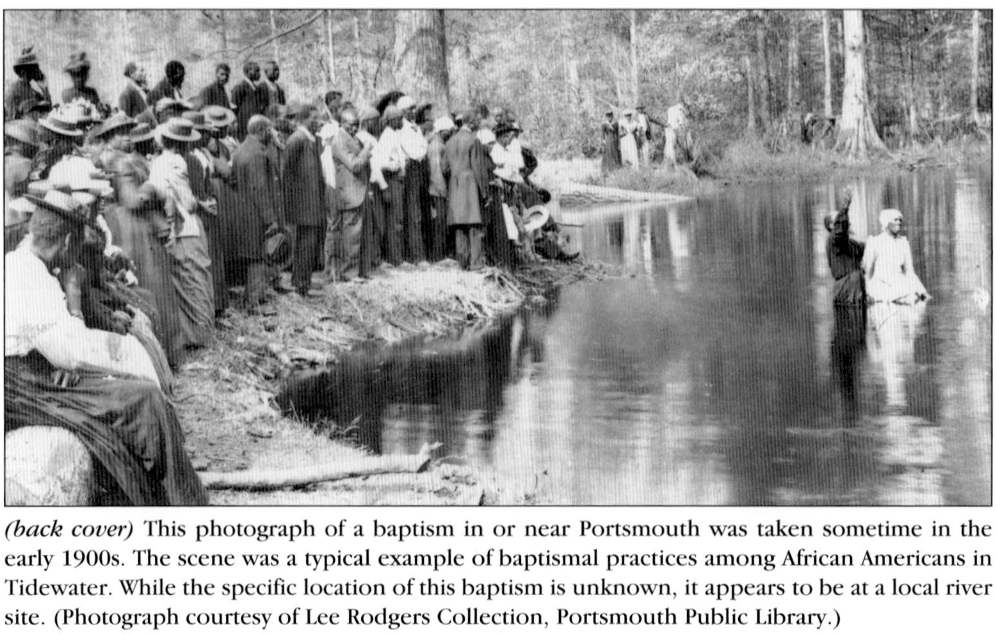

(back cover) This photograph of a baptism in or near Portsmouth was taken sometime in the early 1900s. The scene was a typical example of baptismal practices among African Americans in Tidewater. While the specific location of this baptism is unknown, it appears to be at a local river site. (Photograph courtesy of Lee Rodgers Collection, Portsmouth Public Library.)

Black America Series

Portsmouth Virginia

Cassandra Newby-Alexander Ph.D., Mae Breckenridge-Haywood,
and the African American Historical Society of Portsmouth

ARCADIA
PUBLISHING

Copyright © 2003 by Cassandra Newby-Alexander Ph.D., Mae Breckenridge-Haywood, and the African American Historical Society of Portsmouth
ISBN 978-0-7385-1581-6

Published by Arcadia Publishing
Charleston, South Carolina

Printed in the United States of America

Library of Congress Catalog Card Number: 2003110639

For all general information contact Arcadia Publishing at:
Telephone 843-853-2070
Fax 843-853-0044
E-mail sales@arcadiapublishing.com
For customer service and orders:
Toll-Free 1-888-313-2665

Visit us on the Internet at www.arcadiapublishing.com

CONTENTS

Acknowledgments		6
Introduction		7
1.	The Religious World	9
2.	Striving for Education	17
3.	Employment	27
4.	Organizing a Community through Neighborhoods	49
5.	Politics and the Fight for Freedom and Equality	75
6.	Music and Entertainment	93
7.	The Boy Scouts	115
Endnotes		125

ACKNOWLEDGMENTS

The history of Portsmouth's African Americans might have passed into obscurity had it not been for the careful work of Jeffrey Wilson and Lee Rodgers who kept copious notes recording the accomplishments of African Americans of their era. However, even their efforts would have remained in relative obscurity had it not been for the dedicated work of Mrs. Bertha Edwards whose mammoth efforts have not been properly praised.

We would like to thank Mr. Dean Burgess, the Portsmouth Library director, who was instrumental in initiating the preservation of most of the material, and Mrs. Sue Burton, director of the Portsmouth Public Library, for her ongoing support of our efforts to preserve the history of African Americans in Portsmouth. Without her support, we would not have been able to display many of the photographs and illustrations presented in this book. She has also graciously lent us many materials that made it easier to accomplish this task. Similarly, the Rev. Lonnie McClain, pastor of Emanuel AME Church, graciously opened the doors and records of the church to allow us access to vital resources.

Additionally, we are indebted to the members of the African-American Historical Society of Portsmouth. They endorsed this project enthusiastically and worked diligently to collect pictures and give help whenever needed. Members of the society are Patrice L. Beale, Mae Breckenridge-Haywood, Beulah S. Carey, Christine Davis, Bertha W. Edwards, Dr. Deborah Edwards, Joseph M. Ellis, Iva Foust, Howard Foust, Bernard D. Griffin, Jeffrey M. Herring, Charles E. Johnson, Neva C. Langston, Genevieve LaFargue, Earnest Marshall, Bettie Jo Matthews-Martin, Floyd R. Myrick, Dr. Cassandra Newby-Alexander, Marlene Randall, Jacqueline Rasberry, Bessie B. Richards, Stanley Semple, Eunice Semple, Lottie C. Short, Pearl B. Stowe, Edna Sugars, Marion Turner, Charles B. Whitehurst Sr., Rebecca H. Williams, and the Rev. E.M. Woodard. Their efforts and support were a tremendous asset to the completion of this project.

We would be remiss if we did not acknowledge the early work of Marshall Butt, Alfred Mapp, and Robert Wentz. While focusing primarily on the white community in Portsmouth, they did provide a good framework in which to evaluate the world in which African Americans lived. Of course, the work of the authors of *Readings in Black and White: Lower Tidewater Virginia* (Tommy Bogger, Sarah Hughes, Terry Jones, and William Paquette) was invaluable in highlighting the unique world of Portsmouth's African Americans from slavery to the protest movements of the 1960s and 1970s. Also, the work of Norfolk State University history majors, especially those who researched topics related to African Americans in Portsmouth, has proven priceless. We are indebted to them, particularly Sherri Butler and Scott Thompson, for their thorough research on the black theaters and Truxtun. We would be negligent if we did not thank the editorial work of William Alexander, professor of history at Norfolk State University, and Bertha Edwards. Their careful reading and input proved to be central to our efforts.

It is because of the work of all these individuals that we have a starting point from which to present an overview of this extraordinary history—the history of a people who lived and worked in a city called Portsmouth, Virginia.

Introduction

Historians have long viewed the Tidewater area as a southern metropolis whose history has been one of fierce contention between the cities—primarily Portsmouth and Norfolk—and outside forces. The city also had to battle demons from within. A typical southern seaport, historians have witnessed Tidewater's development of urban slavery; its repression of free blacks; its behavior as a military base; its relations with the African-American, Native-American and foreign-born communities; and its struggle to become a thriving seaport. Tidewater's politics were heavily dependent upon economic concerns as a seaport town, and its heterogeneous population transformed the community even when social divisions emerged or increased.

Portsmouth, Virginia, traces its history to the plantation of Col. William Crawford who laid out the boundaries of what became a city. As early as 1608, English explorers led by Capt. John Smith journeyed from the James River to the Elizabeth River and took note of a beautiful and bountiful area that would be later known as Portsmouth. Because of the plentiful pine and fir trees and numerous tributaries that ran into the river and then into the Chesapeake Bay, the travelers thought it would be the perfect site for a shipbuilding and commercial area. It would take over 200 years before that would become a reality. In 1664, Capt. William Carver, a ship owner and master mariner who also served in the House of Burgesses, patented the lands with the expectation of creating an 860-acre plantation. By 1716, Carver's lands, which had been forfeited to the colony after Carver was hanged for treason during Bacon's Rebellion in 1680, expanded to include an additional 269 acres. These lands were transferred to Col. William Crawford, a wealthy merchant, ship owner, Norfolk County judge, and House of Burgesses delegate. In 1752, Crawford followed a typical pattern of English aristocrats by carving out a town from part of his extensive land holdings. With 65 acres, Crawford had the land surveyed and named after the great naval port and dockyard in England. He sold the half-acre lots of most of the 65 acres, but set aside the four corners of High and Court Streets for public use.

Initially, Portsmouth was settled as a plantation community that would require large numbers of cheap labor. Moreover, Scottish merchants who operated ship stores across the river in Norfolk relocated to Portsmouth in the early 1750s. This newly established town gave these merchants more land on which to build their wharves and warehouses and more opportunity to dominate the industry in that town. Most of the residents in Portsmouth lived on small lots and made their living as tradesmen, merchants, and common laborers. However, there were some plantation owners who lived in town for convenience. This enabled Portsmouth to witness the emergence of a small but growing African and later African–American population, most of whom were enslaved. Many of the blacks in Portsmouth during those early years worked in the shipping industry in some capacity. The growing shipping industry, based primarily on riverboat trading in the interior, the ferry service between Norfolk and Portsmouth, and the port commerce, provided a plethora of jobs for enslaved African Americans. Additionally, domestic, skilled, and unskilled labor kept those not directly connected with the shipping industry occupied. From this small town the beginnings of a community, black and white, would thrive in part because of the social and commercial interaction of its residents.

Throughout their presence in this country, African Americans were cognizant of the need to look primarily to their own community for assistance—whether it was to facilitate the pre–Civil War escape through the Underground Railroad or raise an orphaned child or provide shelter for an elder widow. The era from the 17th to the end of the 19th centuries was not easy for African Americans, particularly in Portsmouth. Slavery was the single defining institution that dominated life for blacks. Even if free on bond, the established laws made it a given that blacks were slaves. Therefore it was incumbent upon anyone not bound to that institution to prove his or her claim to freedom. This reality made life for free blacks even more difficult as they struggled with employment discrimination, job displacement from white immigrants, environmental segregation, and exclusion from enjoying the privileges of society. Disparity was forced upon the black community in every aspect of their lives. Following the Civil War and passage of the 13th Amendment abolishing slavery, lynching and other forms of violence and intimidation against blacks were common tactics used to enforce white dominance and black segregation. Furthermore, blacks suffered from low employment opportunities and pay, inadequate schooling, overcrowded neighborhoods, substandard housing, limited recreational facilities, and few health care facilities, if any.

By the turn of the century, Jim Crow was a part of the marrow of American life. The economic and political achievements of the Reconstruction and Redemption era began being swept away by the construction of a harsh system of segregation. While segregation was nothing new, the hope inspired by the radical Republicans began fading as it became increasingly clear that white America would not allow African Americans to integrate and incorporate themselves as active members in American society. To African Americans, this attitude was clearly evident. When the Supreme Court declared segregation constitutional in *Plessy v. Ferguson* (1896), the rights of African Americans were relegated, once again, to second-class citizenship enforced with terror, violence, and intimidation. Following the *Plessy* decision, numerous states incorporated disfranchising clauses in their constitutions. So, for many African American leaders, the need to build a strong and viable community within the larger American community became even more necessary because white leaders made it abundantly clear that they would not allow blacks to become full-fledged, participating members in American society.

Consequently, African Americans in Portsmouth had begun building a strong, insulated community. They responded to segregation, discrimination, and exclusion by creating a world that provided the social and economic outlets denied to them in mainstream American society. It was during the time of Jim Crow, as segregation hardened, that black educational efforts bore fruit, as illustrated in the rise of a small number of black professionals in the fields of law, medicine, and education. Between 1900 and 1960 Portsmouth's African Americans forged a "place" for themselves within their own "home" sphere—their communities. This included the creation of middle class communities that became the fraternal, political, and financial models for blacks in and around Portsmouth. Under the leadership of such individuals as Dr. William Reid, Thomas Newbie, James Choate, William T. Hall, Nancy T. Wheeler, Jeffrey Wilson, Harvey N. Johnson Sr., J.A. Overton, I.C. Norcom, the Rev. E.G. Corprew, Samuel Fisher, Lee Rodgers, and countless others, Portsmouth emerged as a center for black business activity in Tidewater, at times even eclipsing Norfolk's thriving black communities' development. The actions of the African–American community epitomized the political, social, and economic landscape changes in Portsmouth. They reflected not only their cultural heritage but also what occurred throughout America and in the South. These changes were best illustrated by the emergence of an economically independent professional elite in the black community who galvanized the economy through their work and through the businesses and organizations that catered specifically to the black community and professional classes.

One

The Religious World

Col. William Crawford provided a site for a parish church in 1752 that became a reality when the Elizabeth River Parish was divided. The old parish in Williamsburg, established in 1640, had become too inconvenient because as the area expanded, the numerous waterways made travel difficult. In 1761 three new parishes were created in Virginia, the Portsmouth parish being the only one in Hampton Roads. It would eventually be known as Trinity Episcopal Church, built in 1762 at the corner of High and Court Streets. Keeping with the traditions of that period, Trinity segregated its black members and even reserved black painted pews for the house slaves of its prominent white congregants.[1]

According to the testimony of a later minister, Rev. George M. Bain, a congregation of Portsmouth's black Methodists worshipped on Washington Street prior to the Nat Turner episode of 1831. Thereafter, they were constricted to worship with the white Methodists, though seated in the galleries, at the old church on Glasgow Street. The latter built a new church in 1834, now Monumental Methodist, and gave the Glasgow Church to the African-American congregation "with Rev. George M. Bain, pastor, in 1839, where they continued to worship as a separate congregation, with a white pastor, until September 26, 1856. It was then set on fire and entirely consumed, 'the work, no doubt, of some wicked hand.'" Through largely the efforts of free and enslaved African Americans, the congregation bought the lot on North Street in 1857.[3]

Thus, an important agency for maintaining group cohesion and rendering self-help was the church. Although church membership was increasing, the attention to problems of segregation, intimidation, fear, and violence were not addressed. Instead, attention to ones sins—another otherworldly approach—still dominated. This resulted in the black church being challenged in primarily northern urban areas by a rising progressive order. Many blacks began abandoning the traditional Baptist and Methodist denominations and joined Congregational, Presbyterian, Episcopalian, and Catholic churches that seemed to have a more flexible attitude toward the reforms. Many of their members insisted on attention being directed to the immediate societal problems at hand. Furthermore, African Americans began organizing their own denominational groups and religious organizations, for example, the National Baptist Convention and R.H. Boyd's National Baptist Publishing House, as a way of insuring self-determination.

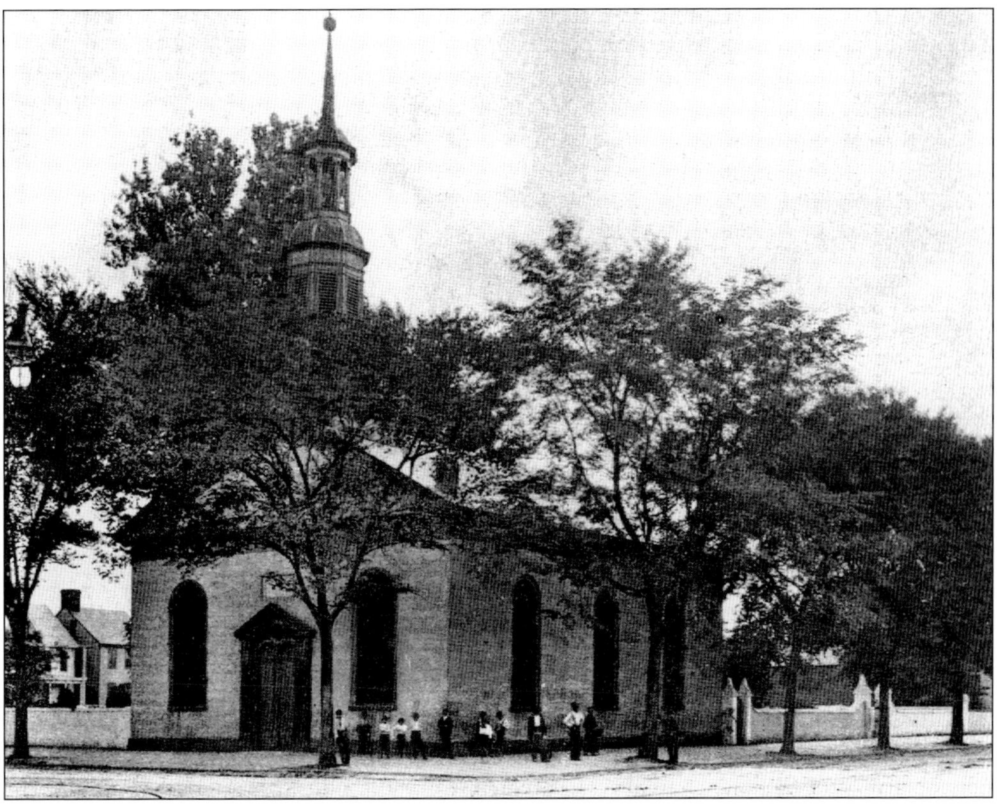

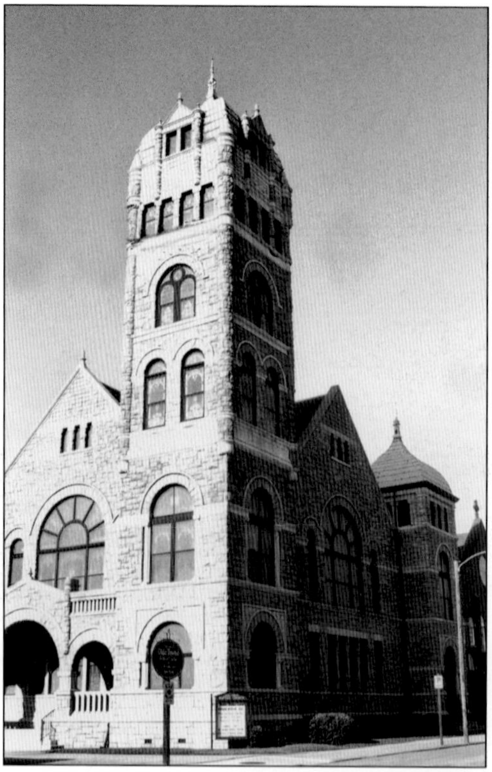

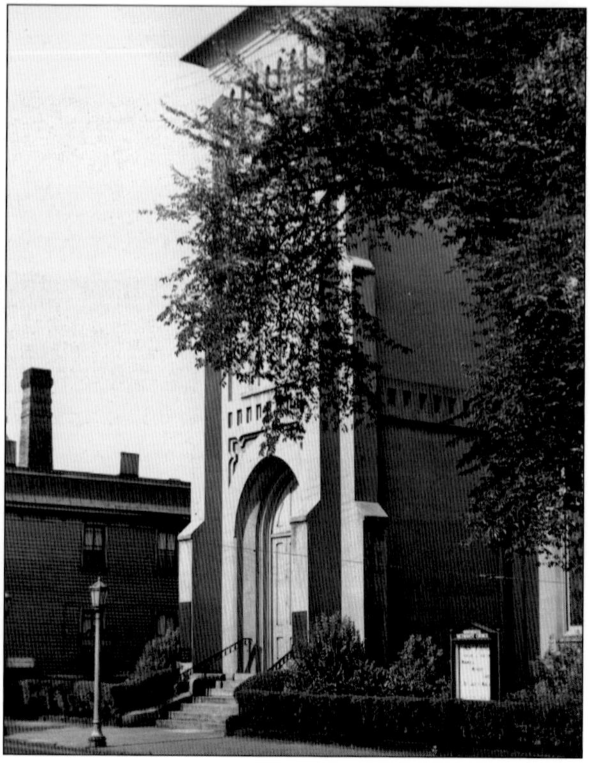

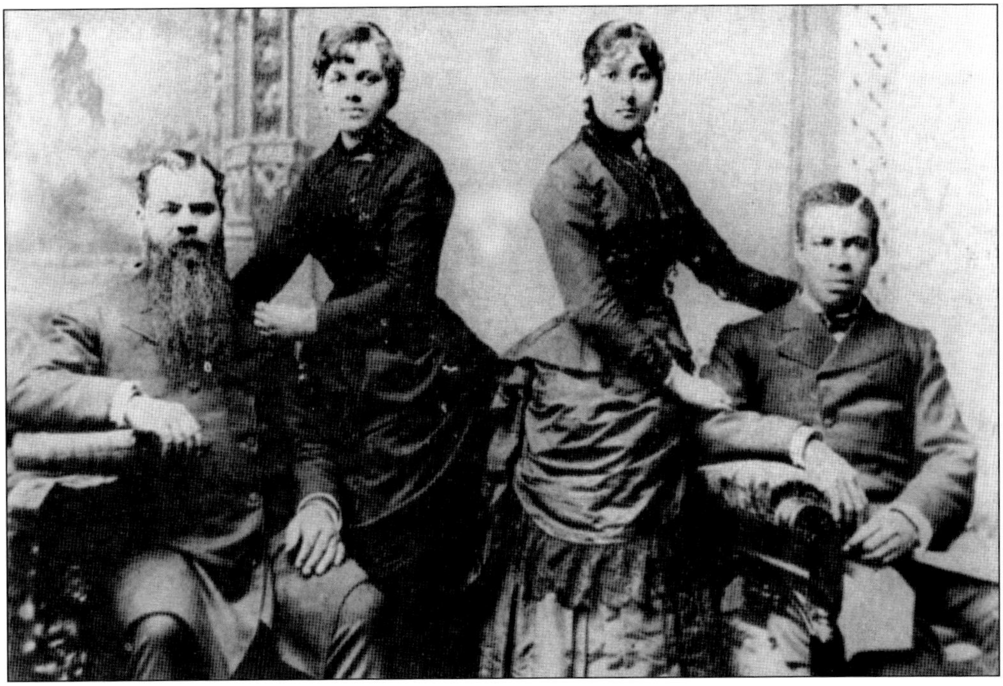

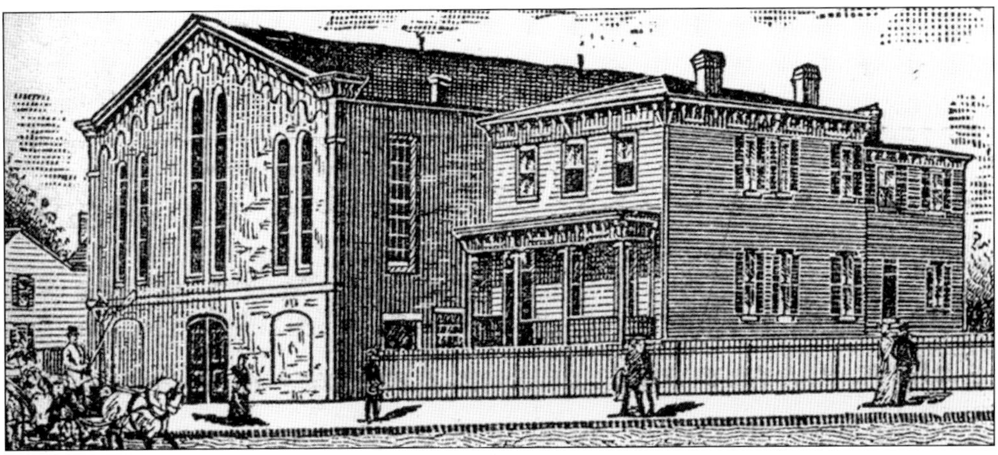

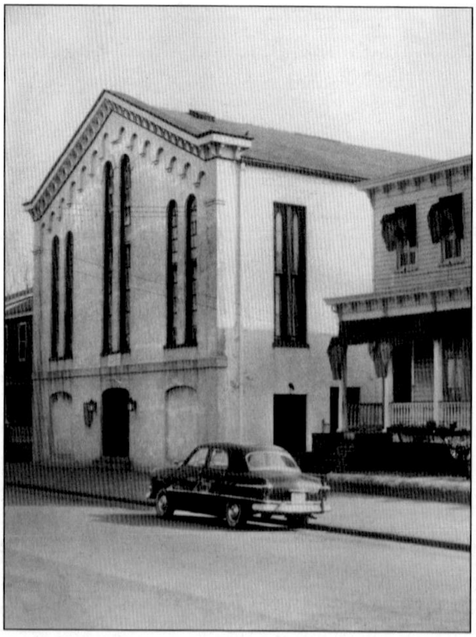

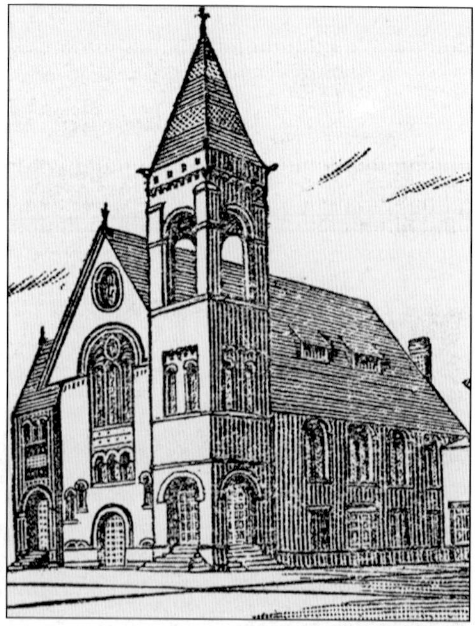

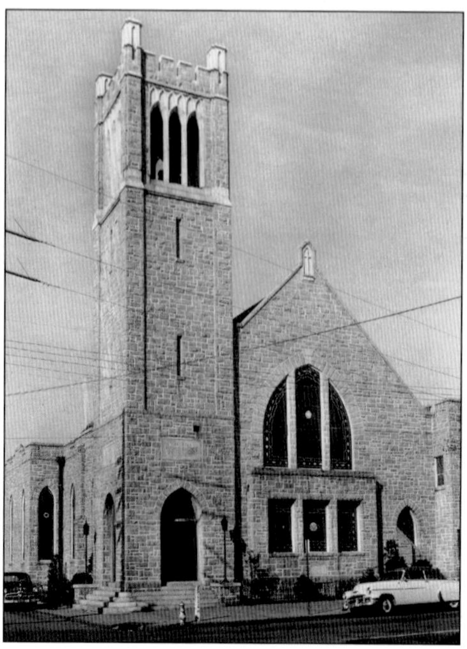

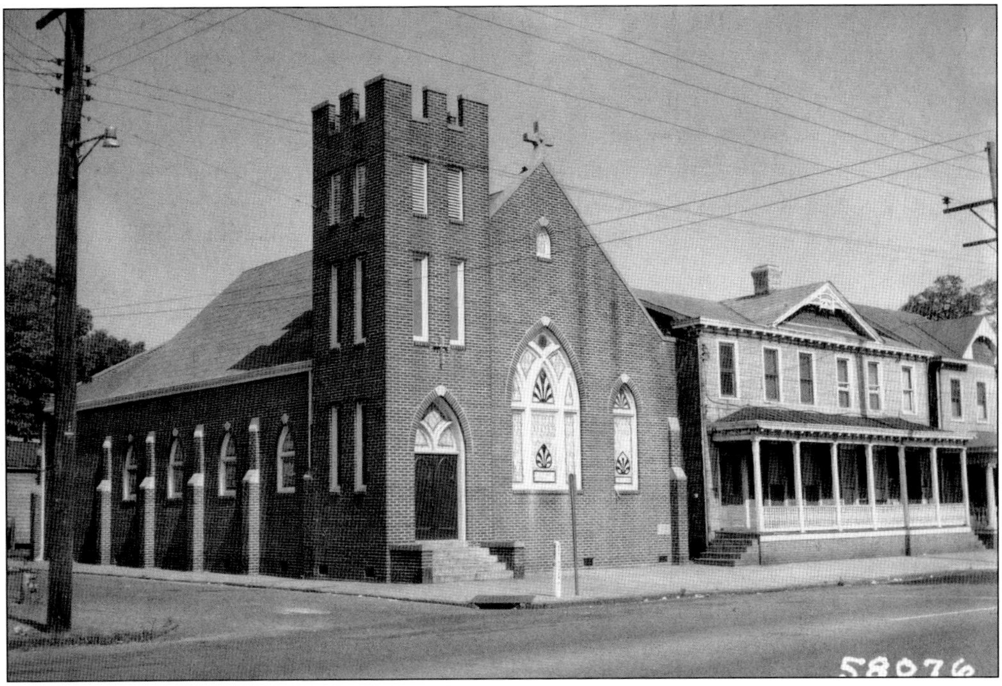

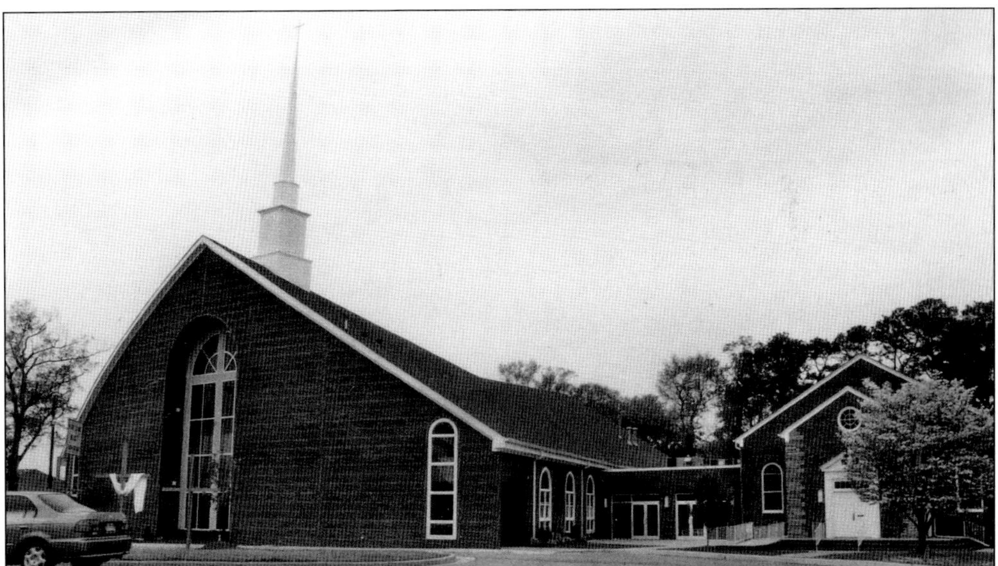

Grove Baptist Church had its beginnings on November 4, 1825, when the Rev. M. Woodson organized a religious gathering in the school building on Craney Island. So successful were the meetings that an edifice was built and named Sycamore Hill Baptist Church. Blacks joined the congregation shortly after it was built, but by 1840 they began worshipping in a separate facility. Mrs. Elizabeth Wright, one of the members of Sycamore Hill, assisted this group by donating land on which the present Grove Baptist Church now stands. (Courtesy Mae Breckenridge-Haywood.)

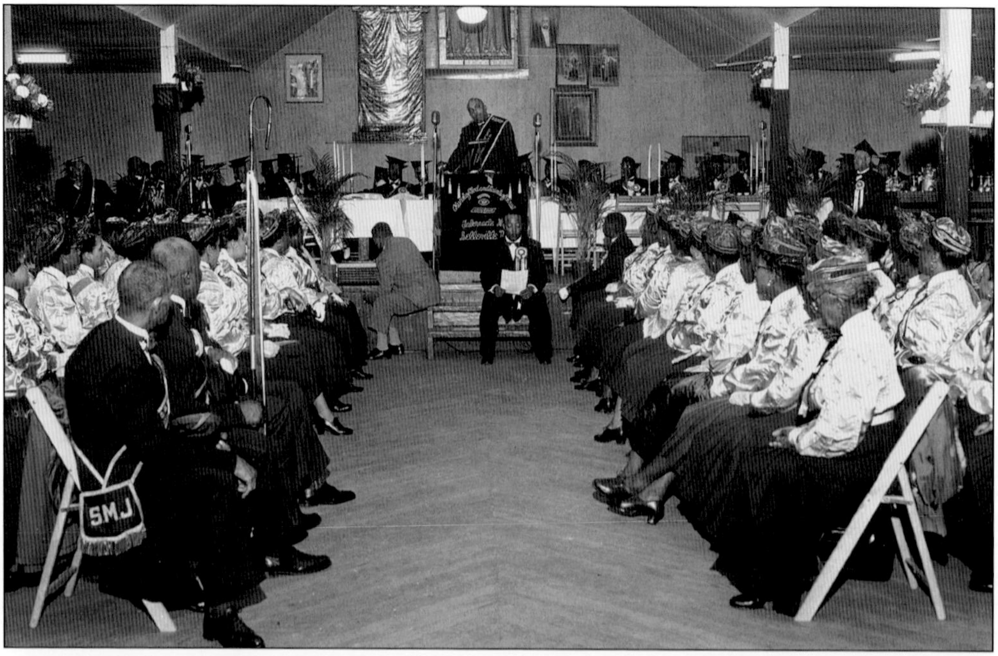
5MJ

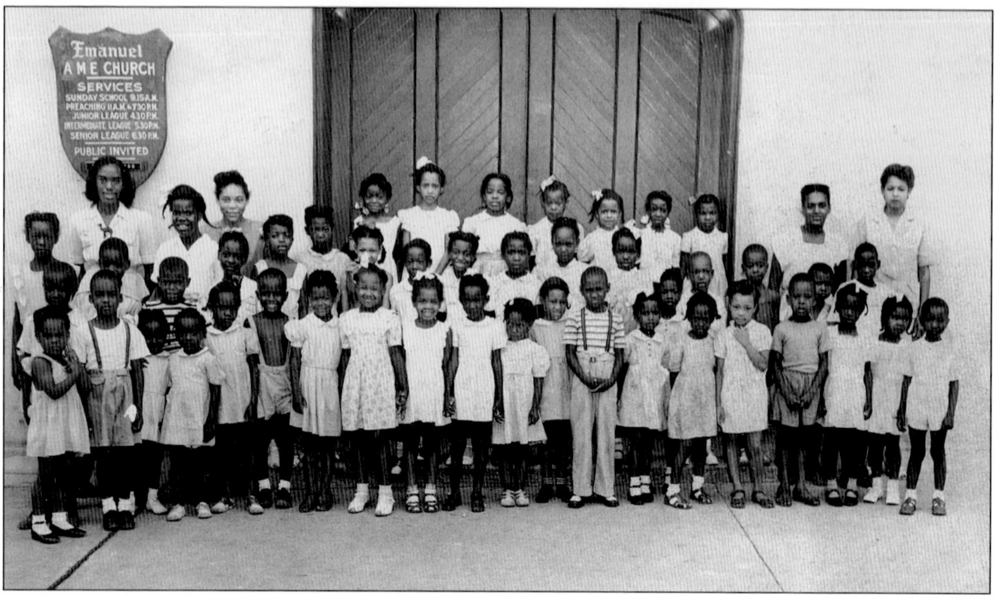
Emanuel
A M E CHURCH
SERVICES
SUNDAY SCHOOL 9.15 A.M.
PREACHING 11 A.M. & 7.30 P.M.
JUNIOR LEAGUE 4.30 P.M.
INTERMEDIATE LEAGUE 5.30 P.M.
SENIOR LEAGUE 6.30 P.M.
PUBLIC INVITED

Two

Striving for Education

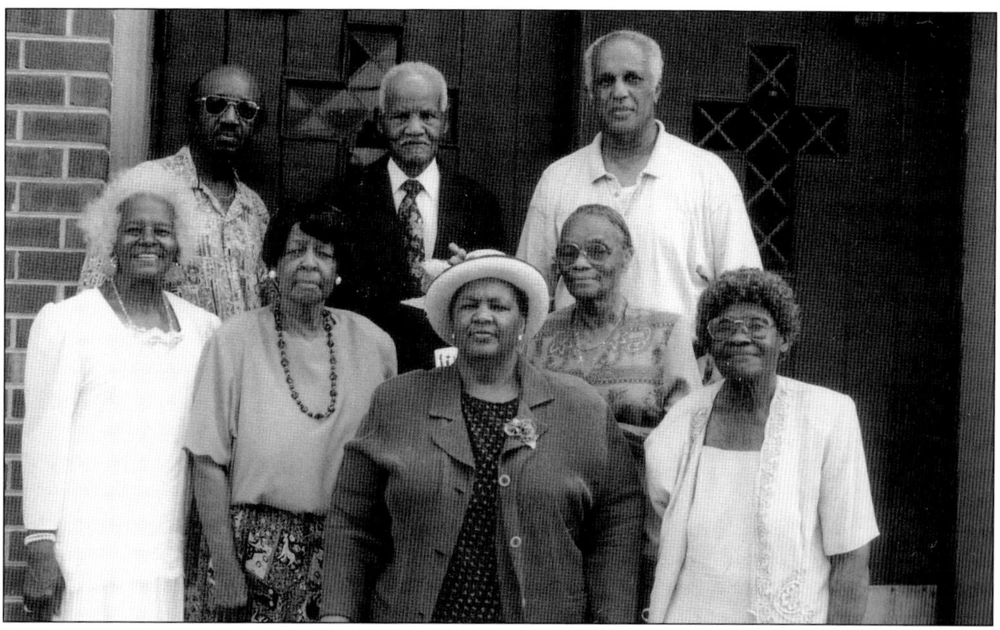

This picture of members of the African American Historical Society of Portsmouth was taken on August 15, 1997 in front of the historic Emanuel AME Church after members had interviewed citizens who were 75 years and older. From left to right are (front row) Dorothy Sharp Faulks, Marian Walker, Mae Breckenridge-Haywood, Lelia Barnes, and Rev. E.M. Woodard; (back row) Thomas Beamon, Mr. Gaines, and Charles Whitehurst (former president.) Mrs. Marion Walker had interviewed Mr. Gaines; he was 75 years old and a runner who resided in the Churchland section of Portsmouth.

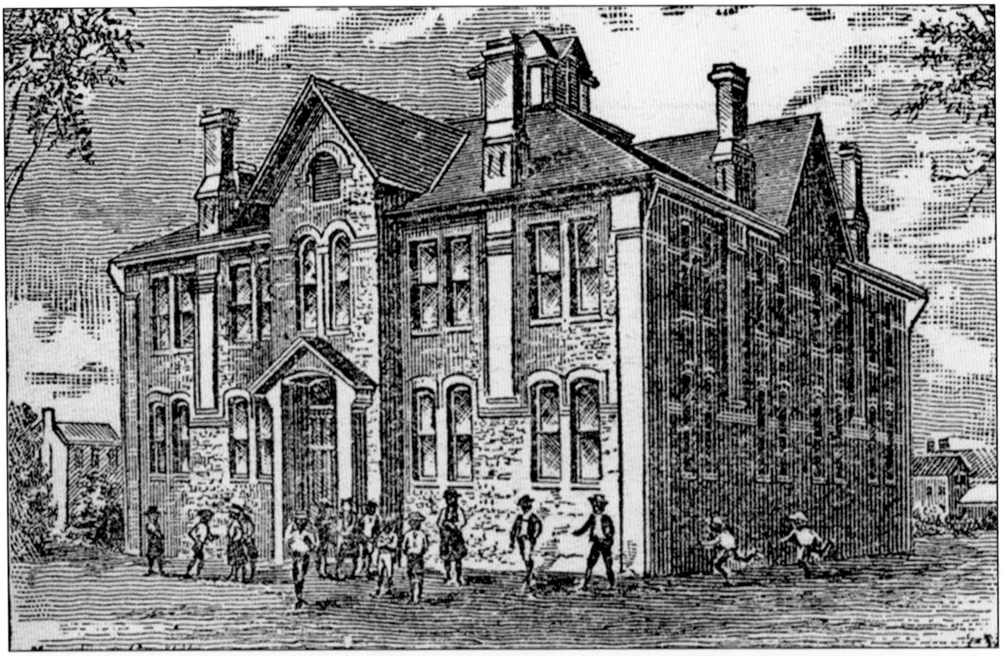

This artist's rendering of the Chestnut Street School, taken from Edward Pollock's *Sketch Book of Portsmouth*, depicted it as it looked when the book was published in 1886. Located at 907–917 Chestnut Street and funded through private donations from the George Peabody Foundation, the school was the first for African Americans in Portsmouth. (Courtesy Portsmouth Public Library.)

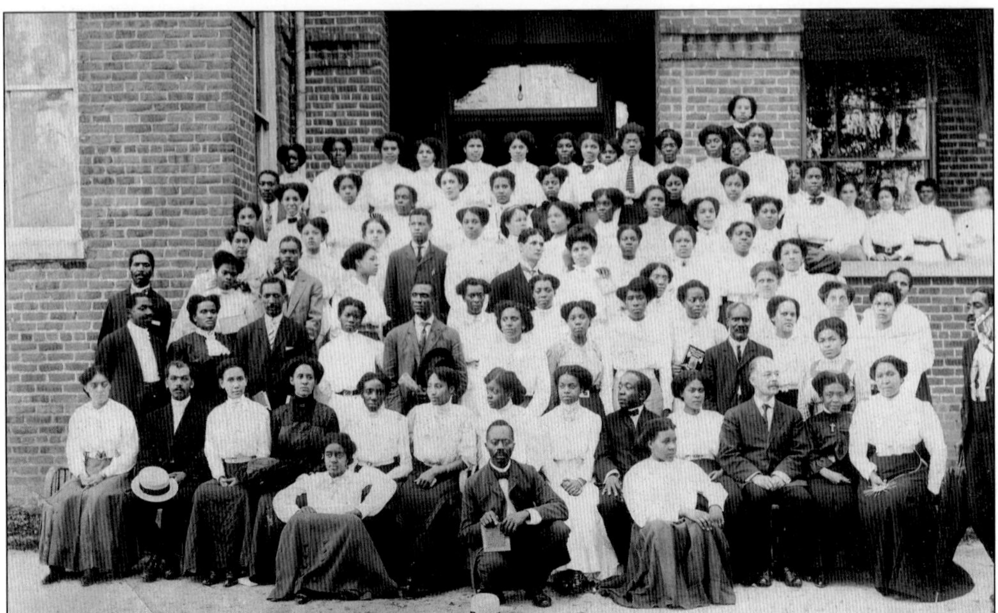

I.C. Norcom High School faculty and students are pictured here *c.* 1900. The photo is from the I.C. Norcom personal family collection. (Courtesy Rachel Norcom-Smith, granddaughter of I.C. Norcom.)

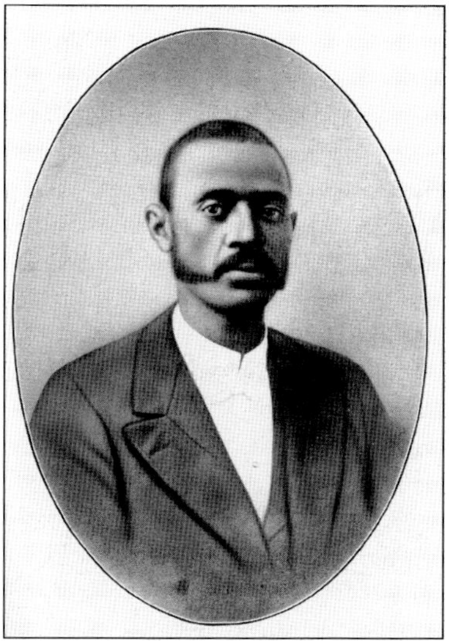

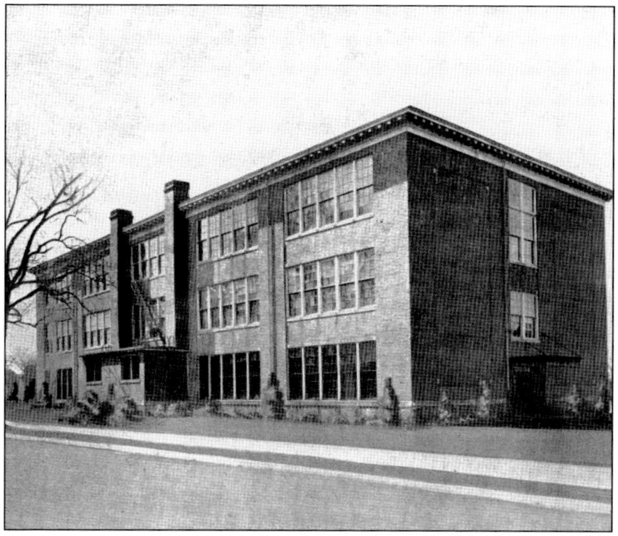

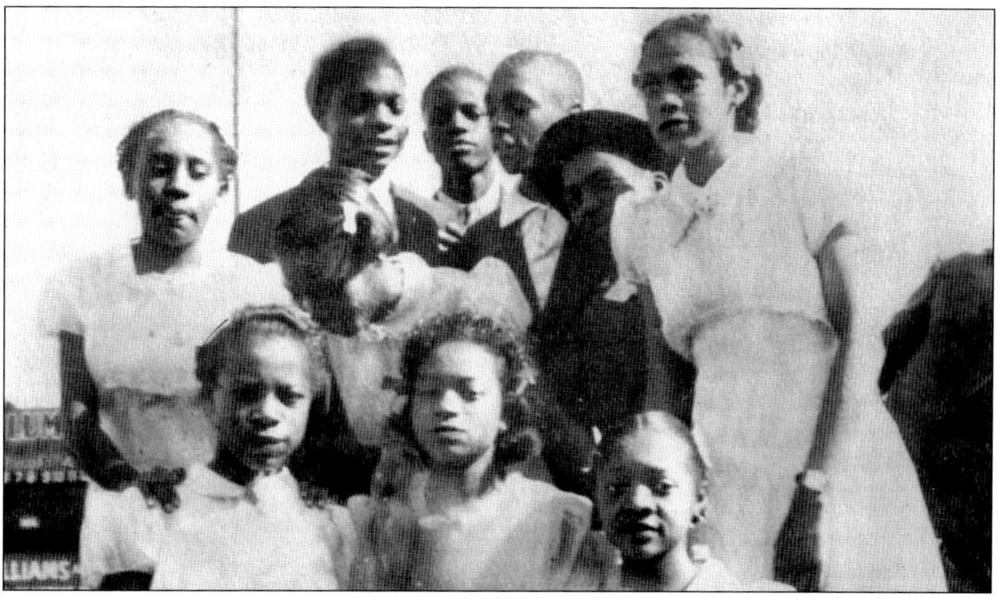

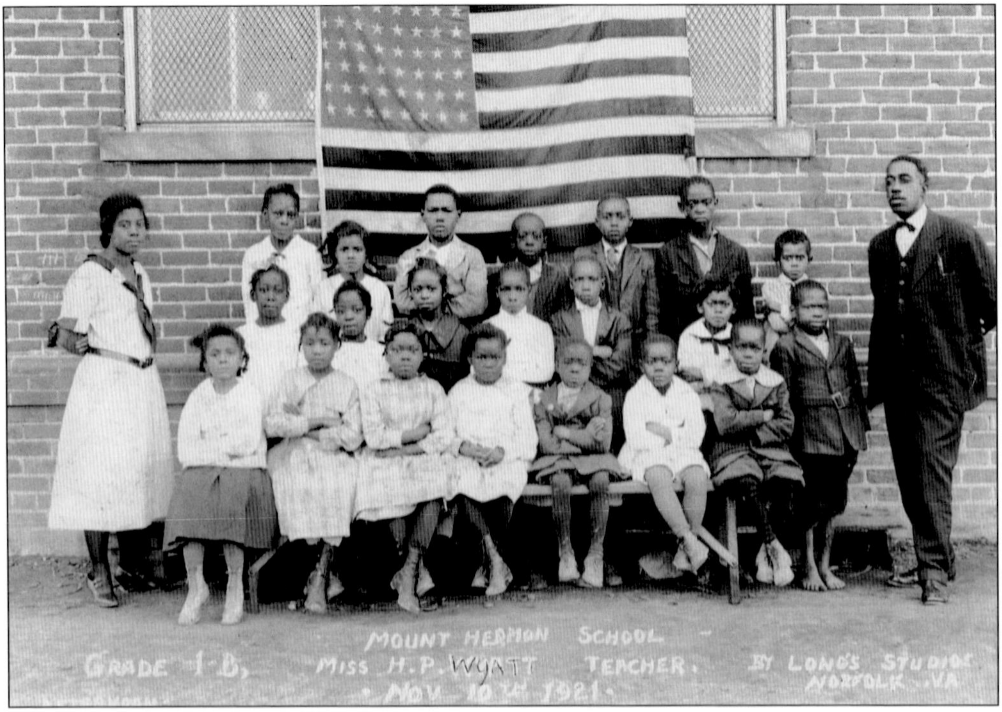
MOUNT HERMON SCHOOL
GRADE 1-B, MISS H.P. WYATT TEACHER.
NOV 10th 1921.
BY LONG'S STUDIOS
NORFOLK, VA

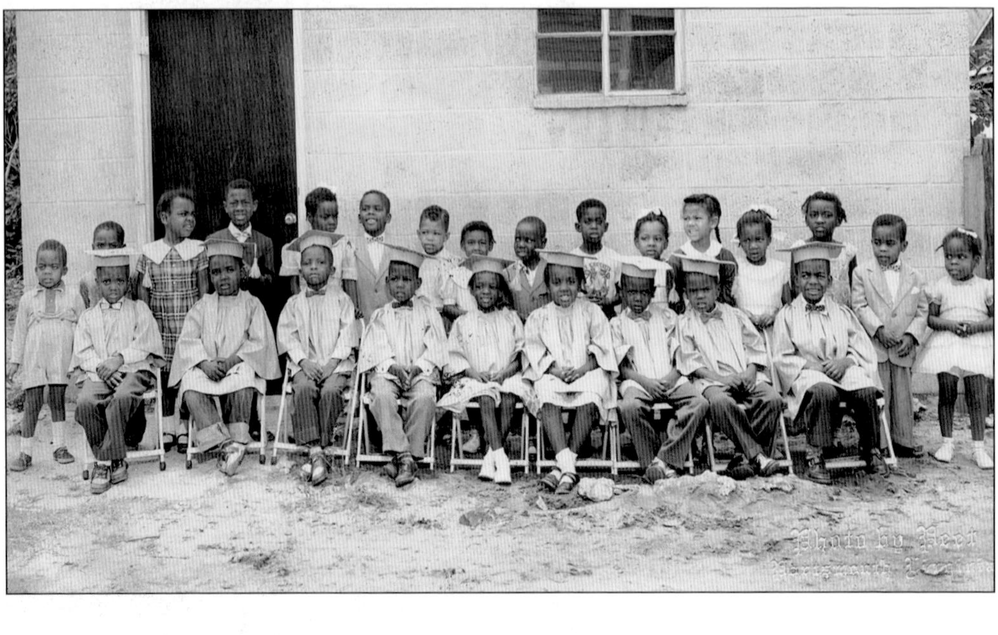
Photo by

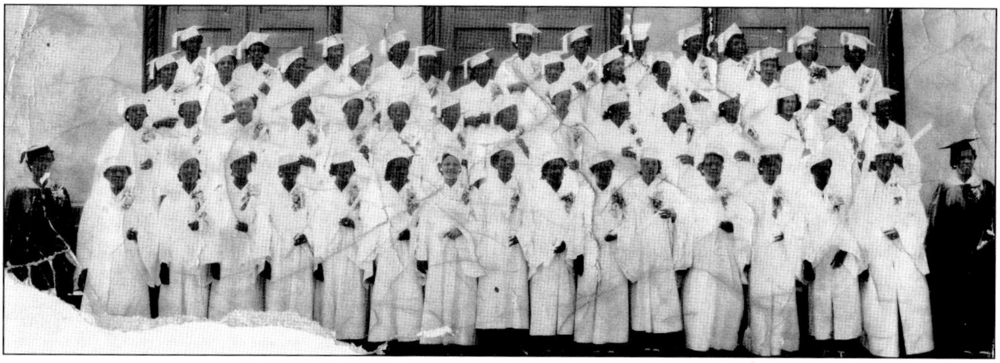

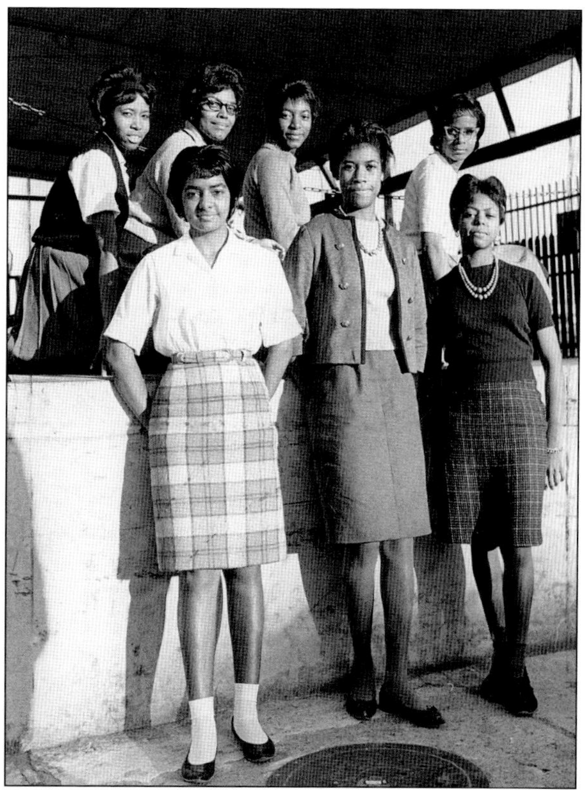

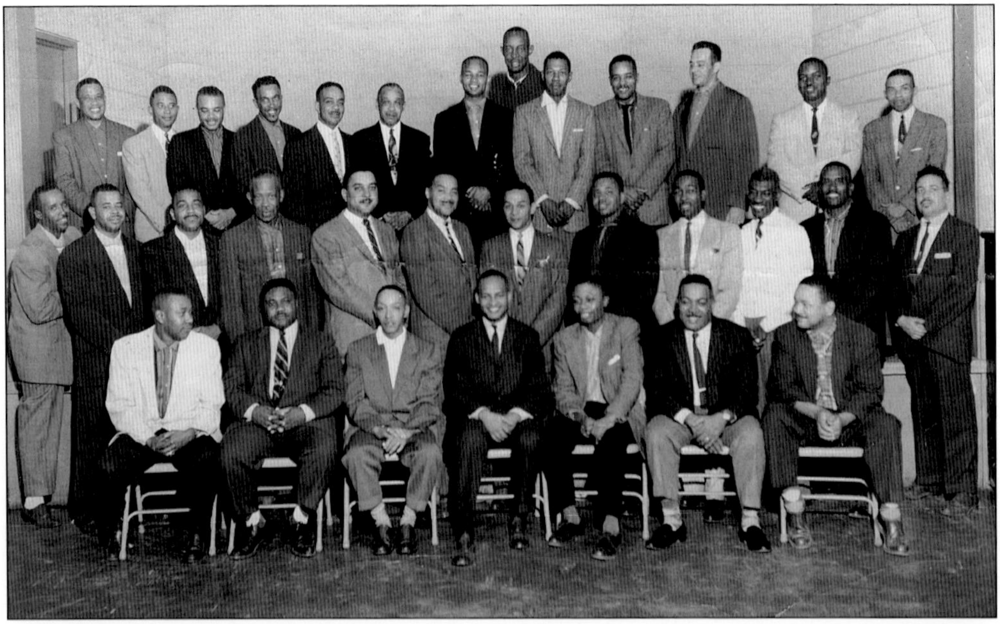

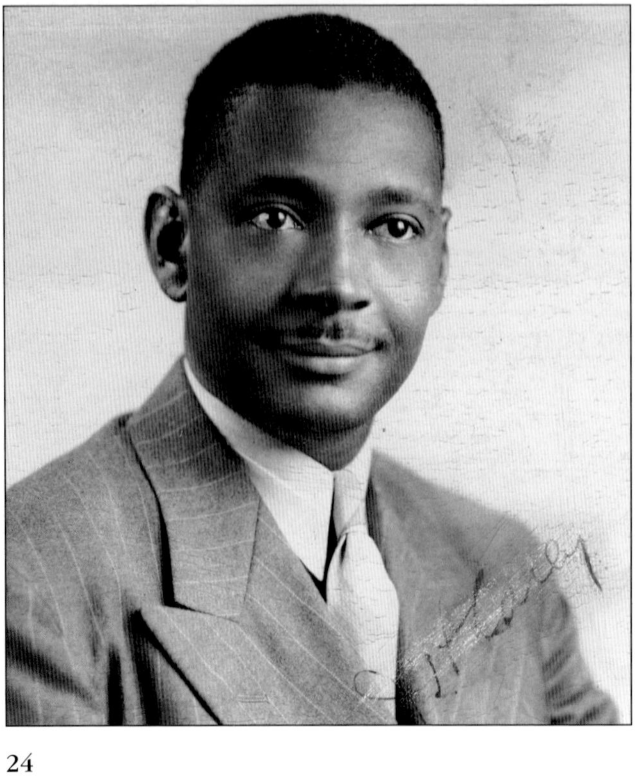

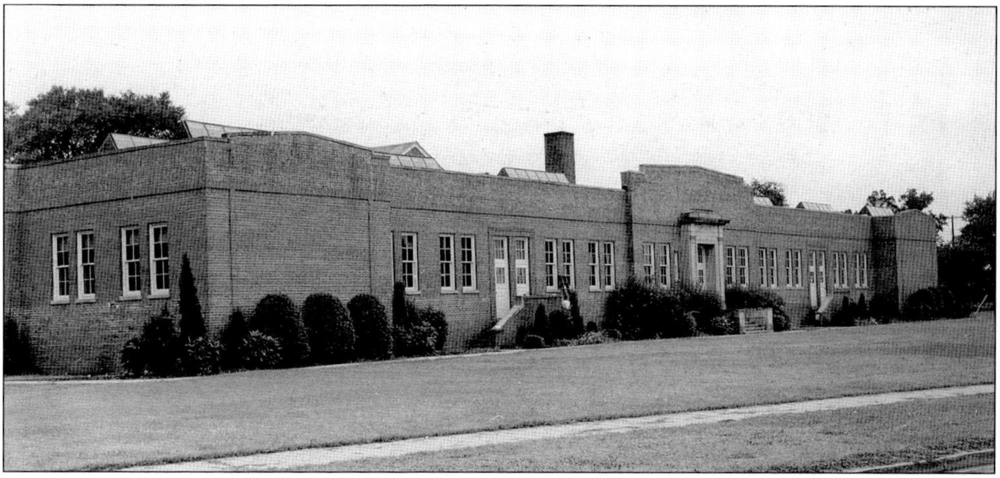

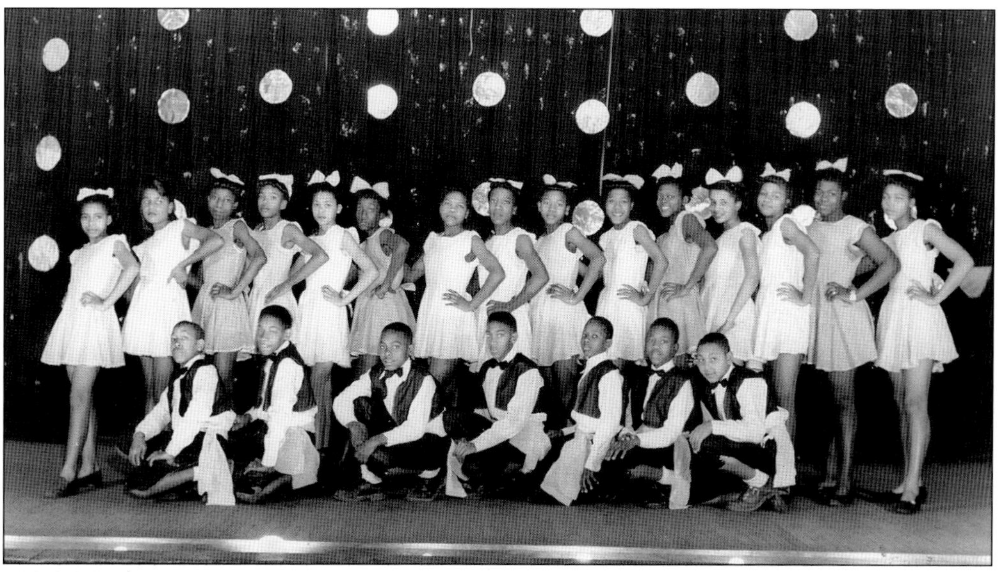

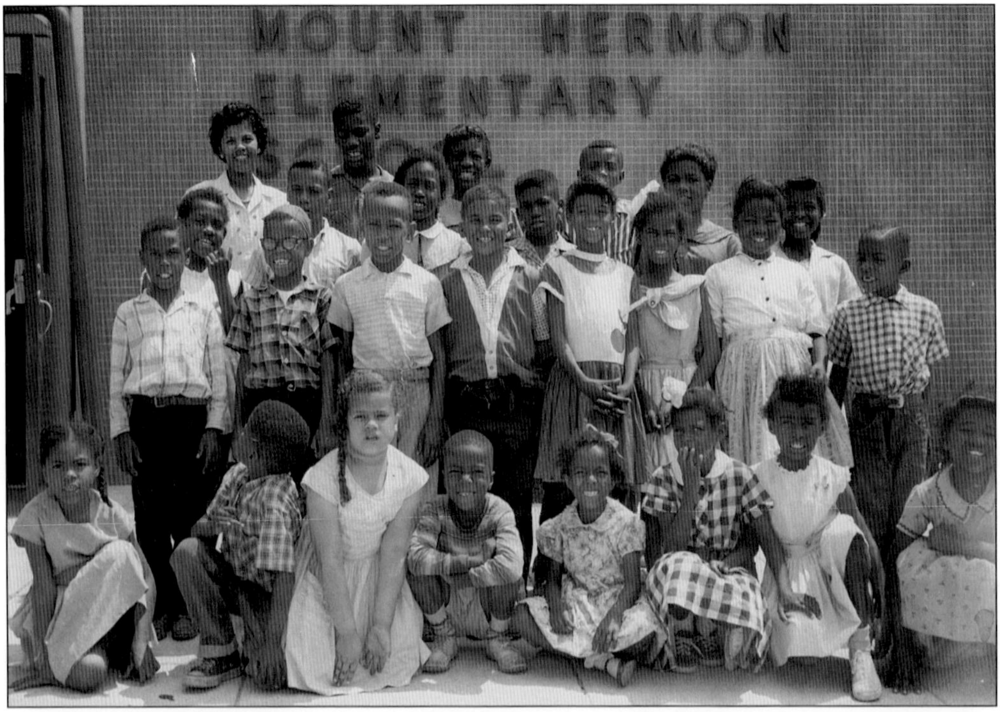
MOUNT HERMON
ELEMENTARY

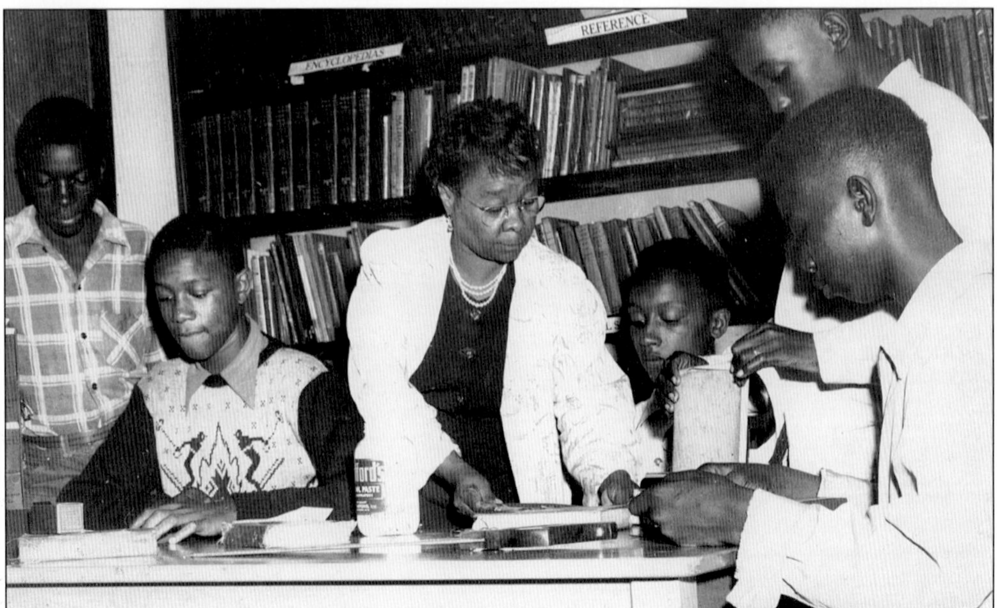
REFERENCE
ENCYCLOPEDIAS

Three

EMPLOYMENT

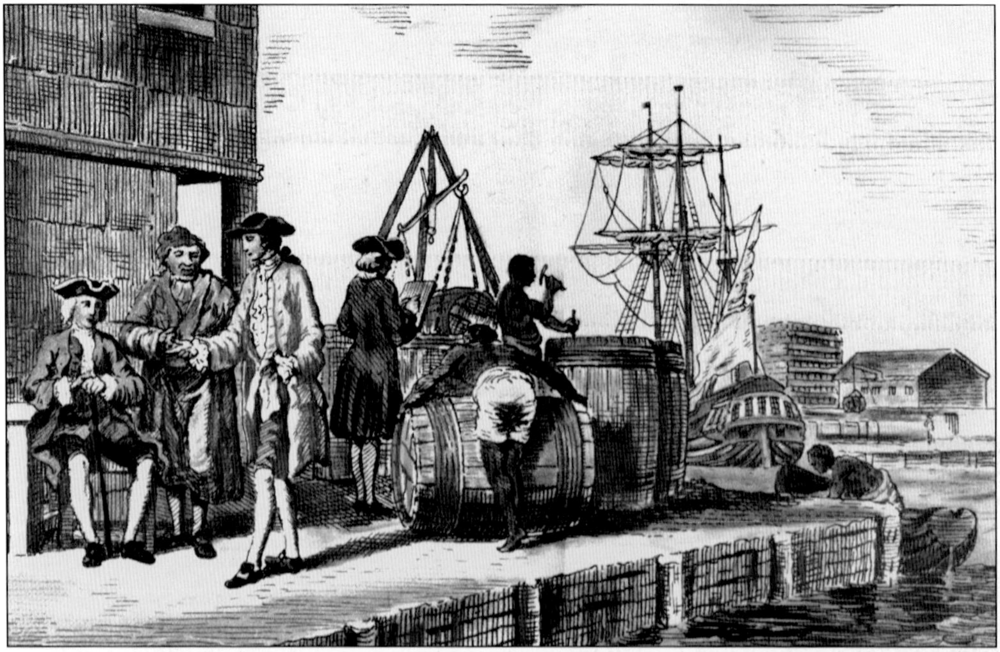

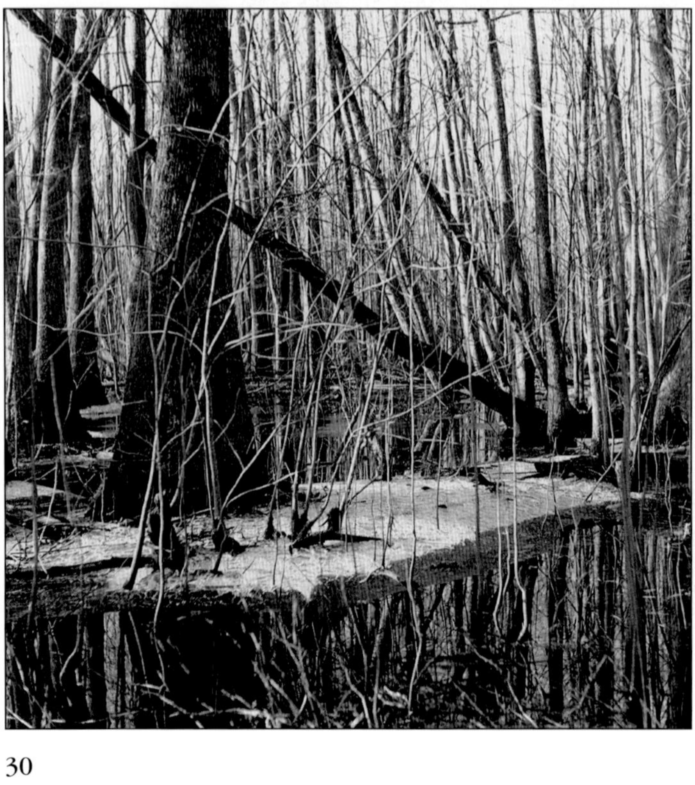

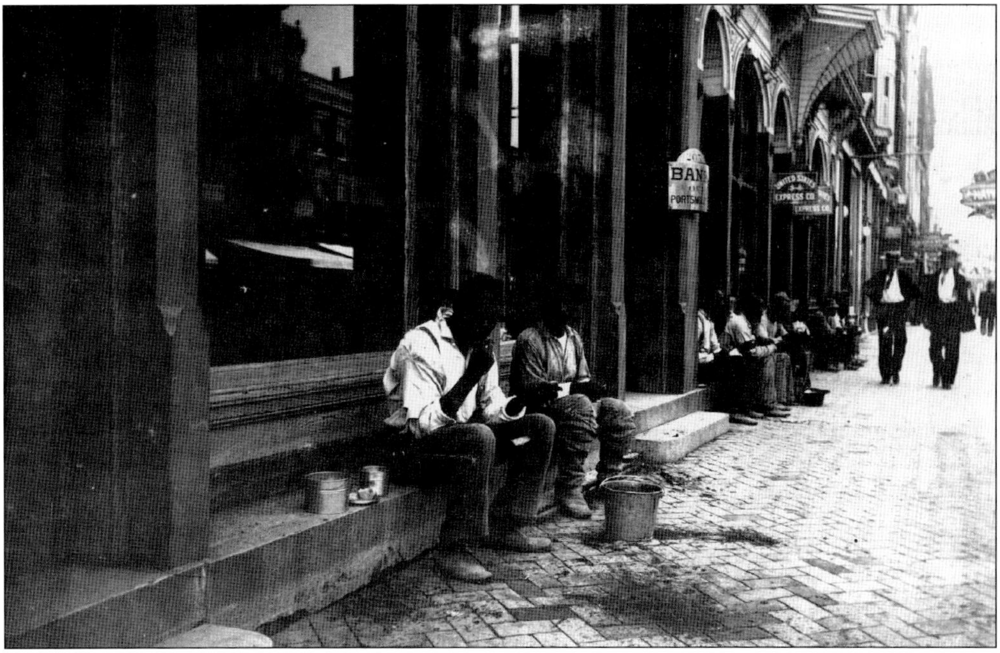

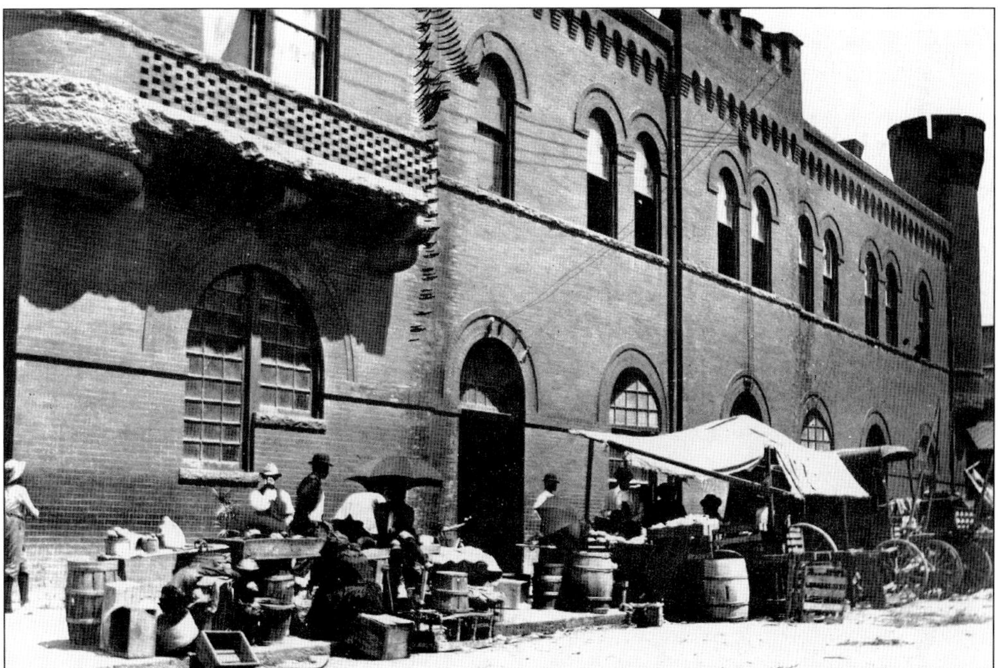

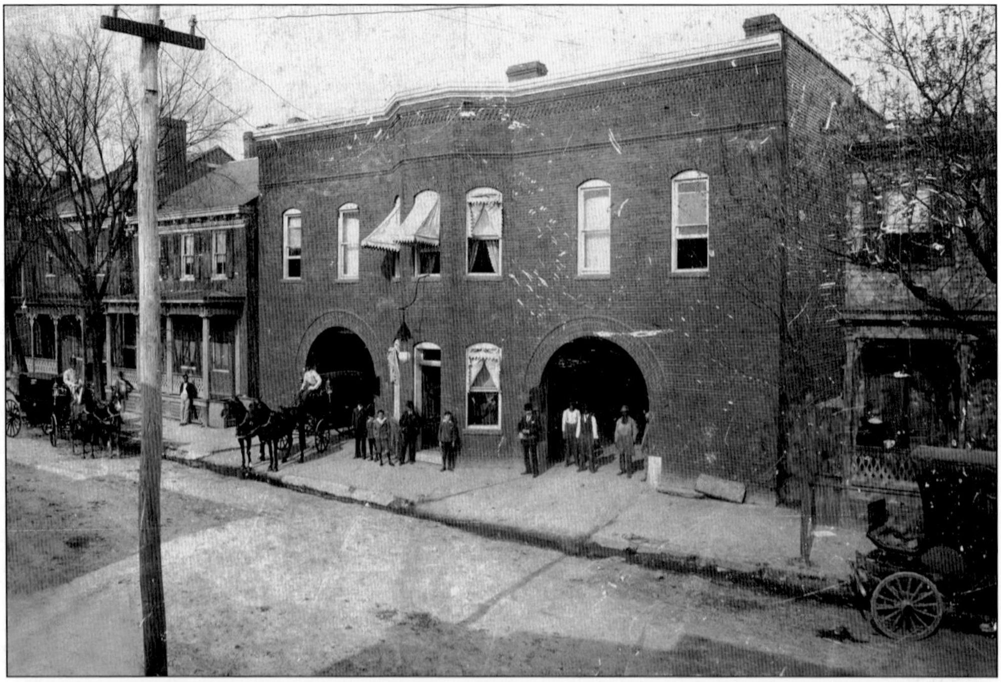

The Portsmouth Burial Company, owned by African Americans, was originally a fire station. The building was located in the 600 block of County Street, behind Columbia Street. In later years, it was used as an apartment building. (Courtesy Portsmouth Public Library.)

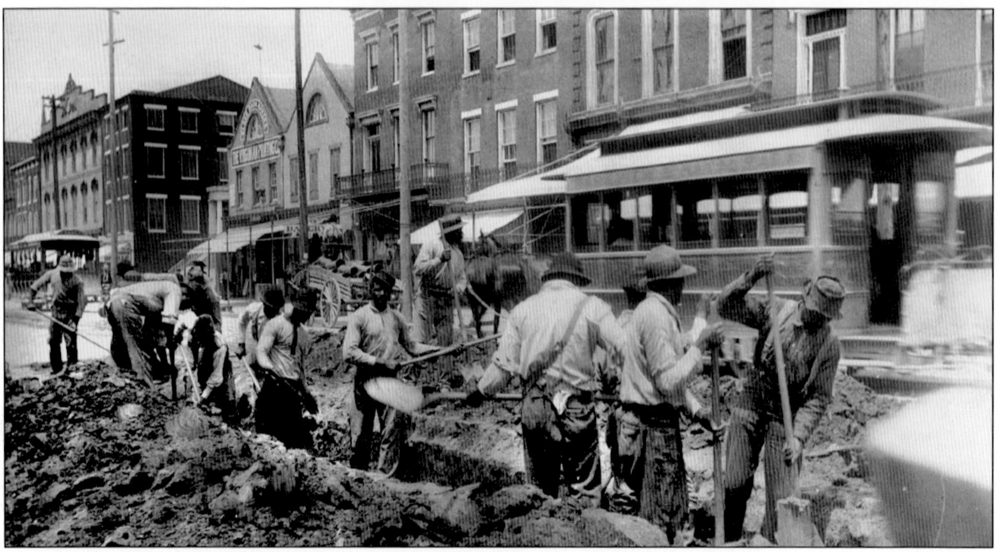

This 1890s photograph was taken of African-American men digging up the north side of the 200 block of High Street to install a sewer system. Ditch digging, streetcar rail construction, and other forms of unskilled manual labor were often the only jobs available to black men in the late 19th and early 20th centuries. Behind the men were the horse-drawn streetcars, which were commonly used during this period and ran from the downtown area to the suburbs of Park View and the Naval Hospital. By the turn of the century, electrical streetcars replaced horse drawn cars. (Courtesy Olde Towne Collection, Portsmouth Public Library.)

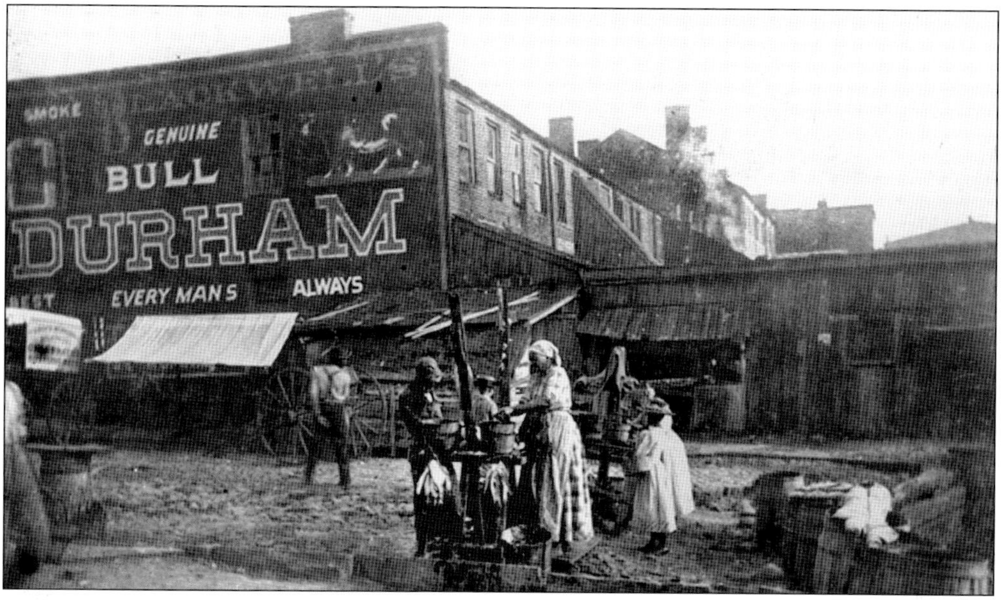

This photograph depicts a woman cleaning fish at the Fish Market, located in the 100 block of County Street in 1900. According to Jeffery Wilson in a December 11, 1924 article in the *Portsmouth Star's* "Colored Notes," "The old colored butchers of slavery days were Moses Turner, Sam Hodges, Robert or Dennis Sneed, Chas. Thompson, Jeffrey Tatem, Jr. David Edwards. Of course they did business for their masters. There were others occupying stalls in Portsmouth and Norfolk markets. We had fresh killed meats every day. No packinghouse meats from Chicago, Omaha, and other western cities came then, and it was good meat, not preserved by embalming fluids, etc. When the city market was on Crawford Street, fronting on High Street, the police station was over the market, a two story structure with cells." (Courtesy Olde Towne Collection, Portsmouth Public Library.)

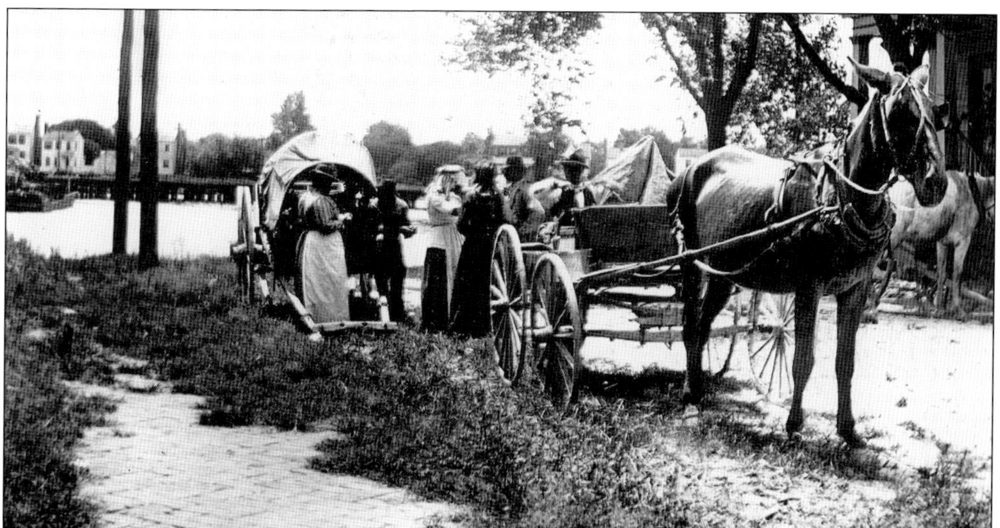

These people are crossing at Gander Creek, also known as Crab or Gosport Creek, with their market wagons at the south end of Middle and South Street sometime around the turn of the 20th century. (Courtesy Olde Towne Collection, Portsmouth Public Library.)

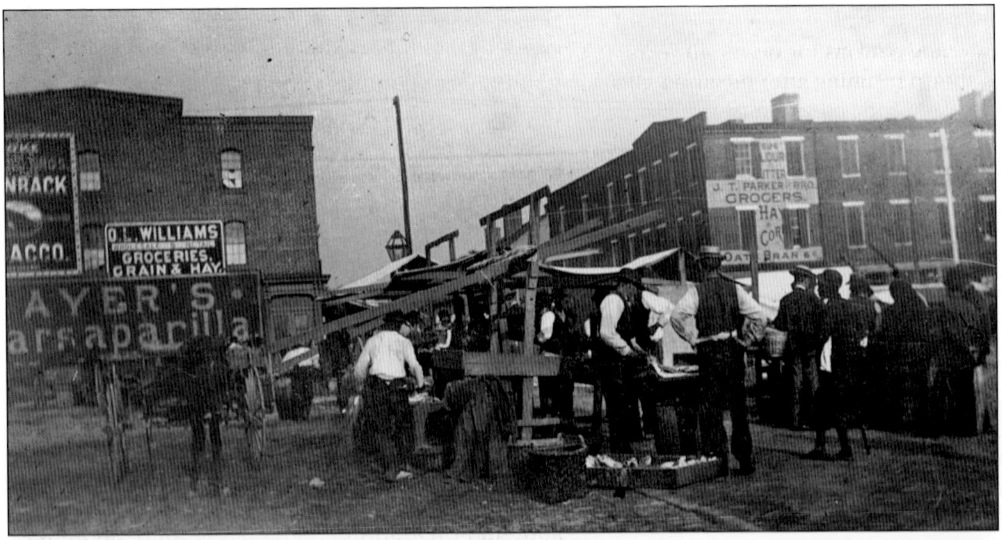

This was a turn of the 20th century open air market located on the west side of Crawford Street at the County Street intersection. It was in the public sphere of the commercial market place that the intersection of young and old, rich and poor, black and white typically occurred. (Courtesy Olde Towne Collection, Portsmouth Public Library.)

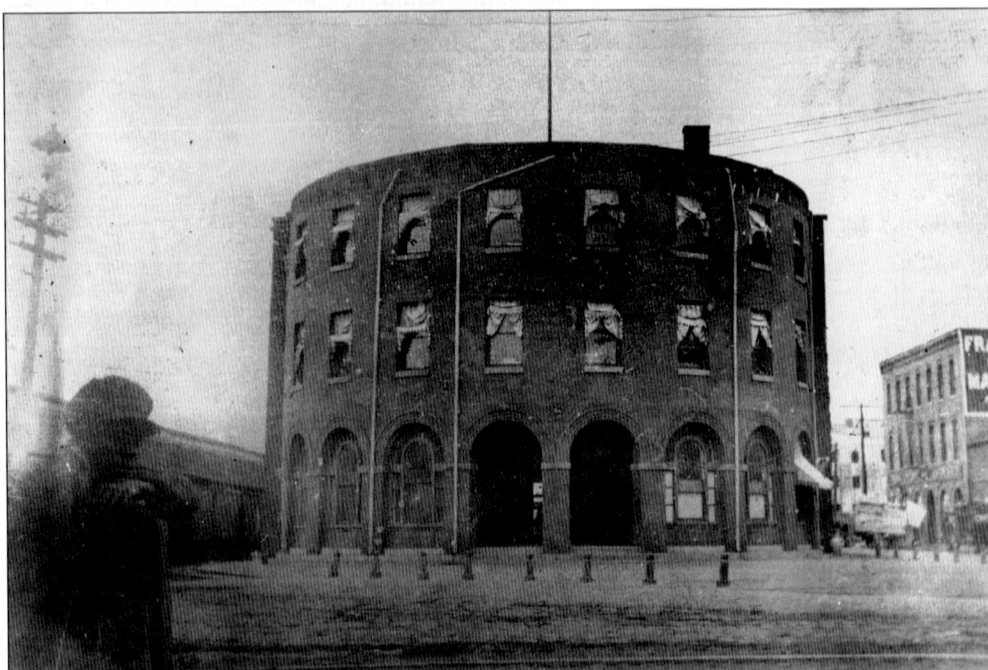

This is how the Seaboard Airline Railway Building once looked, pictured sometime between 1906 and 1920. Located at 1 High Street, the building was the train station and headquarters for the railway company. Its location was just south of the ferry terminal that provided travel between Norfolk and Portsmouth. (Courtesy Olde Towne Collection, Portsmouth Public Library.)

Willie C. Jones, who served Seaboard's traveling patrons for nearly 40 years, is shown beaming after receiving gifts from admiring co-workers, associates, and friends at the Seaboard Station in Portsmouth Thursday, January 16, 1958—the day after his official retirement. Jones had the reputation of a model red cap porter because of his service and neatness. Red Caps at Seaboard Station were crucial to the operation of the railroad. A keen mind for detail, the red cap provided passengers with the assurance needed as they hurried to their varying destinations by knowing all arrival and departure schedules to the minute. (Courtesy Lee Rodgers Collection, Portsmouth Public Library.)

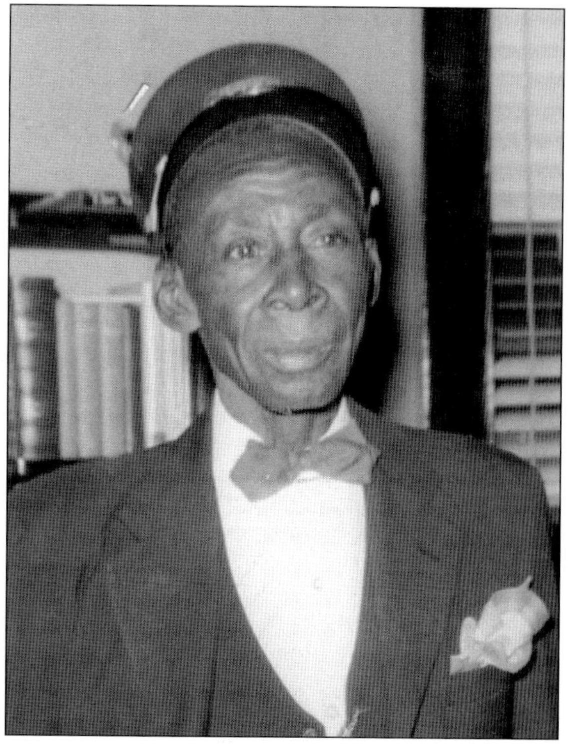

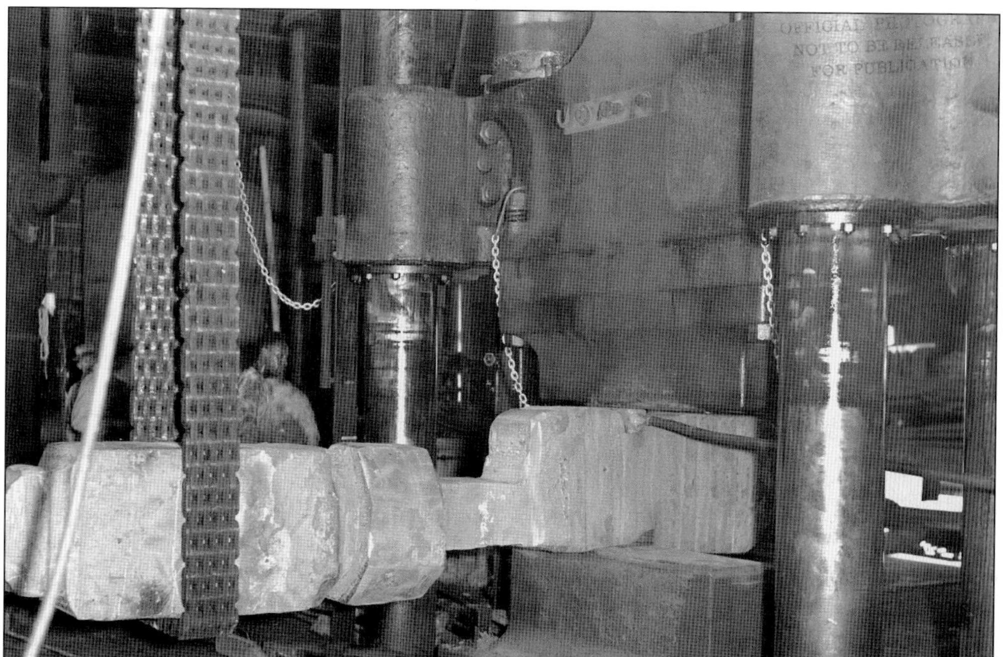

Some skilled industrial positions became available to African Americans during World War II, such as forgings in the Prescott Company and the Fulton Iron Works. ("Rounding for Hauge," July 1943, Courtesy Portsmouth Public Library.)

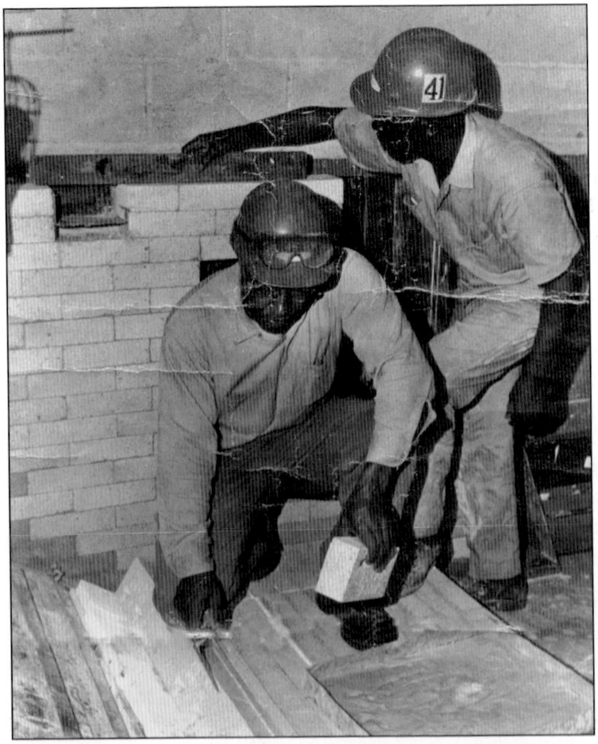

Navy Yard workers are pictured in this photograph. The man standing is Henry Hunt who lived at 1422 Wirt Avenue, the Brighton section of Portsmouth, and worked at the shipyard as a pipe fitter. Mr. Hunt was so dedicated to his trade that he studied the craft of pipe fitting each night. Although the man kneeling is unknown, it is clear that the work being done by both individuals is pipefitting. (Courtesy Barbara Hunt Allen.)

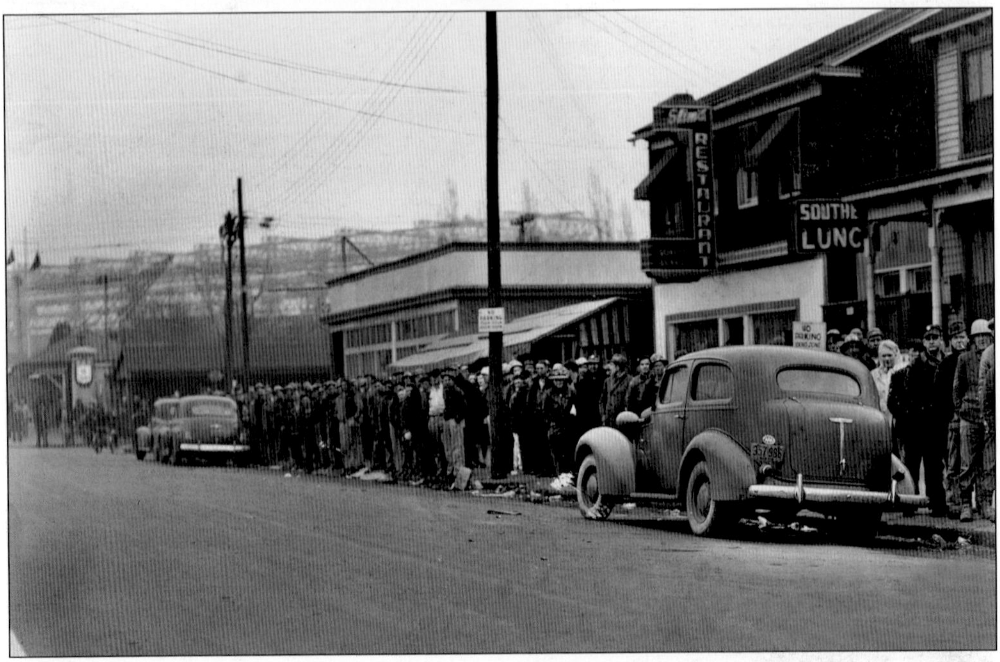

This is a 1944 photograph of Navy Yard workers waiting for bus at Fourth Street gate. Although the majority of positions, especially skilled and supervisory, were reserved for white workers at this time, African Americans were able to gain some employment during this period as unskilled laborers. (Courtesy Olde Towne Collection, Portsmouth Public Library.)

This photograph was taken of Charles Bond on his wedding day. Bond worked at the Navy Yard and in the late 1930s. A Works Progress Administration worker interviewed Charles Bond, a machinist at the Norfolk Navy Yard, for the Writers' Project. In recalling his experiences at the Navy Yard, Bond said, "I have been working there since 1935. I went to Portsmouth High School and then to Hampton Institute for my training. I have lived in Portsmouth all my life in the Lincolnsville section, named for the President . . . . My family has made a go of it in Portsmouth since the time of the Civil War. Once the Yankees took control of Norfolk, my grandfather ran away from the plantation in North Carolina to get his freedom. It seems that wars are pretty important to these cities, with the Navy and all being here." Bond later worked as a teacher at Booker T. Washington High School in Norfolk but continued living at 3019 Elm Avenue in Portsmouth. (Courtesy Miriam Jiggetts.)

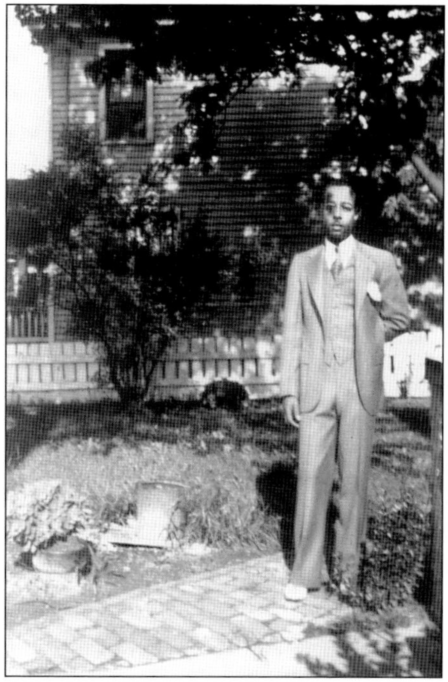

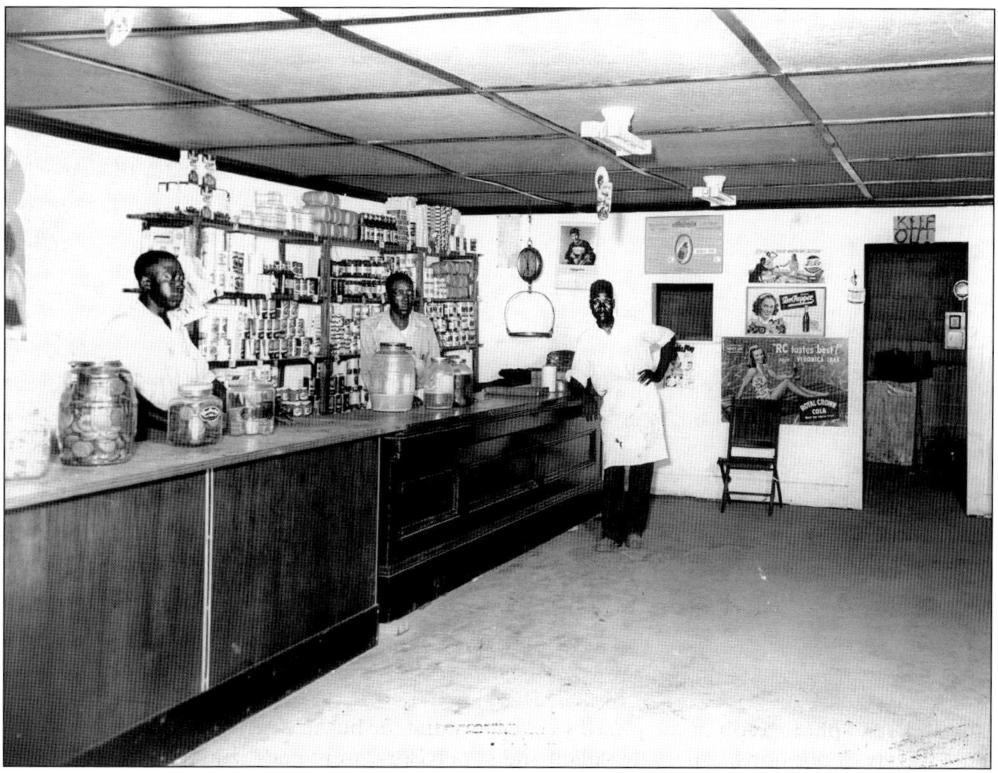

Pictured is Southern Paradise, a popular restaurant in Portsmouth, taken on August 16, 1947. (Courtesy Lee Rodgers Collection, Portsmouth Public Library.)

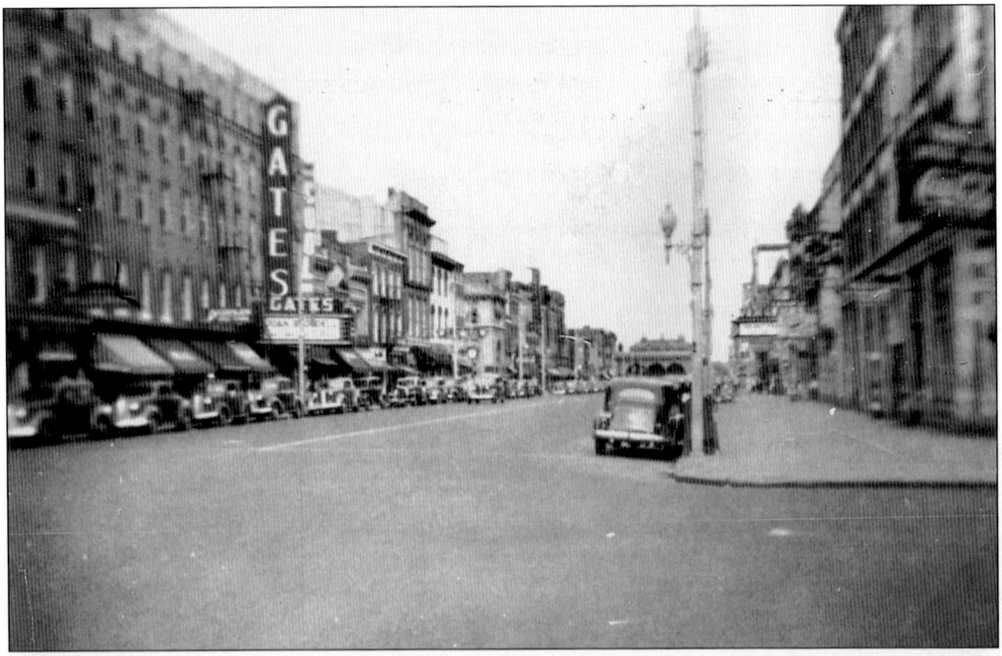

Trant's Drug Store at Court and High Streets on July 23, 1939 is shown here. (Courtesy Portsmouth Public Library.)

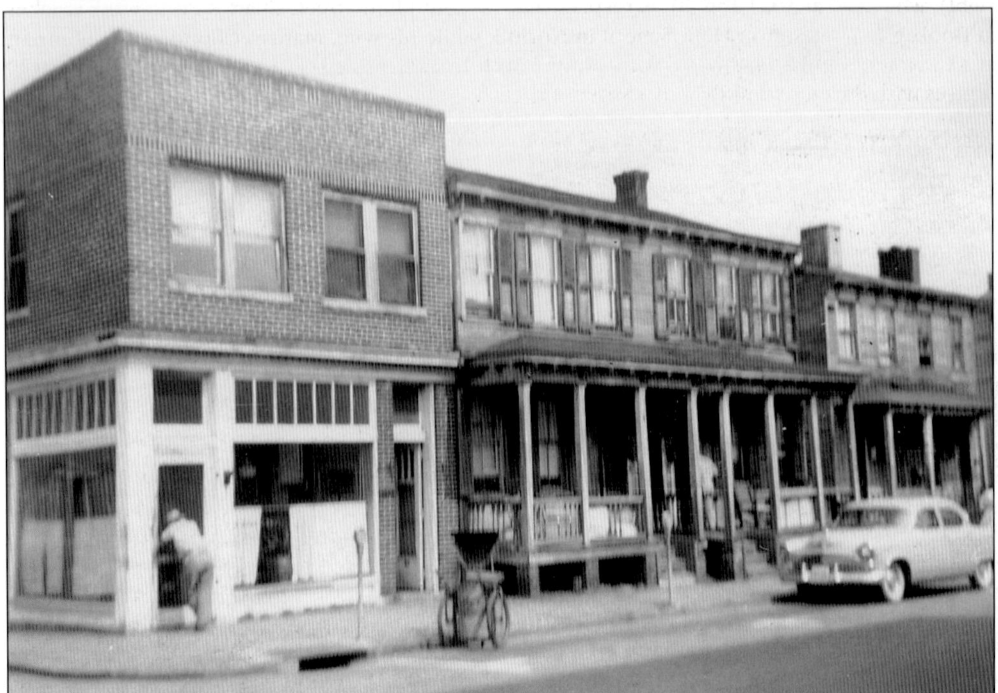

Victor Small's Funeral Home was located in the downstairs building at the corner in the 400 block of Green Street, while Dr. Frank Elliott's office was located upstairs. This photograph was taken sometime in the 1950s. (Courtesy Bertha Edwards Collection, Portsmouth Public Library.)

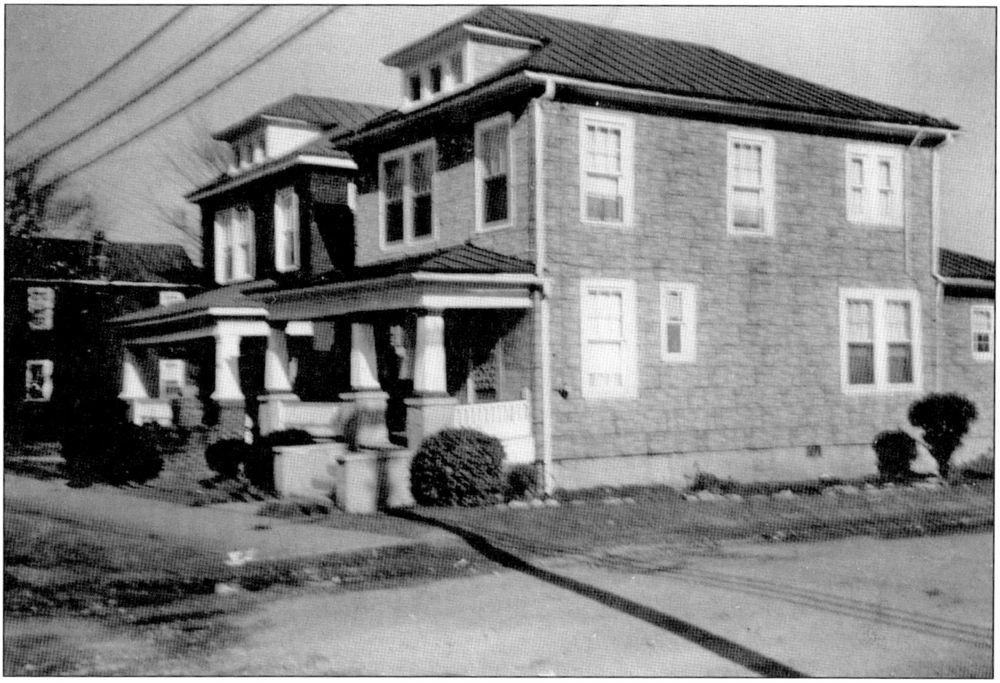

These are homes of Richard T. Bolling (far right) and Mr. and Mrs. Charles C. Bond (second from right), who lived at 3021 and 3019, respectively, on south Elm Street. Charles Bond was a teacher at Booker T. Washington High School in Norfolk while his wife, Margaret Bond, was a librarian at I.C. Norcom High School in Portsmouth. Both houses were very similar in style—two-story houses with dormer window and a spacious porch.

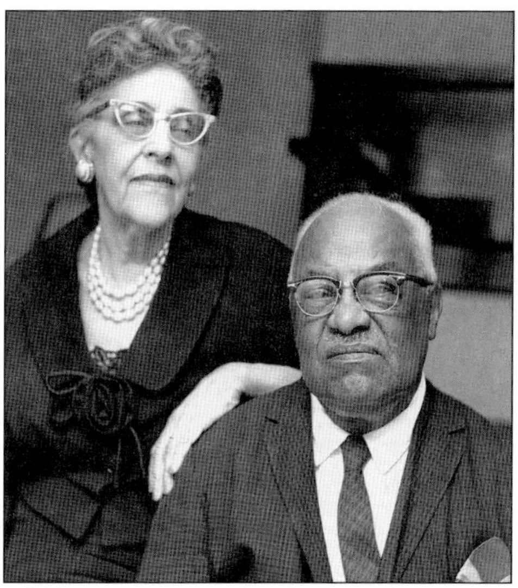

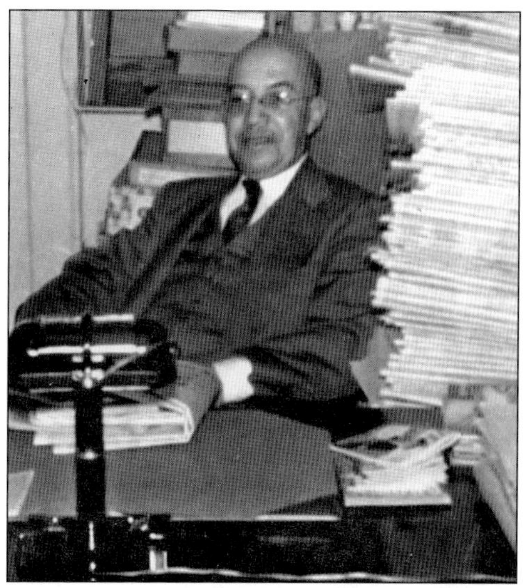

(left) Dr. and Mrs. Frank G. Elliott are shown in the 1950s. Dr. Elliott was one of the prominent physicians practicing in Portsmouth while Mrs. Elliott was heavily involved in a number of social organizations. (Courtesy Lee Rodgers Collection, Portsmouth Public Library.) *(right)* This is a photograph of Richard Bolling busy at work in his office. (Courtesy Lee Rodgers Collection, Portsmouth Public Library.)

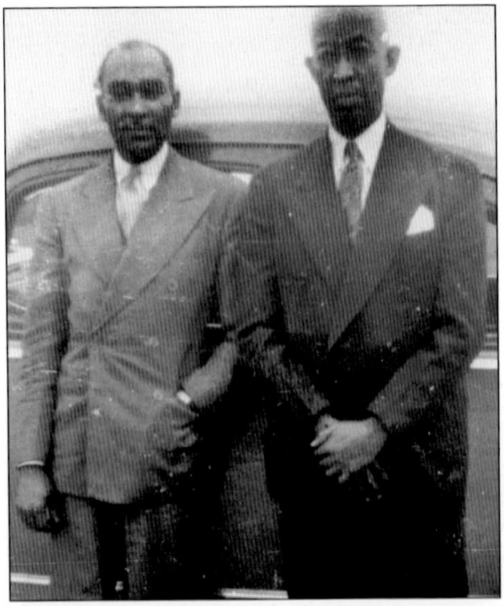

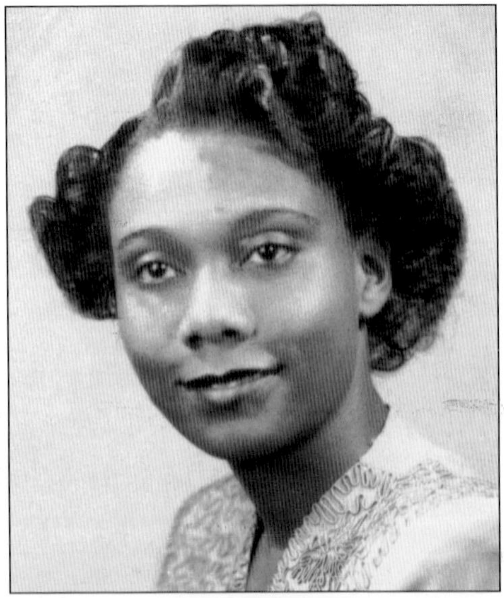

(left) Black physicians were important parts of the black elite. As professionals and independent businessmen and women, physicians were the leaders of the community, especially in helping to found organizations such as the NAACP, black-owned banks, and the like. Pictured here are Mr. George Walker and Dr. J.D. Barnes sometime in the 1950s. (Courtesy Lee Rodgers Collection, Portsmouth Public Library.) *(Right)* Dr. Helen Mewborn Watts was the first black female physician in Portsmouth. A graduate of I.C. Norcom High School, Dr. Watts was a rare commodity in Tidewater, being the only black female physicians for many years. (Courtesy Portsmouth Public Library.)

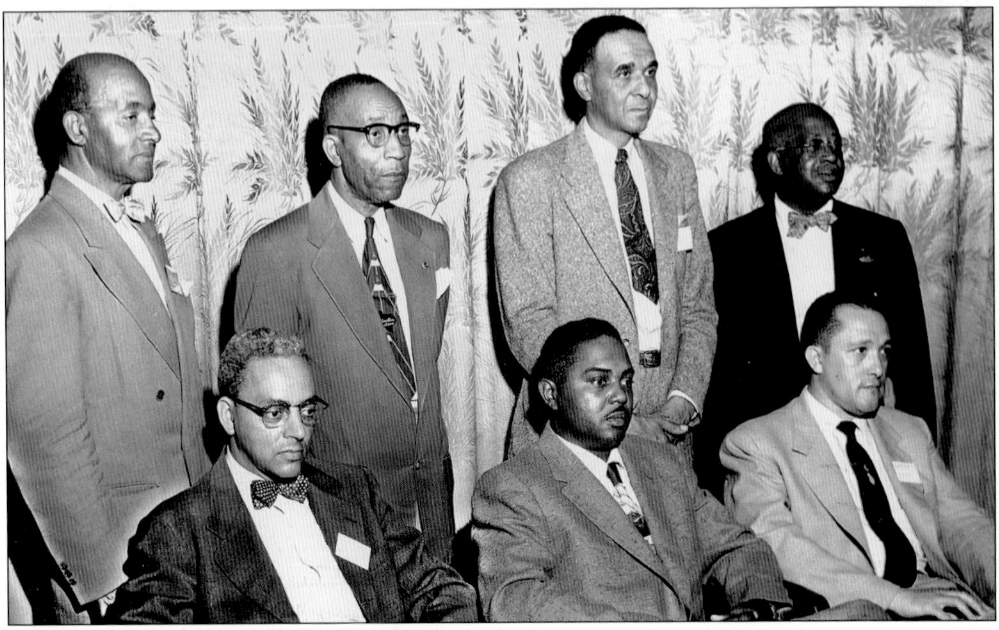

The Old Dominion Dental Society is shown in May 1954. This was a statewide African-American dental association of which all Portsmouth's black dentists were a part. (Courtesy Lee Rodgers Collection, Portsmouth Public Library.)

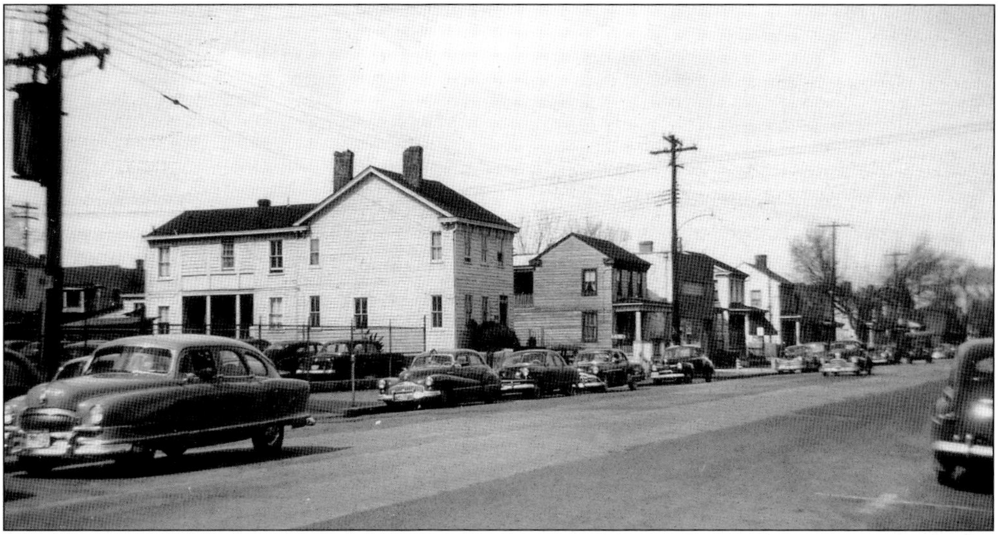

Dr. John Jackson's office building, located at 401 Effingham Street, is the first building on the left. Mr. Holmes had a dental supply office that was upstairs in the Jackson building and made dentures for Drs. McGriff, Hugo Owens, and John Jackson in the1940s and 1950s. Holmes's wife, Mrs. Rafae Holmes, was the elementary school supervisor in Portsmouth during the 1960s and 1970s. (Courtesy Bertha Edwards Collection, Portsmouth Public Library.)

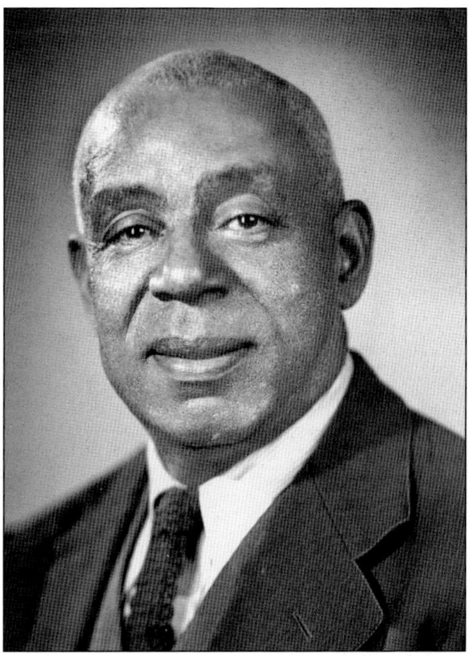

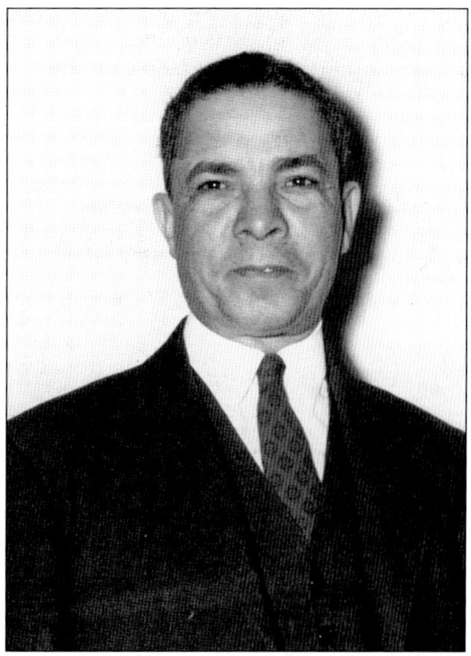

(left) Victor Small, a prominent funeral director, is pictured here on October 9, 1948. (Courtesy Lee Rodgers Collection, Portsmouth Public Library.) *(right)* Thomas H. Reid was a prominent Portsmouth attorney who was active in city and political affairs. He was also involved in a number of fraternal societies including the Beacon Light Lodge No. 34 of Elks, in which he served as the exalted ruler. This photograph was taken on October 18, 1945. (Courtesy Lee Rodgers Collection, Portsmouth Public Library.)

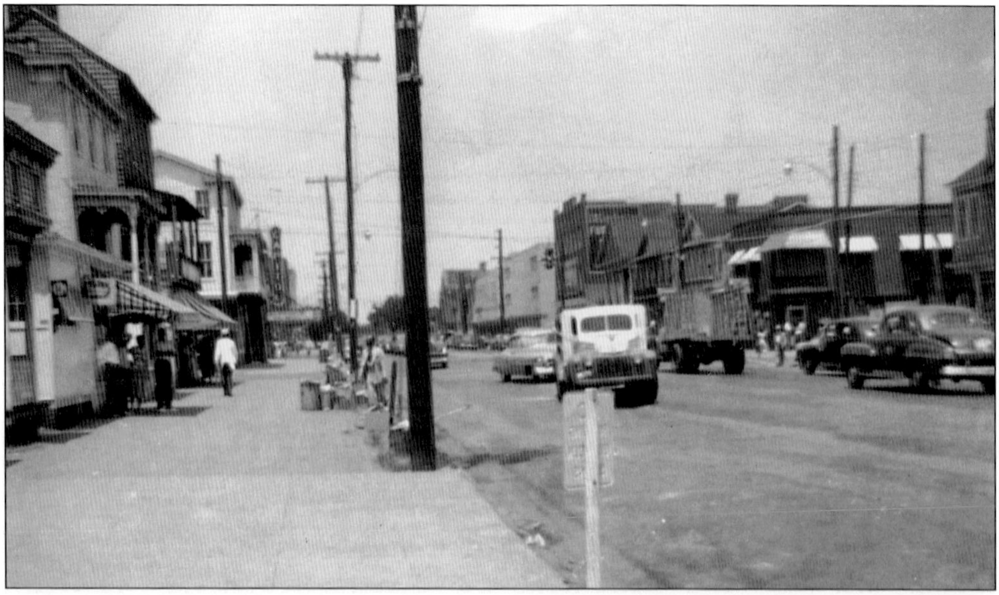

This was the business end of the 700–800 block of Effingham Street, at the corner of Effingham and County Streets, *c.* 1950. The Jones Drug Store building was at the left corner. (Courtesy Portsmouth Public Library.)

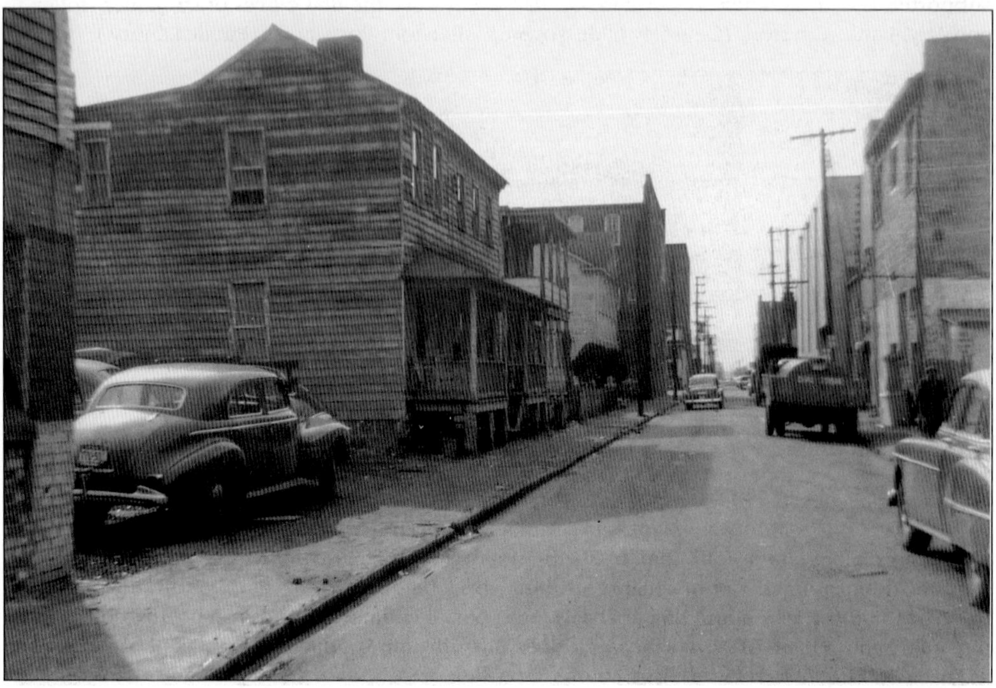

This was the residential end of King Street, *c.* 1950. All of the residences depicted were dilapidated wooden structures. Dr. Hugo Owens' dental office is the far left building (left of the car) in the photograph. His office building is still in existence. (Courtesy Portsmouth Public Library.)

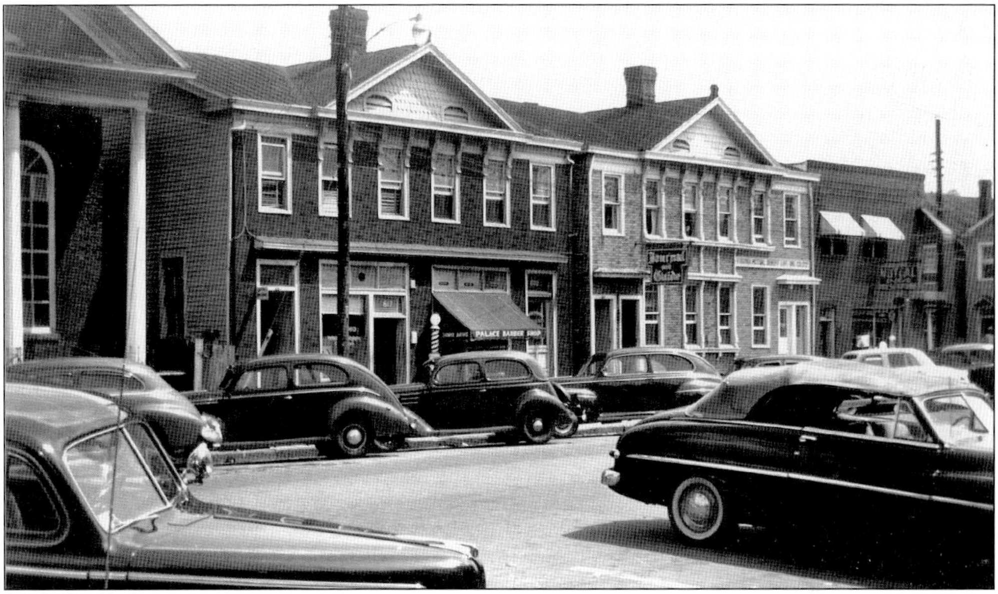

Here is the 600 block of Effingham Street, the main center for black businesses in Portsmouth. In the 1930s and 1940s, the Portsmouth office of the *Journal and Guide* newspaper was located on Effingham Street. Norfolk State University (NSU) named two streets after Portsmouth residents: Mrs. Maude Blow Davis, who worked at NSU for many years, and Mr. John Q. Jordan, a strong NSU supporter, editor, and newspaperman. On this street were the first offices of Dr. James Holley III and Atty. James Overton. (Courtesy Olde Towne Collection, Portsmouth Public Library.)

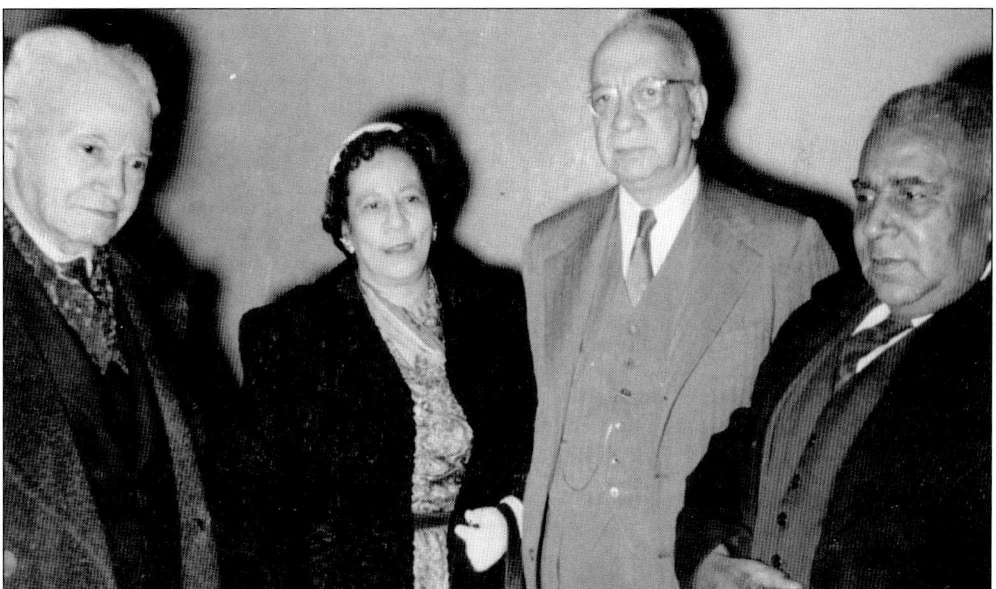

John C. Minkins (far left), Mr. and Mrs. Plumber Bernard Young (center), and John Brown (far right), stand for this photograph taken in 1956. P.B. Young was the founder, owner, and publisher of the Norfolk *Journal and Guide*. (Courtesy Lee Rodgers Collection, Portsmouth Public Library.)

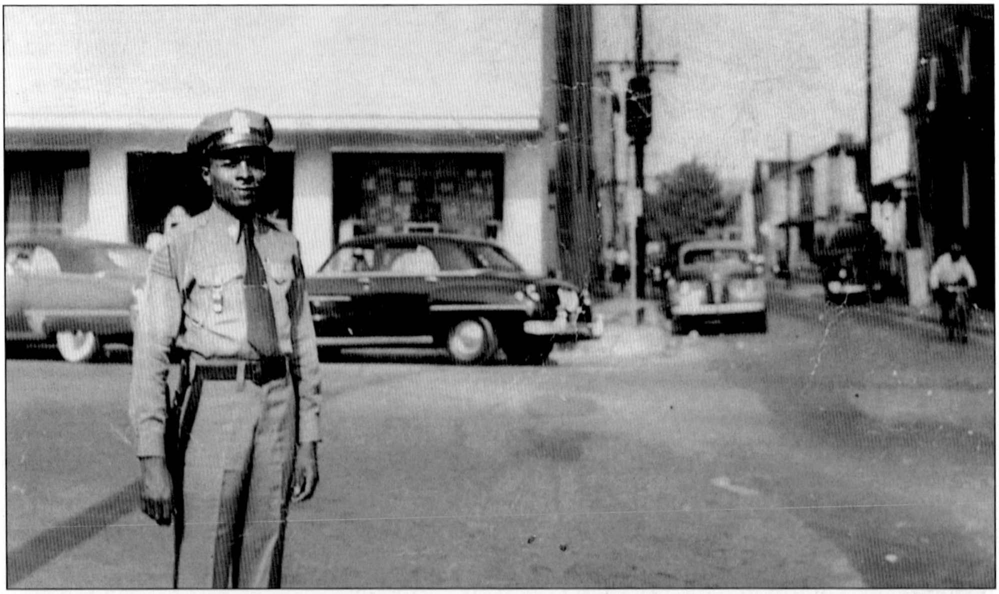

Arceleous Elliott was the first black policeman in Portsmouth after John L. Wilson, who was killed while on duty in 1871. Elliott did not carry a gun; he applied for the job after passing police tests and serving in the U.S. Navy. Elliott graduated from Churchland High School—formerly a black, Norfolk County school. He was assigned to patrol black sections of the city in the 1950s. Elliott is standing at the corner of Effingham and King Streets. (Courtesy Mae Breckenridge-Haywood.)

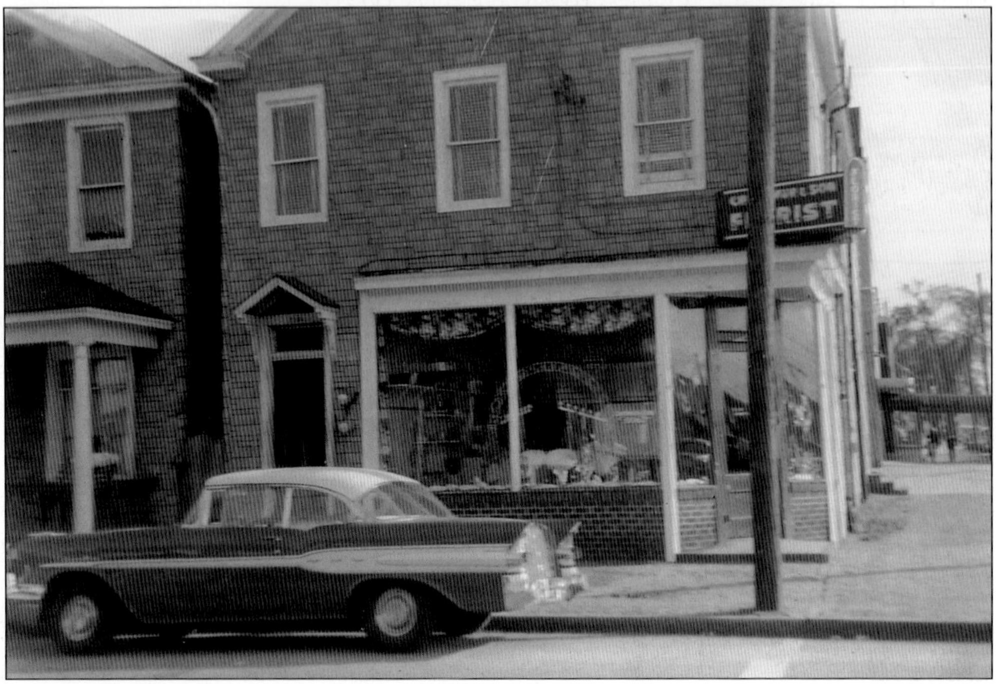

This 1960s photograph was taken of the Creekmur Florist shop located at 2019 Effingham Street at the corner of Lincoln Street. Upstairs was Dr. Jesse Hoax Brown's office. (Courtesy Portsmouth Public Library.)

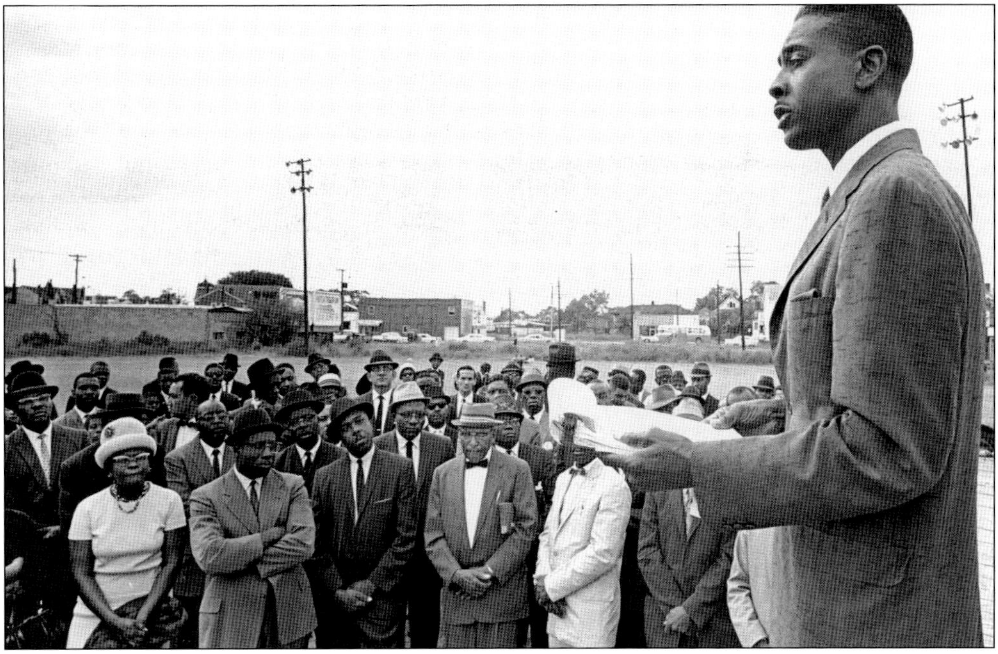

Dr. Hugo A. Owens is a popular dentist and activist. He was born in Norfolk County—an area later annexed by Portsmouth—and after establishing his practice, became active in politics, advocating for the rights of African Americans. During the 1960s, Dr. Owens was president of the local chapter of the NAACP. (Courtesy Portsmouth Public Library.)

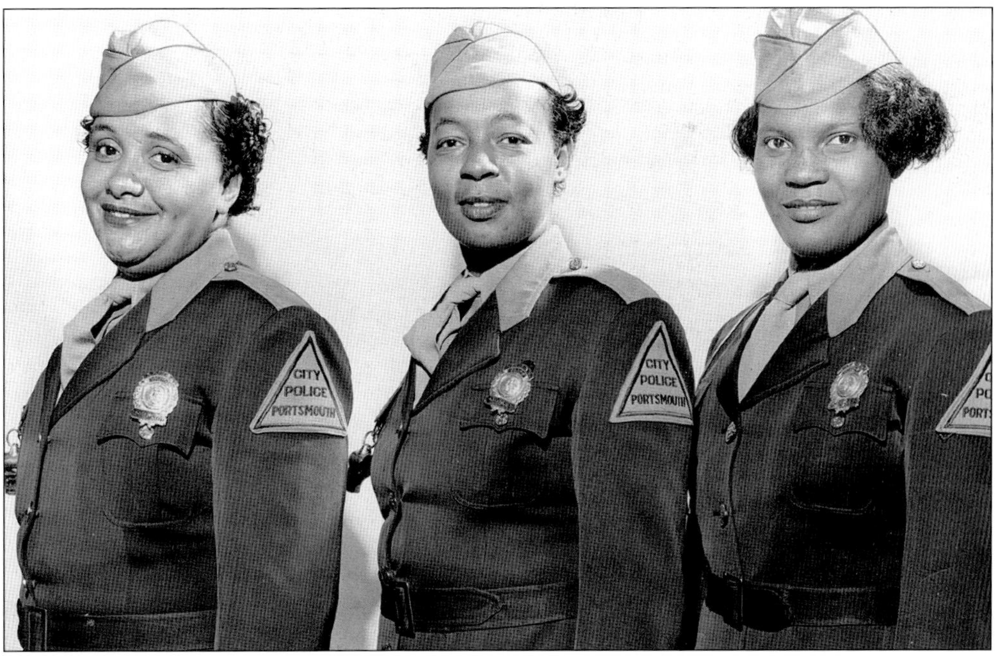

Cecelia Canady, Marion Brown Horne Walker, and Dorothy Edwards McGriff were three African-American Portsmouth city policewomen, *c.* 1960. (Courtesy Lee Rodgers Collection, Portsmouth Public Library.)

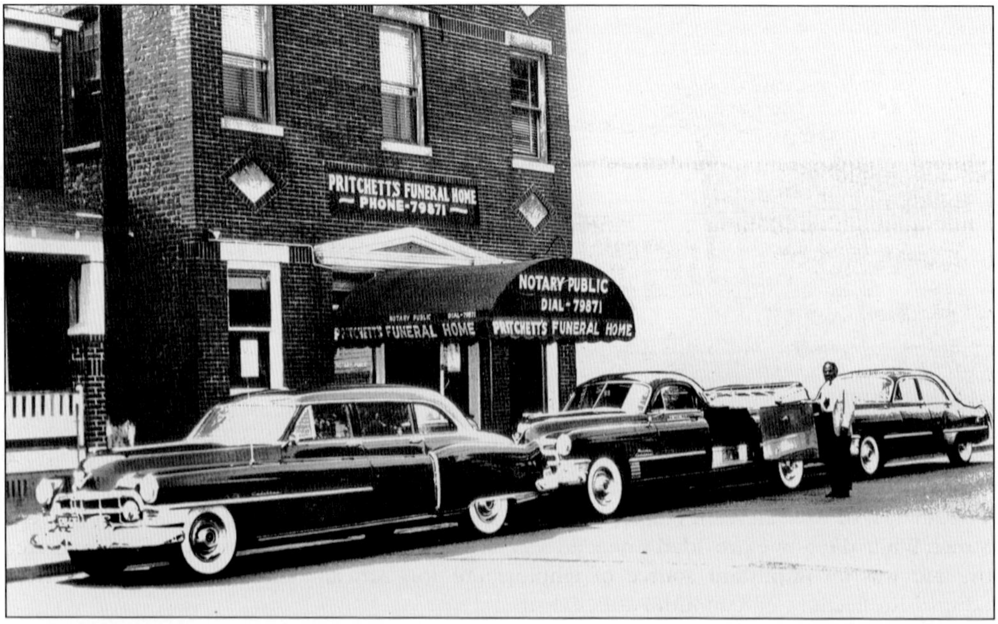

Pritchett's Funeral Home, *c.* 1949, was located in the 800 block of London Street. Like many businesses in the black community, this funeral home had a multi-purpose function. Part of the first floor was Grogan Hall, which sponsored dances. Other entertainment was on the second and third floors. The Hall family home was located next door. William Grogan, a prominent mortician, had formerly owned the funeral home. This was the reason the first floor was known as Grogan Hall. (Courtesy Portsmouth Public Library.)

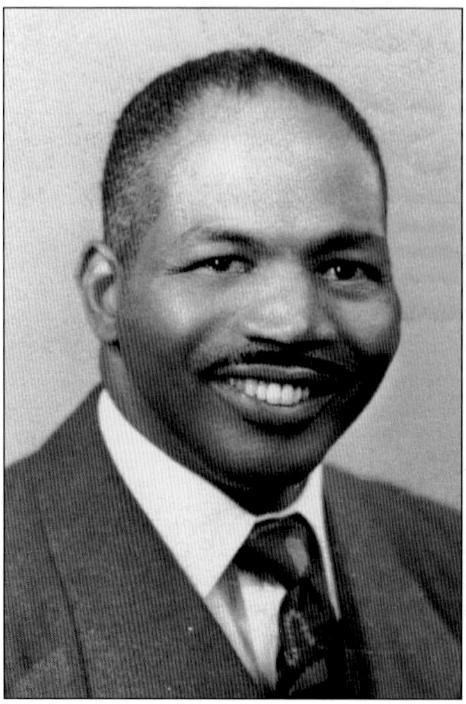

Walter Pritchett, undertaker and owner of Pritchett's Funeral Home, is pictured *c.* 1950. (Courtesy Lee Rodgers Collection, Portsmouth Public Library.)

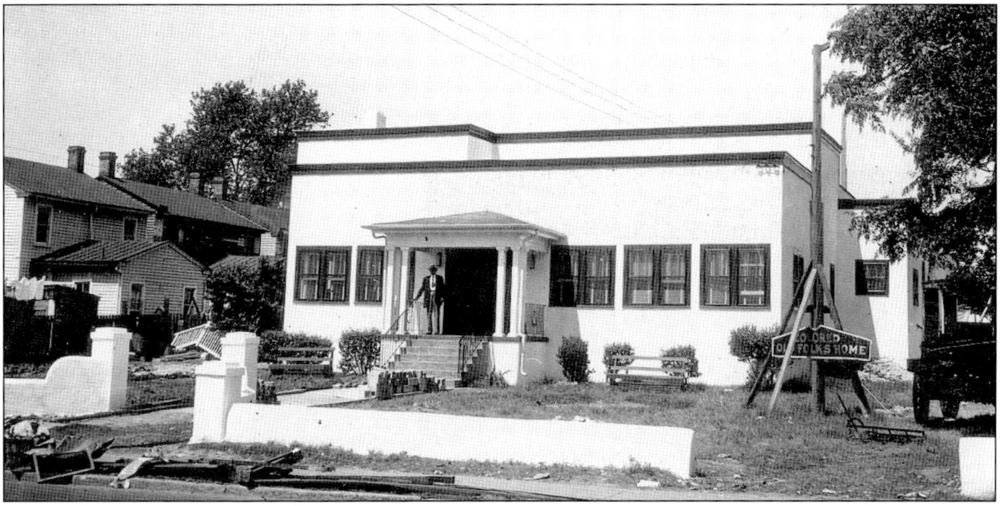

William T. Hall Convalescent Home, formerly called the "Old Folks Home," is shown on Green Street. While the home provided a needed service to the community, it was owned and operated by, and was an important source of employment for, African Americans. (Courtesy Bertha Edwards Collection, Portsmouth Public Library.)

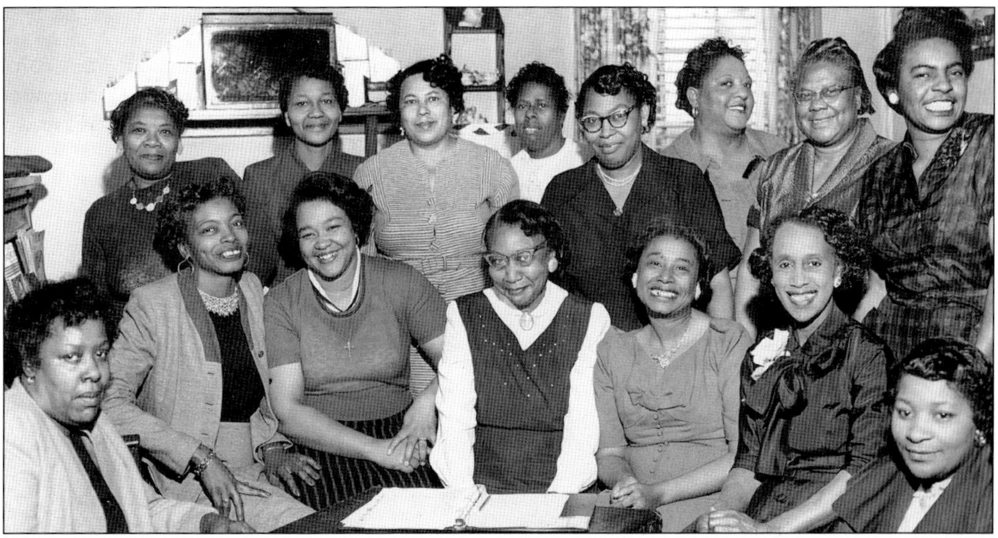

According to an article that appeared in the "Colored Notes" column of the *Norfolk Ledger-Dispatch* and the *Portsmouth Star* newspapers on March 14, 1957, the Portsmouth Registered Beauticians' Association made preparations to play hostess to the Virginia State Beauticians Association's Seventh Trade Show and Annual Convention. This event was held at the Chestnut Street Branch YMCA from April 28 to May 1. Members of the local association, pictured left to right, are the following: (front row) Mrs. Mae Tazzell; Mrs. Louise Dillard; Mrs. Mary Buffalo, assistant treasurer; Mrs. Mabel D. Jackson, treasurer; Mrs. Mable S. Jackson, vice president; Mrs. Otelia Griffin, president; and Mrs. Mary Johnson; (back row) Mrs. Katie C. Perry, chaplain; Mrs. Rebecca Brown; Mrs. Mamie P. Stalling; Mrs. Helen Davis; Mrs. Etta Roberts; Mrs. Arnetta Champlin; Mrs. Mamie V. Dixon; and Miss Margie Steadman. Not present for the photo were Mrs. Annie Frink, secretary, and Mrs. Blanche Jackson, reporter. (Courtesy Lee Rodgers Collection, Portsmouth Public Library.)

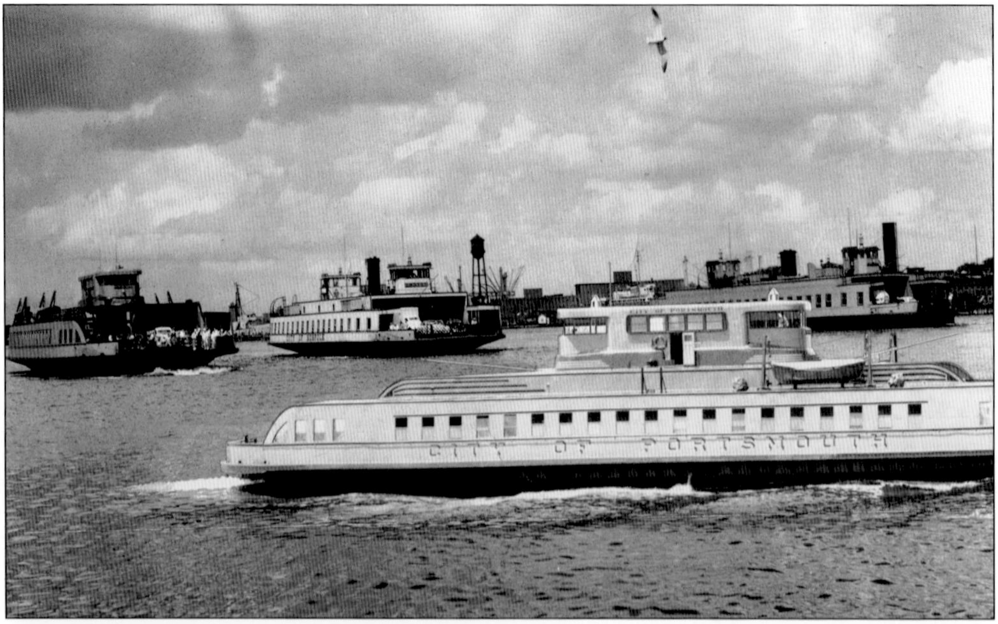

Portsmouth Ferry Service transported passengers between Portsmouth and Norfolk. Many of the people traveling on this ferry lived in Portsmouth and worked in Norfolk. (Courtesy Bertha Edwards Collection, Portsmouth Public Library.)

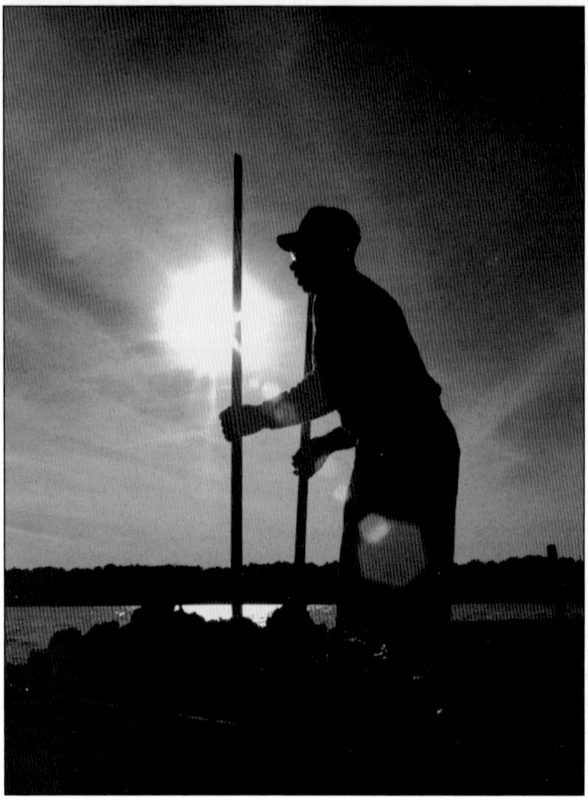

This photograph, taken of Francis Merrill who works as a tonger, illustrates how watermen traditionally gathered oysters in local waters. This age–old practice of harvesting oysters in Hampton Roads was an occupation often dominated by African-American men for centuries. Many still harvest oysters in this manner. (Courtesy Portsmouth Public Library.)

Four

Organizing a Community through Neighborhoods

For most of the 19th century, what is today considered "Old Town" Portsmouth represented not simply a neighborhood but the total extent of the city. Slaveholders in the city tended to have their slaves live on their owner's premises, unlike Norfolk, which allowed many slaves to live in the "black section" of town. This prevented the development of segregated districts prior to the Civil War—allowing free blacks to rent houses or rooms anywhere in the city. Even though blacks and whites lived in close proximity, such illegal activities as makeshift schools and the Underground Railroad flourished.

Emanuel Baptist Church was reportedly the focal point of many activities including the education of its congregational members and participation in the Underground Railroad. Oral accounts stated that many of these escapes were organized near the Navy Yard and Emanuel M.E. Church. According to a WPA report recounting a brief history of blacks in Portsmouth written by Thelma Dunston, large tubs of water were placed outside the building where these meetings were held to inform potential runaways where they were to assemble in preparation for their escape aboard a ship docked in the Portsmouth harbor.[29]

The retreat from advances promised at the conclusion of the Civil War did not catch the black community of Portsmouth unprepared for freedom or unaware of the pressing needs of thousands of destitute freedmen who had migrated to the city since 1862. Black leaders worked to organize the community and to provide for the needs of the people. Antebellum churches and post-bellum businesses were located near the heart of the city in and along the High Street corridor. However, in the post-Reconstruction years, Portsmouth's banks, businesses, day care centers, and middle-class neighborhood would locate on the fringes of the expanding city limits.[30]

Snead's Coach Factory, located at South and Effingham Streets, was the chosen location as a church and lodge room for the Masonic and Odd Fellows Societies. It burned down on October 7, 1869. The fire originated on the first floor of the building in the Masonic Lodge, caused by the explosion of an oil lamp. Lodge officials denied this claim, stating that there had been no light used there for days. The newspaper speculated that the fire might have been intentionally set. The property was owned by Arthur Emmerson and Herman Matthews and was insured by Richmond Mutual for $3,000. On November 30, a similarly suspicious fire destroyed Zion Baptist

Church—at Green and King Streets. The church, built in 1864, had been one of the largest in the city at that time. The congregation, who had formerly worshipped in the basement of the Court Street Baptist Church, immediately commenced to rebuild the church as a brick structure.[31]

Black self-help groups in Portsmouth performed welfare and social functions through many church-affiliated organizations, providing its members with sick benefits and burial fees. Committed to self-help, the churches' benevolent and mutual aid societies served as agencies for the improvement of social and moral conditions among African Americans primarily by promoting education and encouraging members to become Bible readers. Choirs and quartets performed at benefit concerts and religious services, while churches organized sewing circles, established missions in the slums and jails, founded and supported homes for the aged and orphans, and generally contributed to the overall improvement of black living conditions in Portsmouth. Self-help institutions did not emanate just from churches. As the black middle class emerged in the post–Civil War years, so did secular organizations, especially the secret lodges and fraternal and sororal groups. The Independent Sons of Liberty was one of the earliest such groups to arise in Portsmouth. Organized in 1865 by 25 men, this group, like many that emerged at this time throughout the nation, offered insurance against sickness and death, aided widows and orphans of deceased members, and provided opportunities for social intercourse. This kind of community spirit remained the bedrock of the African–American community, especially as segregation and exclusion continued to be white society's policies as America entered the 20th century.

Concurrent with the emergence of self-help groups were others with social orientations. The Silver Thrift and Charity League Club, a benevolent Portsmouth group, highlighted the changes marked by the emergence of Portsmouth's black middle class. Initially the Silver Thrift held ritualistic meetings. Many of the women members, however, were anxious to have news of their meetings publicized in the newspaper in their quest to imitate high society. In an attempt to mimic the upper classes, black and white middle class societies publicized formal entertainment and meetings held in well-furnished homes of members, which substituted for their organizations' secret rituals. This reflected the emergence of professionals within Portsmouth's middle class African Americans. Black attorneys, such as William M. Reid, and physicians, such as William Troy and J.J. France, were part of this small but growing black leadership. These blacks became educated, worked hard, accumulated money, and started businesses; there was an effort among what E. Franklin Frazier called the "black bourgeoisie" to create a mirrored society in their effort to imitate white society.[32]

The first black benevolent society of the post–Civil War era was the Independent Sons of Liberty, founded with 25 men. John W. Barnes, nationally known as the "Father of Fraternal Orders" started the Arabia Temple Oasis in 1904. James Choate founded the Buffaloes, Sons of Portsmouth, Sons of Virginia and Reindeers. Other groups included the Beacon Light-Lodge of Elks #34, Arabia Temple—Shriners, Masonic Order, and the Knights of Pythias.[33]

Efforts to combine financial resources in the 1870s and 1880s were accompanied by a notable rise, albeit temporary, in black property ownership and a middle class. The gain in financial prosperity saw also an increase in skilled, semi-professional, and professional occupations. Ironically, the greatest single contributing factor to the development of these black communities was the infusion of immigrant former runaway slaves and free blacks, and the emancipation of independent urban slaves in the community. In the years following emancipation, African Americans demonstrated a consistent desire to create their own world free of discrimination, prejudice, and injustice. One of those avenues chosen was the creation of a middle class neighborhood with many of the same amenities available in the white community but without the harassments and prejudice. Beginning in the late 19th century, Portsmouth would see the formation of four major communities that would provide its upwardly mobile middle classes with modern living facilities and an accompanying business community. Lincolnsville was Portsmouth's first middle class African-American community. Truxtun would follow in the 1920s, Cavalier Manor in the 1950s, and Crystal Lake Estates would be the most recent, developing as an upper middle class neighborhood in the 1980s.

Lincolnsville was the first community set aside for blacks in 1890 in an area that would later be annexed to Portsmouth. It would be the forerunner to Truxtun, a federally funded black community for the Norfolk Naval Shipyard workers. The community had its roots with the Hatton and Neimeyer families whose former plantation lands became part of the city (in 1890.) The community was about 30 acres in size and ran north of North Street; west of Washington Street, Green Street and the Gas House; south of Emmett Street; and east of Fort Lane and Cedar Grove Cemetery. The history of the name "Lincolnsville" has been, over the years, debated endlessly by local residents. However, the explanation that it was named in honor of President Abraham Lincoln has the most historical validity. Although Lincolnsville was primarily a residential community, there were a number of key black-owned businesses and organizations that provided for the commercial and social needs of its inhabitants Locals and immigrants were the mainstay of the Lincolnsville community, especially those who were employed at the shipyard or were professionals such as teachers, lawyers, and physicians. Not surprisingly, the community was seen as very closely knit. Blacks in Lincolnsville controlled their own civil and economic affairs, organizing to serve the needs of the citizens. Early in its history, Sam David and Henry Wilkins got the mail for Lincolnsville's black families and distributed it on Sundays at Emanuel AME Church. Moreover, blacks served in official capacities: Tom Davis served as the magistrate and John Riddick worked as the constable. The community formed lodges and social clubs, building three halls. Moreover, these halls—Love and Charity, Norcom, and Hodgson—were multipurpose facilities with one hall's second floor used as a skating ring. All monies collected for the use of these facilities were used for building maintenance. Quite naturally churches played a major role in the community. Emanuel AME, Zion Baptist, Ebenezer Baptist, Mount Hermon Temple, and Grove Baptist Churches drew Lincolnsville residents as members. However, when an economic downturn occurred, and they were frequent in Hampton Roads until the 1950s, the black community was the first and hardest hit. Lincolnsville was no exception. In the late 1950s, Portsmouth's city council chose the community as its first urban renewal project. Residents were prohibited from improving their residences. Instead, the city chose to level this community that functioned as a city within a city with its own professional, trade, and working classes.[34]

Until the late 19th century, blacks tended to be renters instead of landowners in much of Portsmouth—with the exception of the Lincolnsville section. David Owens, for example, owned a large tract across from Emanuel AME Church. That property would later be divided and purchased by several families, including the Holley family.[35]

The increase in professionals in early 20th century American society also was the impetus for the birth of private and public service–oriented organizations. In part, technology demanded a more educated population, requiring a rudimentary schooling. School attendance became mandatory, and public services such as hospitals, orphanages, libraries, and recreational facilities were established. However, segregation and discrimination resulted in African Americans being excluded from access to these facilities. This was especially hard hitting in the provision of health care. Discrimination against or exclusion of black patients and physicians was so widespread that major cities throughout the state established private hospitals to care for the underserved black population. For Portsmouth's African–American residents, the closest health care facility was Norfolk Community Hospital.[36]

The First World War, which increased the availability of jobs in these and supporting industries, created a sudden economic boom for the region, energizing more industry and immigration. With a lack of preparation for this tremendous population increase, the federal government stepped in with a progressive-minded idea, funding the first self-sustaining housing communities in Portsmouth and Newport News.

Truxtun was America's first community built by the United States Government exclusively for African Americans. Created in 1919 by the United States Housing Corporation (USHC), a government agency, it was constructed as a result of the Navy's mobilization effort in WWI. Tasked with building homes for war workers in critical industrial areas, the USHC built the community of Truxtun to provide housing for black workers at Norfolk Naval Shipyard. A total of 250 homes were created for these workers with many still remaining—it is now recognized as a historic district.

The Truxtun community provided relief for black workers in a Portsmouth community that had little housing for blacks and their families and was plagued by unscrupulous, rent-profiteering landlords. The USHC constructed houses, a school, and a town center somewhat comparable to those found in many working-class towns throughout the United States. The original design of the town included a school, a YMCA, building, stores, a movie theater, and a church. But unlike the situation in similar white communities, cost-saving procedures were used in Truxtun, including substandard building materials and no hot water. In addition, funding to provide the town with a YMCA or a movie theater was lacking. Despite these drawbacks, Truxtun was self-sufficient and boasted a town manager, an elementary school, social organizations, and democratic participation by its citizens. Moreover, Fred McCracken had the distinction of being the only black town manager in the U.S. He enjoyed this title from the time of Truxtun's inception to 1921 when Truxtun and Cradock were combined and both communities fell under the supervision of Cradock's town manager. McCracken was designated by the USHC to directly supervise the sale of houses in Truxtun. He was responsible for collecting rent and providing general guidance for the town. Resident Jerry Hinton said, "when I first come there, Truxtun was a, just a forest . . . a beautiful place. And the sidewalk would come right to you and right back close up to your door . . . Truxtun, wan't in Portsmouth then. Twas a government reservation, and we had to provide our own garbage and everything ourself. We had one black policeman and the rest were white. On Deep Creek Boulevard, we had stores right dere . . . They had grocery stores, and clothing stores, and all like that. They're all torn down now, sometime before the Second World War."

Hinton, born in 1897 in Raleigh, North Carolina, moved to Truxtun shortly after arriving in Portsmouth to work as a general helper at the shipyard. Although he would keep this position until retiring, he worked in skilled positions such as mechanic and fork lift operator. Hinton remarked about how Truxtun changed over the years. When he first moved in, the town did not have a church. Instead, residents met in the mess hall until an edifice was constructed and became Mount Carmel Baptist Church. It also did not have a school until Truxtun Elementary School was built. However, the community united in numerous ways including the Truxtun baseball team that played games with local teams in the 1920s and 1930s.[37]

Ora Churchill, a former teacher in the Portsmouth Public Schools, recounted that, "At the outbreak of WWI, the Norfolk Navy, Naval Shipyard, in Portsmouth, Virginia, was in need for housing for the workers. They, in turn, began to make plans to build homes for blacks, and homes for whites. They homes for the whites were built in Cradock, south of the Naval Shipyard, and the homes for the blacks were built, north of the Naval Shipyard, and that community is called Truxtun. It received its name from uh, war hero, an unsung war hero, by the name of Truxtun, Admiral Truxtun, and they held onto this name. They thought it was a good name. Now Truxtun began to thrive after uh, the persons, the residents moved in, and they began to uh, feel at home being the first real home that they had had. New home. And uh, they began to organize among themselves, and they organized to the extent they had police, four policemen, uh, a town house, they called, they had a manager, city manager, the town manager, they called himself, and they had uh, uh secretaries and what-not to work in this office, they, they chose in the area...The people in Truxtun became very close-knit, and they became almost "his brother's keeper." They could leave home and leave the doors open, even go downtown, and no one would bother, uh, the neighbors looked out for each other."[38]

Many organizations helped African Americans adjust to city life. Prominent among them were religious organizations such as the church, the YMCA and YWCA, and various settlement houses scattered throughout the nation. The YMCA was the center of intellectual and social life in various cities in America. It was a place where lectures were given, plays and music were performed, and classes in liberal arts and industrial skills were offered. In 1888, Norfolk's blacks established the oldest continuously operating all-black YMCA in the United States. The Hunton

YMCA, under the leadership of the Reverend William G. Hunton, offered religious study, literary and debating societies, educational classes, recreational programs, and athletics. Not until 1946 would Portsmouth's African Americans population, establish a YMCA, located on Chestnut Street near I.C. Norcom High School.[39]

Portsmouth's black women also launched several self-help organizations in the aftermath of the Civil War. These clubs provided orphanages, retirement homes, nursery schools, kindergartens, educational assistance and day care centers to fulfill the social needs of the community. The most noted was the Miller Day Care Nursery, established by Ida Barbour and 20 other women in 1911. After initially taking in five orphans, Barbour and 20 other women—known as the Women's League—established the Miller Day Nursery and Home for them and other neighborhood children. This daycare facility became especially important to the Norfolk Naval Shipyard workers during the First and Second World Wars. The Miller Day Nursery, the area's first daycare to take in infants, continues today.[40]

Libraries, recreational and daycare centers were also exclusively the result of effort by black individuals are groups. For example, the New Deal-funded Library for African Americans (1937-1941) was the outgrowth of the Portsmouth Library Association. The Reverend M.B. Birchette, Rector of St. James Episcopal Church, whose core members created this library committee were part of the church's Mission Study Group of Monumental Methodist Episcopal Church. Other leaders of the library committee included Mrs. Lillian Jones, the Reverend W.H. Willis, and Mrs. W.E. Reid. This Library existed in the Parish House at St. James Episcopal Church Library and was financed by the National Youth Administration (NYA), a New Deal agency. Mrs. Willie Mae Sanford was hired as the first librarian for the community library. Although the library served the city's black population as a reading room, it was forced to close after four years because the NYA ceased funding the operation.[41]

In 1944 Reverend Willis, after the suggestion of Reverend Birchette, requested assistance from the Portsmouth City Council for the creation of a library for its black citizens. The City promised to build and maintain a library if a proper location could be secured. Afterward, the Portsmouth Library Association, headed by Mrs. Cornelia Reid, conducted a money-raising drive that resulted in the purchase of two suitable lots for a library building at a cost of $1,800. Support for the Library was widespread with its strongest advocates coming from Portsmouth's black churches and civic organizations. On December 20, 1945, community library became Portsmouth's first public library established for African Americans. The structure, which was erected at a cost of $11,500, was located at 804 South Street. The Library opened with a collection of 3,000 books, 20 magazines, and three newspapers, and Mrs. Bertha Winborne Edwards became the first librarian. It was Mrs. Edwards who began a systematic personal collection of the history of African Americans in Portsmouth as recorded in the *Portsmouth Star's* "Colored Notes," the Norfolk *Journal and Guide*, civic and social organizations programs, church records, and other documents.[42]

The library was multi-faceted, serving the black community as a library, meeting place for various organizations and groups, a clothes distribution center for the poor, and a place where black citizens sought assistance completing employment applications and other forms. The librarian also assisted the citizenry, volunteering her time counseling other school librarians, teachers, and groups interested in utilizing services provided by a library. Also, the library educated the community with monthly newsletters and bibliographies, and served the community with educational displays and interlibrary loan system.[43]

The Old Folks Home for the Colored, founded by William T. Hall of Portsmouth was established to assist seniors in the community. On April 14, 1937 WPA worker Thelma Dunston interviewed Mary Jane Wilson, who was born *c.* 1859, at the Old Folks Home. In the interview, Miss Wilson recounted how her father worked as a teamster in the Norfolk Naval Shipyard and became one of the first African–American landowners in Portsmouth after emancipation. From her descriptions, the house he built was located in the Lincolnsville section. She also noted that her first opportunity to attend school was after the Civil War. Classes were initially held in a church until a building was constructed. That school would later be called Chestnut Street Academy.[44]

Racism and segregation continued to force Portsmouth's African Americans to rely on their own resources in an effort to build a strong, socially self-sufficient community. Segregation also forced the benevolent and self-help societies to expand and form the nucleus of African-American businesses, which included insurance companies, banks, retirement homes, unemployment insurance companies, food and clothing stores, and funeral homes. These organizations would be the mainstays that would help the city's African-American community to thrive until the 1960s. Of course, that is a story for another day.[45]

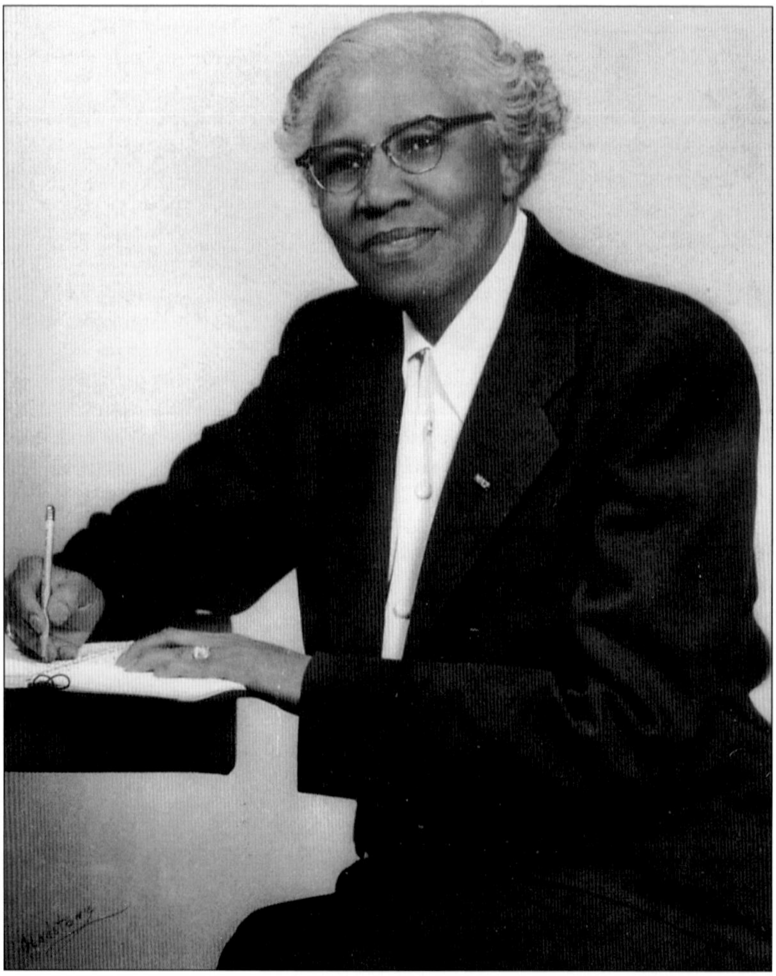

Nancy Wheeler, *c.* 1960, was a prominent funeral director and civic advocate. She was one of the few African-American women to own a business in Portsmouth and was among the first to become politically active. (Courtesy Mae Breckenridge-Haywood.)

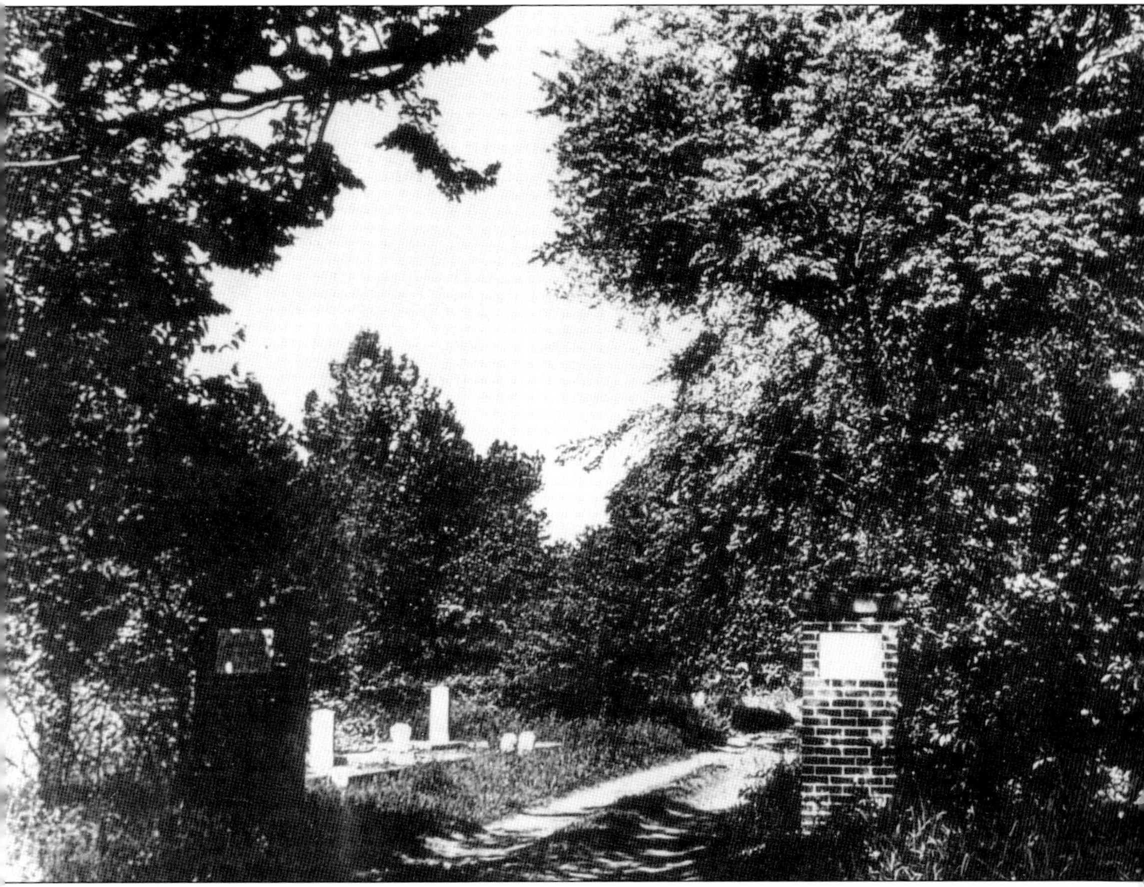

Fisher's Hill Cemetery, *c.* 1970, is the oldest African-American cemetery in Portsmouth. Mount Calvary and Mount Olive Cemeteries were listed as the black Portsmouth cemeteries in 1895 even though they were located a mile outside the city limits on Deep Creek Road. Around the turn of the century, the area was annexed and eventually came to be known as Fisher's Hill Cemetery, even though there were actually three cemeteries separated by ditches. Perhaps the reason it was called Fisher's Hill was that the Fisher Funeral Home owned many of the lots, burying the loved ones of those who used their services on purchased lots in that area. (Courtesy Lee Rodgers Collection, Portsmouth Public Library.)

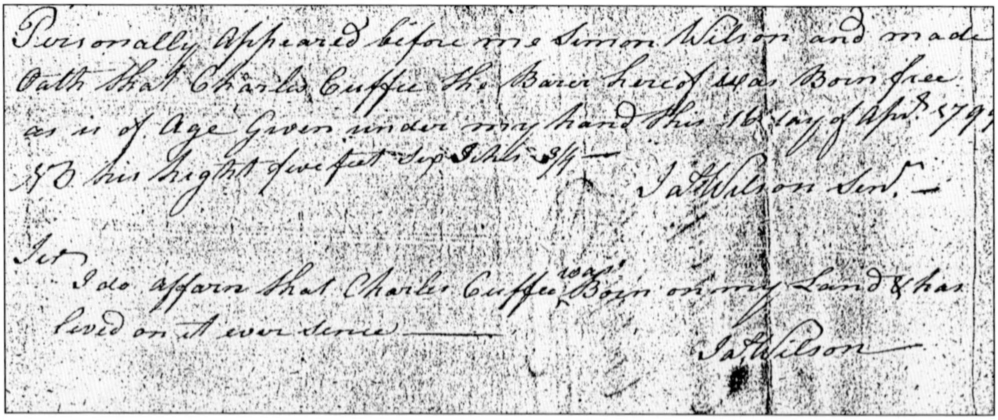
Personally Appeared before me Simon Wilson and made Oath that Charles Cuffee the Barer hereof was Born free as is of Age Given under my hand this 16 day of Apr. 1799 A D. his hieghth five feet Six Inches 3/4 — Ja. Wilson Senr.

Test
I do affirm that Charles Cuffee was Born on my Land & has lived on it ever since — Ja. Wilson

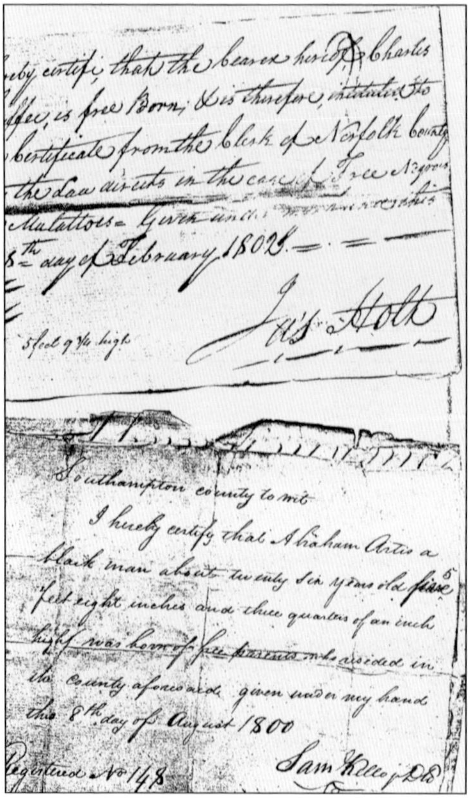
...eby certify that the bearer hereof Charles ...ffee, is free Born; & is therefore entitled to ... certificate from the Clerk of Norfolk County ... the Law directs in the case of Free Negroes ... Mulattoes — Given under ... 8th day of February 1802 —

Jas Hoth

5 feet 9 3/4 high

Southampton county to wit
I hereby certify that Abraham Artis a black man about twenty six years old five feet eight inches and three quarters of an inch high was born of free parents who resided in the County aforesaid given under my hand this 8th day of August 1800

Registered No 148 Sam Kello ...

These free papers of Charles Cuffee, which can be found in the Records Room of the Chesapeake Courthouse, are an example of the kinds of documents free blacks were, by law, expected to have on their persons at all time in Virginia. The documents read: *Personally appeared before me Simon Wilson and made oath that Charles Cuffee the bond hire of was born free as in of age given under my hand this 16th day of April 1799, A.D. his height of five feet nine inches high. James Wilson I do affirm that Charles Cuffee was born on my land and has lived on it ever since. James Wilson I do certify that the bearer here of Charles Cuffee is free born; this therefore intention to a certificate from the Clerk of Norfolk County as the law asserts in the case of Free Negroes and Mulattoes given under my hand this 28th day of February 1802. 5 feet 9 inches high. James Hoth. Southampton County to wit, I hereby certify that Abraham Artis a black man about 26 years old five feet eight inches and three quarters of an inch high was born of free parents who resided I the county aforesaid given under my hand this 8th day of August 1800. Sam Whitfield, Registered No. 148.* (Photograph Courtesy Mae Breckenridge-Haywood.)

Pension records of Joseph Herbert who served in the second Calvary USCT, Company E, from December 25, 1863, to February 12, 1866. Herbert was enlisted at Fort Monroe by Colonel Cole for a three-year term and held the rank of Private. Herbert was aged 19 and was 5' 11" tall and listed as black with black eyes and hair. He was born in Norfolk County in 1844, probably born a slave on a plantation in Berkley, and was listed as a farmer. He was mustered out in Los Brazos, Texas. After leaving the service, he homesteaded somewhere in Virginia for five years. Eventually Herbert came to Norfolk County and married Penelope Old. By 1877, he was residing in the Newtown section that was located by the gate of the Naval Shipyard—the area was later annexed into Portsmouth. Herbert died in 1902. He had seven children with Penelope. Penelope ("Penny") Herbert was listed under the "Midwives" subject heading in the 1925 Portsmouth City Directory. The listing was as follows: "Grimes Bettie L. Mrs. (318 Shell Road), Herbert, Penny (colored, 618 Edwards Street), Moseley, Hannah (colored, 1539 Clifford Street),Smith, Florence (colored, 1017 Palmer)." (Courtesy Rebecca H. Williams.)

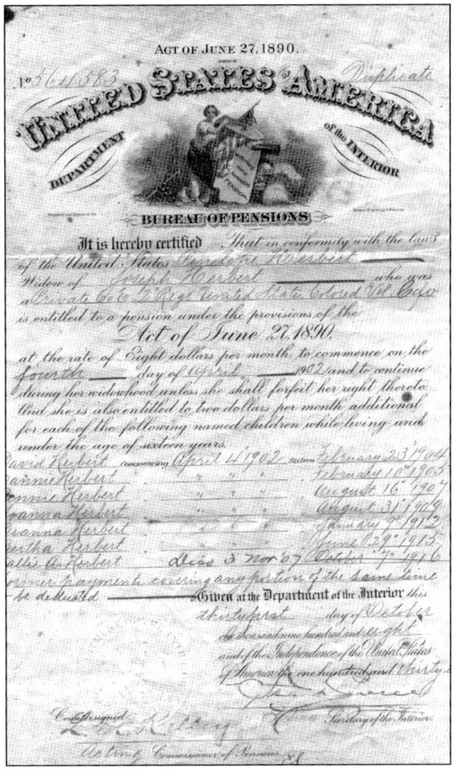
ACT OF JUNE 27, 1890.

No 564583 Duplicate

UNITED STATES OF AMERICA

DEPARTMENT OF THE INTERIOR

BUREAU OF PENSIONS

It is hereby certified That in conformity with the laws of the United States Penelope Herbert Widow of Joseph Herbert who was a Private Co E 2 Regt United State Colored Vol Cav is entitled to a pension under the provisions of the Act of June 27, 1890, at the rate of Eight dollars per month, to commence on the fourth day of April 1902 and to continue during her widowhood unless she shall forfeit her right thereto. And she is also entitled to two dollars per month additional for each of the following named children while living and under the age of sixteen years.

David Herbert	commencing April 4 1902	sixteen	February 23 1904
Fannie Herbert	" " "		February 10 1905
Annie Herbert	" " "		August 16 1907
Joanna Herbert	" " "		August 31 1909
Rianna Herbert	" " "		January 7 1912
Bertha Herbert	" " "		June 29 1913
Allie A. Herbert	Dies 3 Nov 07		October 7 1916

former payments covering any portion of the same time be deducted

Given at the Department of the Interior this thirty first day of October one thousand nine hundred and eight and of the Independence of the United States of America the one hundred and thirty

Secretary of the Interior.

Countersigned

Acting Commissioner of Pensions.

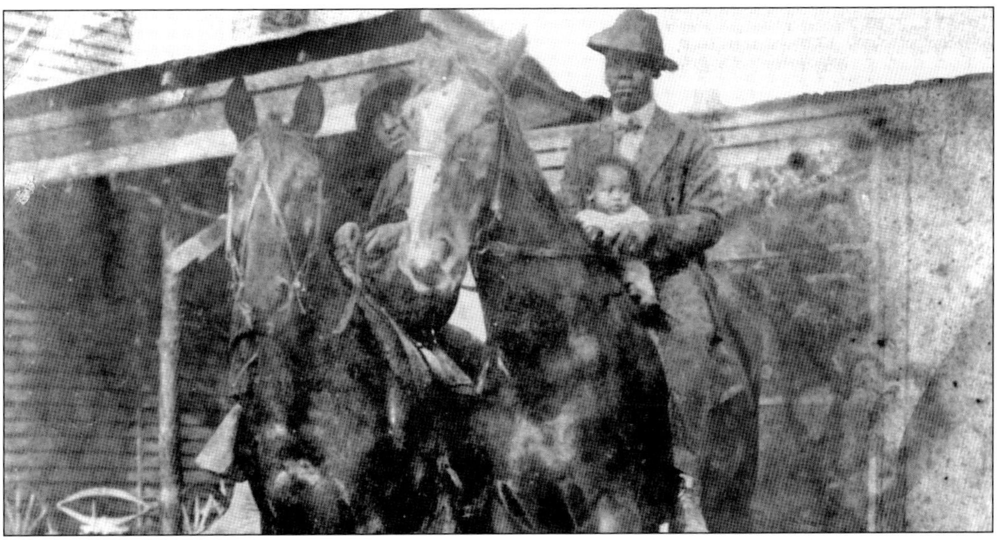

Taken in 1915 in the Newtown section of Portsmouth, this photograph depicts, from left to right, Bertha H. Lenyon, David Herbert, and John Herbert (baby). Bertha Lenyon and David Herbert, sister and brother, were the children of Joseph Herbert, who served in the 2nd USCT Calvary during the Civil War. The baby, John Herbert, is the son of David Herbert. David Herbert, who was married to Pearl Rice Herbert, was a carpenter who worked on all the black historic churches in Portsmouth and was self-employed. The Herberts lived on Edward Street (near the Portsmouth Naval Yard). (Courtesy Rebecca H. Williams.)

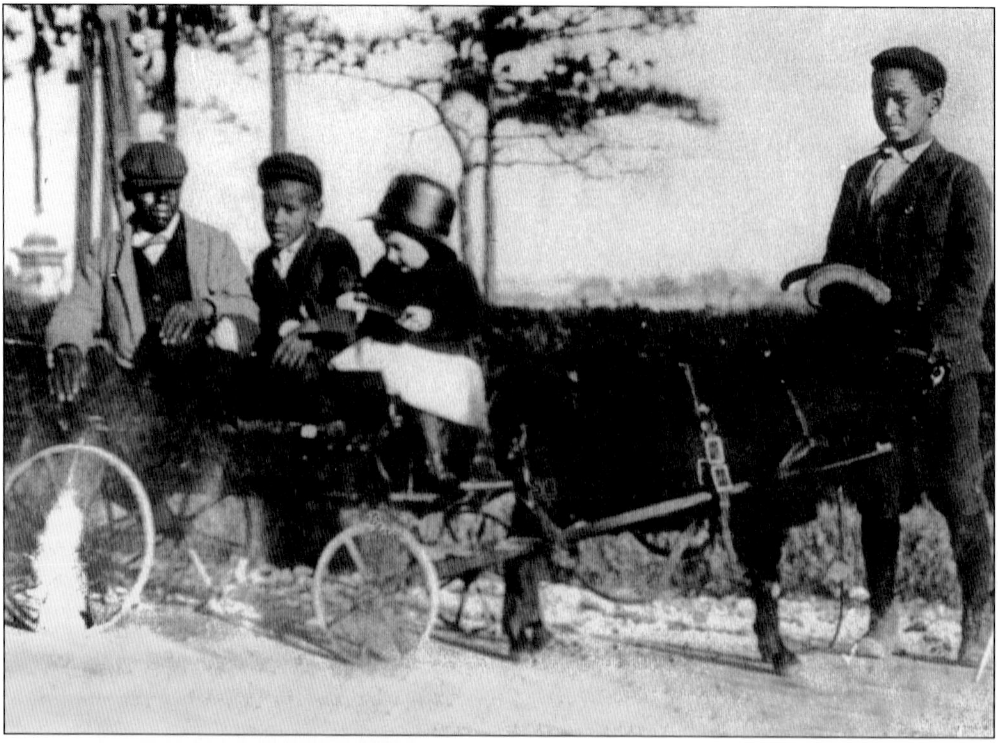

This photograph depicts local children, black and white, playing at the Portsmouth Naval Hospital's playground in Portsmouth, *c.* 1900. Most of these children were from the Lincolnsville community. (Courtesy Portsmouth Public Library.)

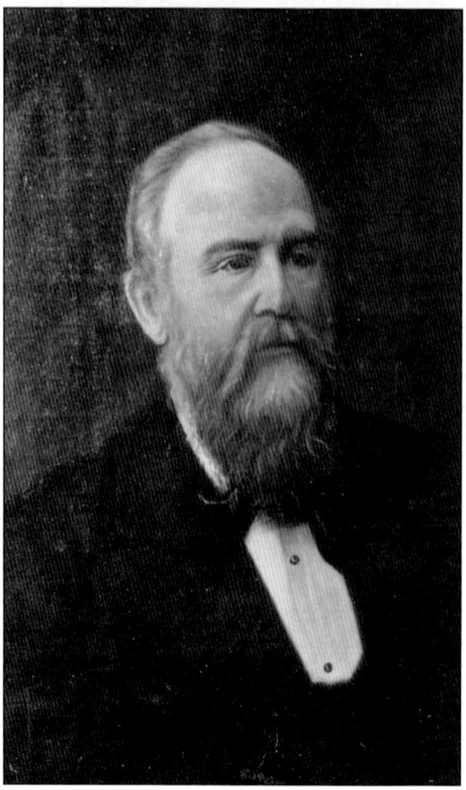

Maj. George W. Grice served as mayor of Portsmouth and was the former slave owner of Jeffrey Wilson, the celebrated newspaper writer. Grice gained some renown as the quartermaster for Gen. Robert E. Lee's army. Jeffery Wilson, author of the *Portsmouth Star's* "Colored Notes," wrote about his travels with Grice and the Confederate army during the Civil War with considerable affection. It was Grice who taught Wilson how to read and write. (Courtesy Mae Breckenridge-Haywood.)

Jeffrey T. Wilson (1843–1929), the newspaper columnist for the *Portsmouth Star,* was a writer with "true grit." Wilson was well respected in the community, and he was a devoted churchman at Emanuel AME Church, often called "Mr. Emanuel." He was married four times, outliving all four wives. He was known for his outspoken and candid writings during the 1920s for the local newspaper. Excerpts from the *Portsmouth Star*, "Colored Notes" follow:

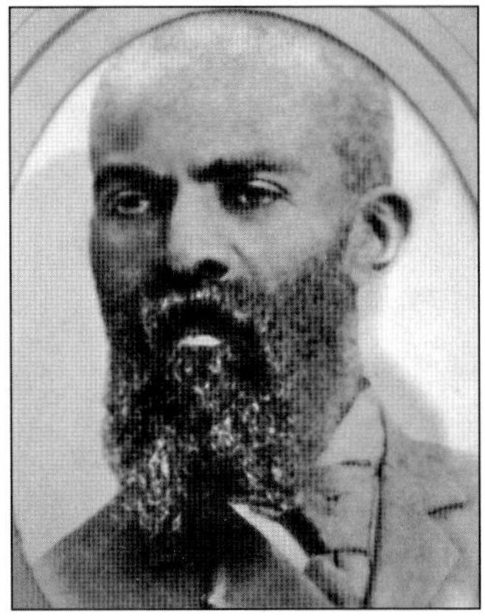

October 26, 1924. The day was when there was only one colored church in Portsmouth, and that was the old African church on Glasgow Street, pastored by the Rev. George M. Bain, grandfather of Judge K.A. Bain of the Hustings Court. The Baptists assembled in the basement of Court Street Baptist Church under the care of Rev. Thomas Hume, Court Street pastor.

October 29, 1924. The gospel ship is moored to the wharf at Immanuel AME Church, North Street and all passengers desiring a safe journey will do well to procure their tickets at once, as the time for its departure is near at hand. No later than Sunday night, at the farthest—get on board little children.

November 4, 1924. In the old time the "Wood Dock" was at the east end of County Street just a little south of the jail and police station. The lighters would bring cord wood for all and sell it by the cord and 1-4 cord. The draymen would haul it and a wood sawyer{?} would follow it and it, and we kids would put it away. Capt. Luke got a fee for measuring it. He died in 1870. Many of us remember when the county and city jails stood at the corner of High and Washington Streets—and that relic of barbarism—the whipping post stood in the yard of the jail... The jail is still held at another location for bootleggers, etc, yea wife beaters. The whipping post ought to be kept for them anyhow.

November 9, 1924. Fifty years ago, John F. Wilson was shot and seriously wounded at the intersection of High and Middle Streets, from which he died. He was a colored policeman, Portsmouth's first.

November 11, 1924. In 1855, the summer of that year a terrible epidemic of yellow fever visited this city and Norfolk. Scores of people—colored and white—died, and so fast they had to bury them in trenches. Coffins could not be supplied by the local undertakers. Coffins had to be shipped here via Baltimore and we have seen them piled up like cordwood. Doctors were brought here from Charleston, South Carolina., and New Orleans, where fever had been before, and from other southern cities, and from other southern cities. People would shut themselves in their homes; be seized with the fever and one could not help the other or get medical attendance. They would die and it would be probably weeks before it was generally known to the public. The doctors were overworked. The preachers, some of them, went away. One who stood to his post and died a martyr. We refer to Rev. Frances Devlin, the Sainted Catholic priest. "Uncle Bob Butt," the old sexton, worked day and night burying the dead.

November 22, 1924. The UGRR before and during the Civil War was a myth. The white folks adopted it to ease their minds or to satisfy themselves how Negroes got away from slavery to freedom and they couldn't catch on to it. The "UGRR" was not real. Coastwise vessels, white peoples, boats, etc. were the "R.R." Their kitchens, barns, cellars and sometimes their very homes, were the hiding places of fugitive slaves. The hired houses of many slaves were hiding places also. We know of a house on County Street between Middle and Crawford Streets, where fugitives were hidden for over a year and made good their escape to Boston, New Bedford and other free cities.

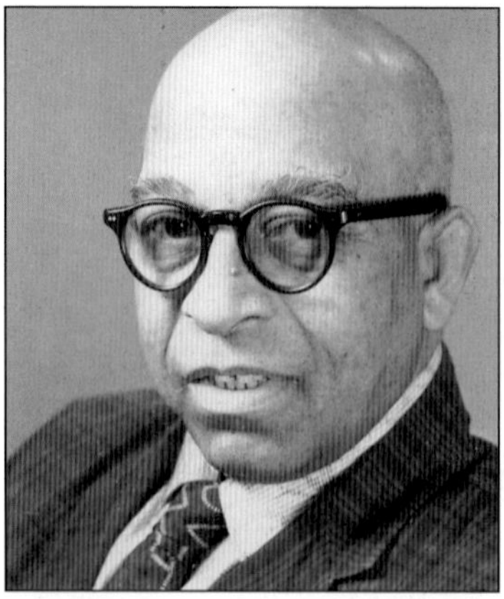

Lee F. Rodgers (1899–1969) was the newspaper columnist who wrote the articles, "Colored Notes" after the death of Jeffrey Wilson. Writing at different times, the two men had very different styles. Lee F. Rodgers was in the first class of graduates from the High Street School (1915), the forerunner of I.C. Norcom High School. Rodgers was the only black member of the *Portsmouth Star* in the 1930s. Here are some excerpts from the articles that Lee F. Rodgers wrote in the *Portsmouth Star,* "Colored Notes."(Courtesy Bertha Edwards Collection, Portsmouth Public Library.)

Plan, Memorial Exercises, April 27, 1939. Preparations are underway for holding annual Memorial Day exercises here, and meetings of the Portsmouth Memorial Association are being held each Saturday at 2 p.m. in the annex of the Ebenezer Baptist Church. The association is not restricted to in membership, it was pointed out, but is organized to include all interested citizens, including representatives from churches, fraternal orders, the various clubs and all other groups here. Moral support, financial support and participation in the Memorial Day events are sought. Rev. A.R. Walker is president of the association, and Lee F. Rodgers is secretary.

Brighton School Operetta, June 1, 1939. Pupils of the Brighton school will appear in the operetta, "The Brownie Land,." Friday night in the Truxton school auditorium under the direction of their teachers. There will be choruses of wood nymphs, butterflies, Gypsy girls, Brownies, and wee-wees. Prof. W.H. Willis is principal of the school

Many Books are Added to Colored Community Library, February 23, 1941. Books that have received a great deal of publicity through the years have been recently added to the Portsmouth Colored Community Library. The Library is the only reading and lending institution of its kind for colored citizens in the city. The library is located on the second floor in St. James Parish House on Bart Street, just in the rear of St. James Episcopal Church. The room has proven to be a rendezvous for students and others in quest of particular books or purposes of research and just for the sheer love of reading any good book.

City well represented Among Colored Officers in the U. S. Army, March 1, 1942. Portsmouth can boast of a number of colored commissioned and non-commissioned officers in the U. S. Army. These officers are stationed in camps scattered over the country, and war time regulations prevent disclosure of the whereabouts of these men and the outfits to which they belong. Portsmouth can boast of a colored nurse who holds a commission, Lieut. Kathryn Y. Bough whose sisters reside on Effingham Street. Portsmouth has one of the highest-ranking colored chaplains in the army, Rev. A. Alfred Watts who is a captain in the Chaplain's Corp. He is the son of Mrs. Annie Watts of Mount Hermon and brother of Mrs. Annie McCoy of Glasgow Street. Sergeant Emmerson Smith is a Portsmouth boy, and son of Mr. and Mrs. Frank Smith of Palmer Street. Sergeant William Walker of Portsmouth is with the Medical Department.

Outing to Ocean Breeze Beach, July 9, 1948. This will be conducted Monday, July 12, by the Portsmouth Chapter of the Elizabeth City State Teachers College Alumni Association, it was announced by the secretary, Mrs. R.T. Bridgers. Buses will leave High Street and Mt. Vernon Avenue at 10 am and from Deep Creek Boulevard and Gosport Road at 10:15. Mrs. Maude Howell is president of the alumni chapter.

Opening the way to Fair Grounds, November 5, 1958. Official ribbon-cutting ceremonies were held Friday afternoon, October 31, at Sunset Lake Park near Deep Creek, opening the road to the grounds of the Hampton Roads Fair. The fair will extend to Sunday, November 9, offering many features, including entertainment and exhibits.

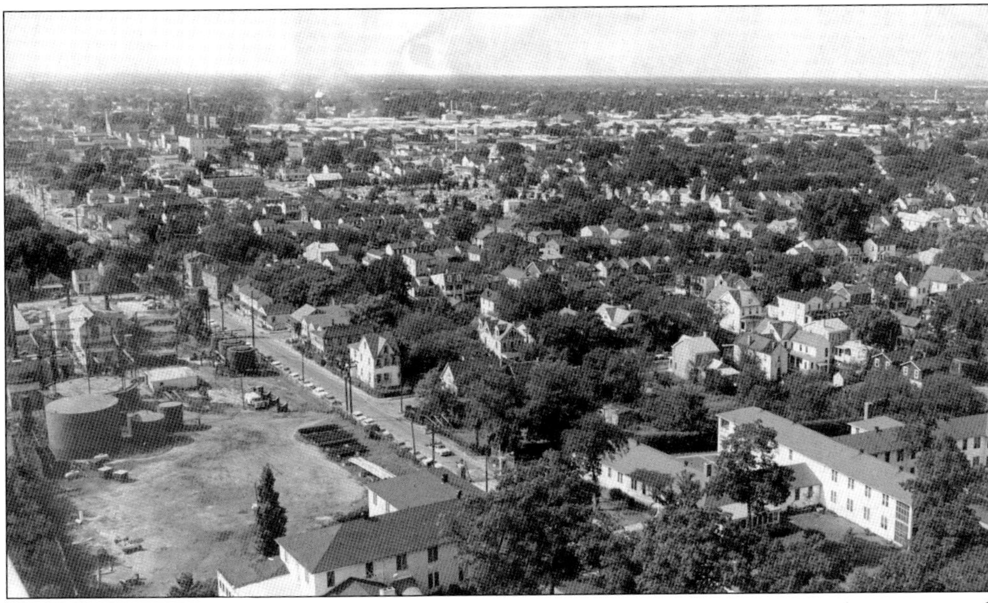

This is a photograph of the Lincolnsville community at the Green Street and the Portsmouth Naval Hospital entrance before the gas works was torn down in 1955. The destruction of the once-thriving middle class community, named in honor of President Abraham Lincoln, was described as "a purely financial venture" "under the guise of slum clearance." (Courtesy Portsmouth Public Library.)

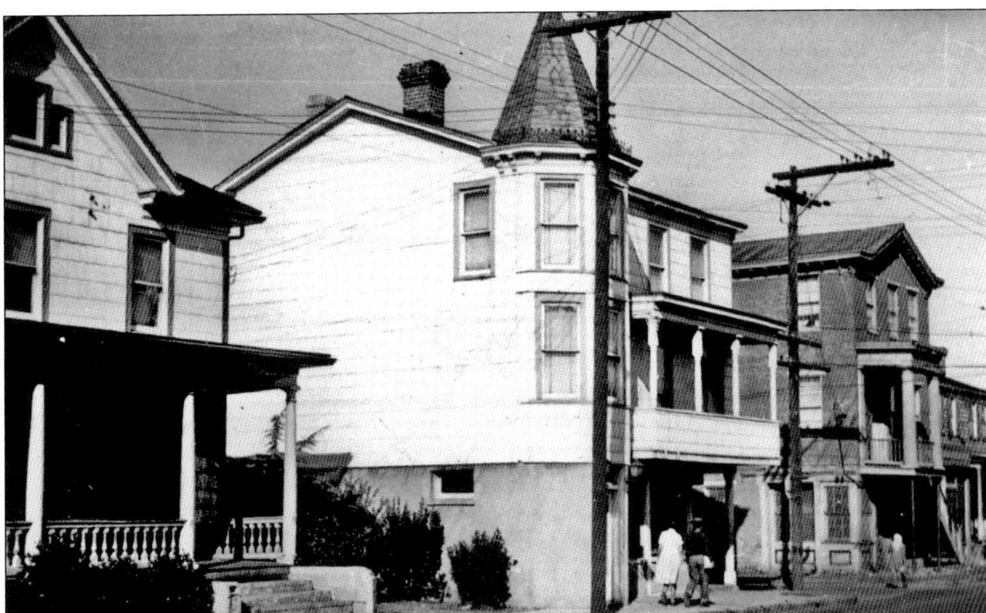

This view shows the west side of Green Street, looking north in the Lincolnsville section in October 1948. The house to the far left belonged to Hiram Simmons, Portsmouth's favorite church hymn composer. To the right of the Simmons house was the Omicron Hotel owned by Bill Myers. Next to the Omicron Hotel was a home belonging to the Lassiters—Emma Jane, Antionette, Margaret, and Pearl. (Courtesy Olde Towne Collection, Portsmouth Public Library.)

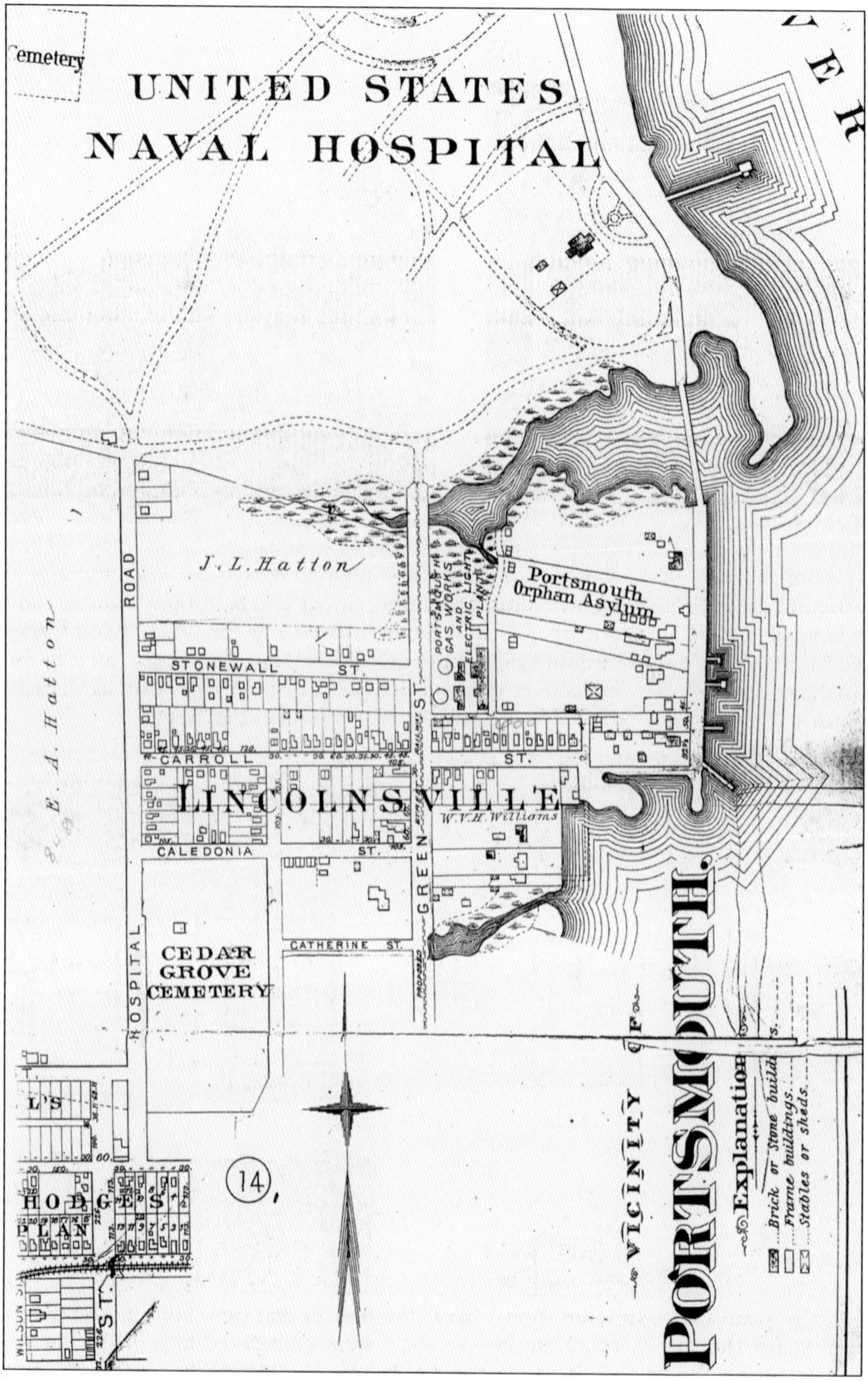

The boundaries of Lincolnsville, and all the surrounding areas, can be clearly seen in this Portsmouth map. Residents, churches, and the Lincolnsville Home Owners League aimed at civic improvement and fought to prevent the destruction of the community, charging that city officials and the housing authority were in collusion. (Courtesy Portsmouth Public Library.)

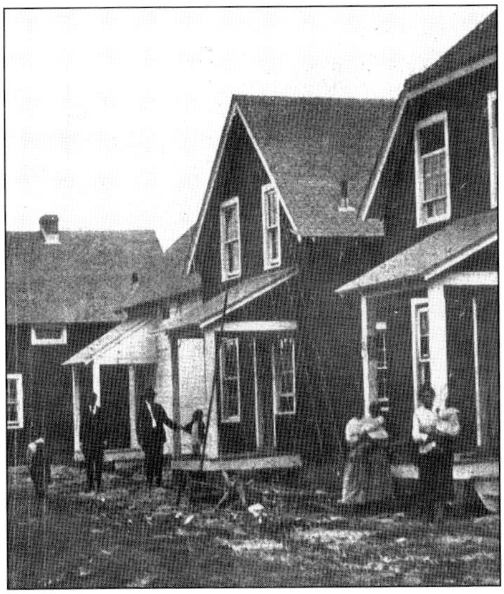

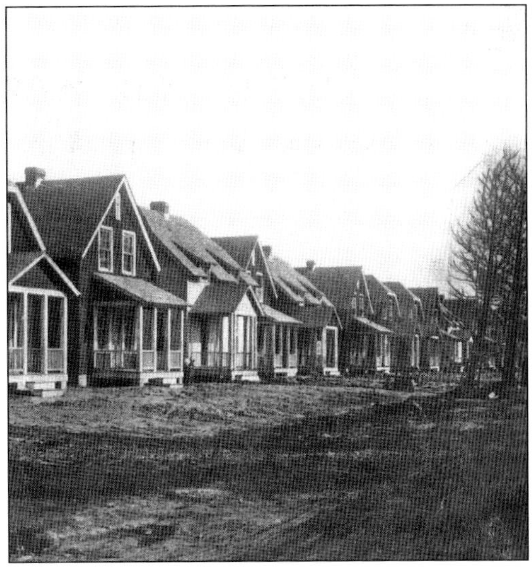

(left) Houses in the town of Truxtun are shown here, *c*. 1920. Those like the one pictured included a living room, kitchen, and a dining room on the first floor, and two bedrooms and a bathroom on the second floor. Each house was outfitted with electricity and bathroom fixtures. (Courtesy Bertha Edwards Collection, Portsmouth Public Library.) *(right)* At the time, Truxtun was often admired as one of the most beautiful black neighborhoods in Hampton Roads. After moving in, many of the residents took pride in their neighborhood by planting extravagant gardens around their houses. (Courtesy Bertha Edwards Collection, Portsmouth Public Library.)

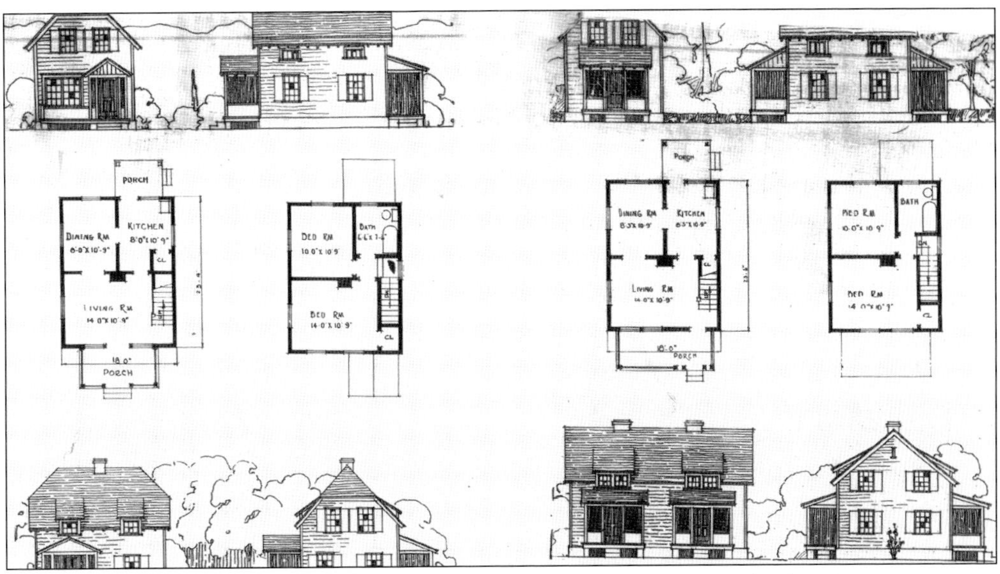

House design plans of Truxtun are shown here. The houses that were built in Truxtun as part of United States Housing Corporation Project 150C were considered high-quality for African-American housing at the time. Each was designed to fit a family of five fairly comfortably. Architect Rossel Edward Mitchell, who designed the town of Truxtun for the United States Housing Corporation, also realized these houses were of superior quality relative to most black housing in this time period and marked a "significant advance in homes for colored workers." (Courtesy Bertha Edwards Collection, Portsmouth Public Library.)

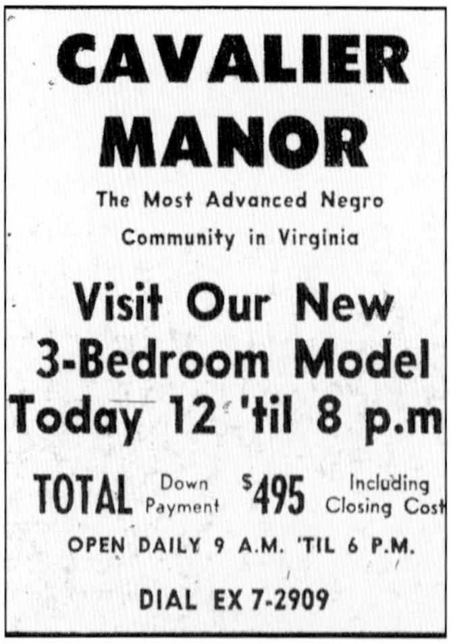

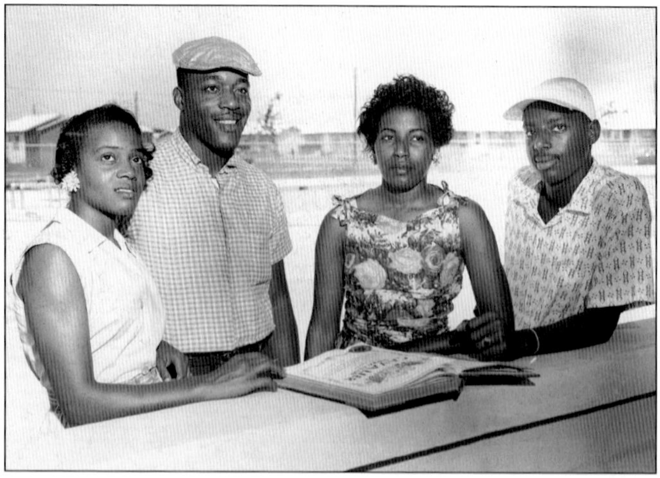

(left) An advertisement in the *Portsmouth Star* of Cavalier Manor shows that these two-to-four bedroom homes were priced from $7,600 to $10,300 in the late 1950s. (Courtesy Portsmouth Public Library.) *(right)* Cavalier Manor Swim Club Committee, *c.* 1960, from left to right are Mr. and Mrs. Vernon (Marlene) Randall, Mrs. Edna Corbett, and Willis Gay. (Lee Rodgers Collection, Courtesy Portsmouth Public Library.)

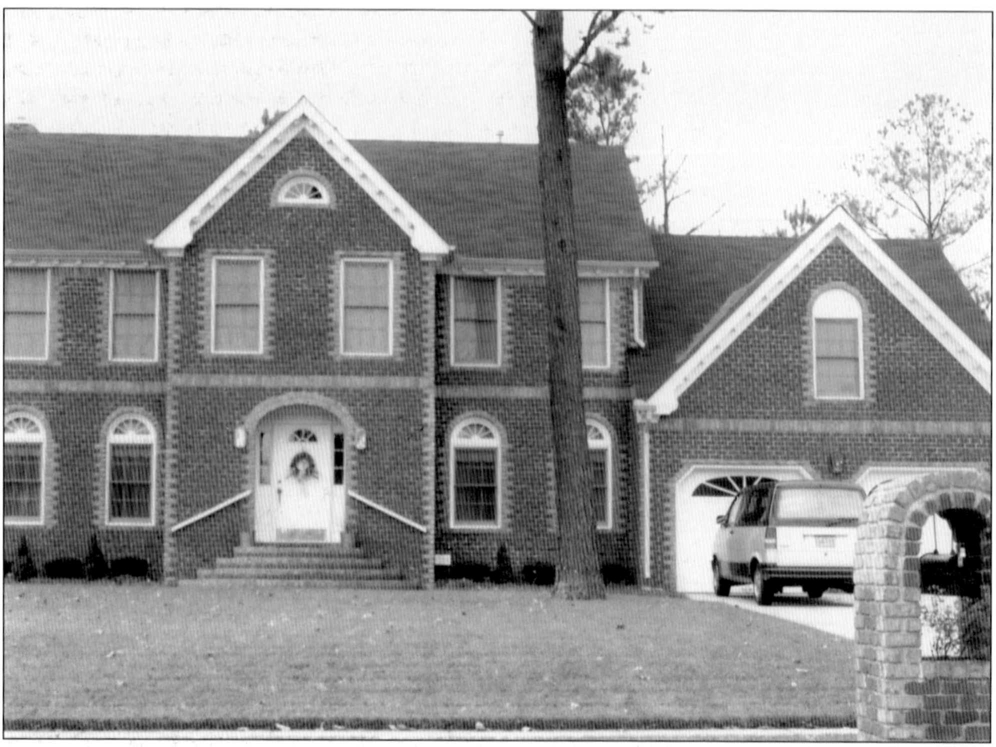

This is a typical home in Crystal Lake Estates, an upper-middle class, predominantly African-American neighborhood in Portsmouth. (Courtesy Mae Breckenridge-Haywood.)

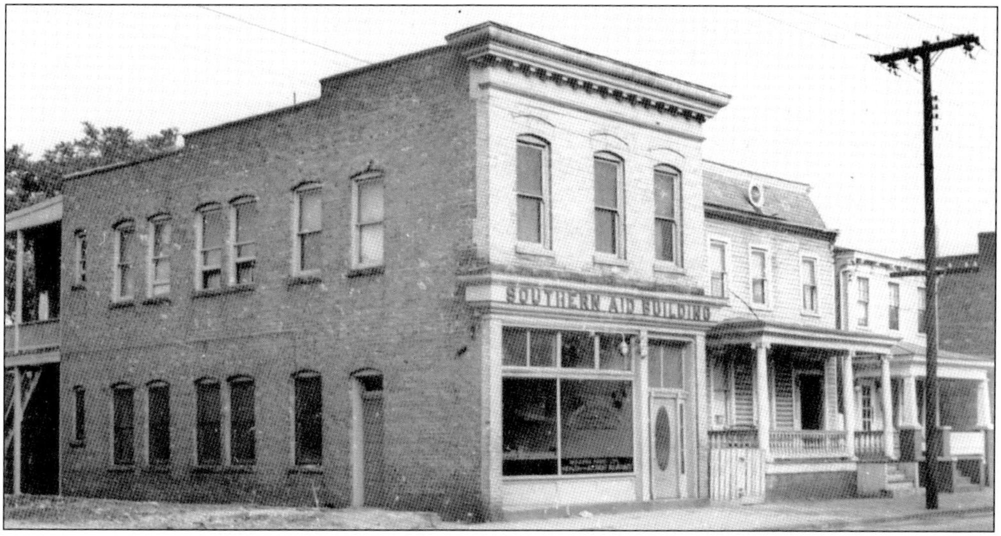

The Southern Aid Building, located on the west side of Green Street, is shown in this May 6, 1951 image looking north toward Glasgow. (Courtesy Olde Towne Collection, Portsmouth Public Library.)

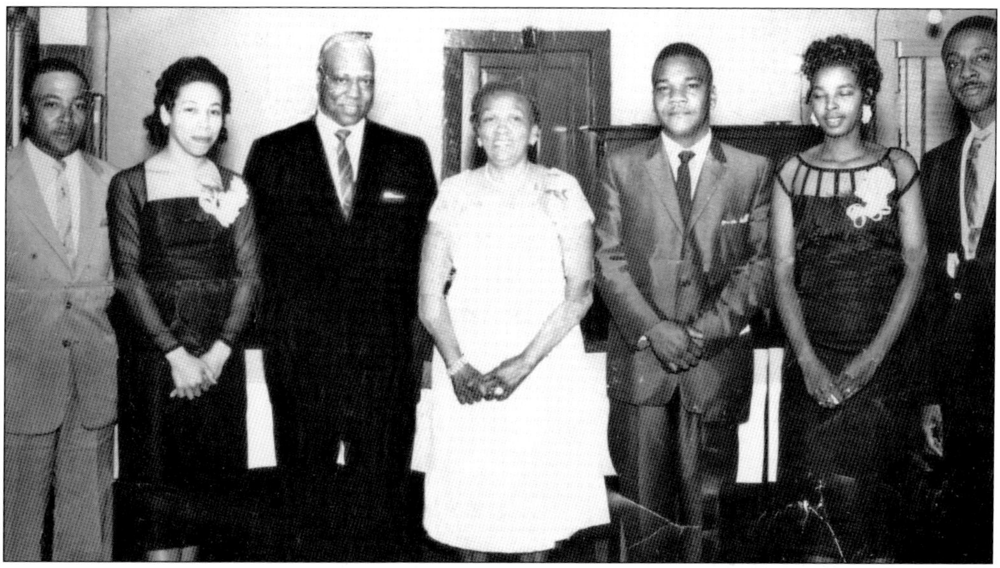

The Club DePorres, sometimes called the "Catholic Club," was founded in 1943. The founders got the idea for a club from the women at St. Joseph's Catholic Church in Norfolk. The first meetings were held on Stonewall Street in the Lincolnsville section. Over the years, the club opened its membership to non-Catholics while continuing its mission as a religious, charitable, and social organization. Originally, the club was known as the Eldorado Club. However, when they incorporated as a non-profit organization, they discovered that a Norfolk group had a similar name. This photograph depicts the club's installation of Matthew Liverman Sr. as its second president, *c.* 1949. Frank Rainey served three terms (two years each) as first president. Pictured, left to right, are as follows: Matthew Liverman Sr., Mary Francis Smith, Victor Ashe, Belle Wood Rainey, Robert Segars, Carolyn Williamson Woodard, and Dr. Hugo Owens. (Courtesy of Bessie Liverman.)

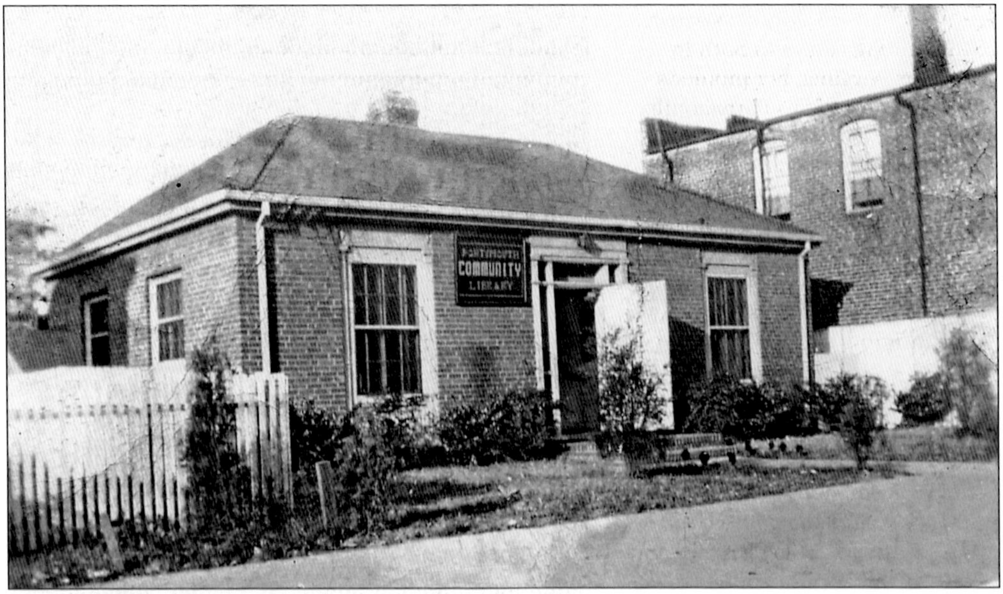

Portsmouth Community Library, 1949–1959, was located at 801 South Street. (Courtesy Bertha Edwards Collection, Portsmouth Public Library.)

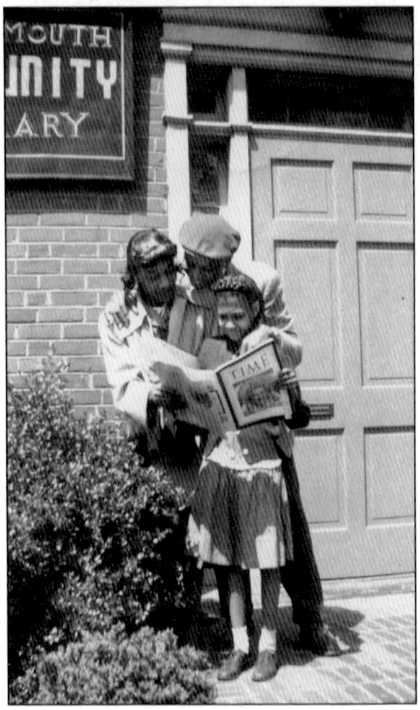

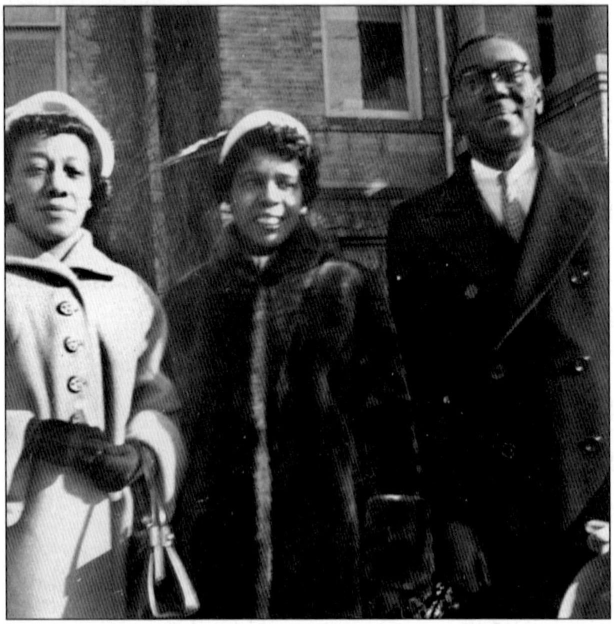

(left) This photograph of the Portsmouth Community Library was probably taken in 1949, shortly after its official opening. From left to right are Mrs. Bertha Edwards (librarian), Thomas Edwards, and Joyce Troy. The library sign was made and donated by George Hardy and Otis Williams. (Courtesy Bertha Edwards Collection, Portsmouth Public Library.) *(right)* Mrs. Bertha Edwards (far left), first librarian of Colored Portsmouth Library, is pictured along with famed musician from Portsmouth, Mr. Colonius Davis (far right). Davis's sister, Miss Rosa Lee Davis, is standing in the middle. The three of them are standing outside Zion Baptist Church in Portsmouth, *c.* 1950. (Lee Rodgers Collection, Courtesy Portsmouth Public Library.)

Mrs. Jane Pyatt was born a slave in 1848. Although she was born in Middlesex, Virginia, her mother's slaveholder moved to Portsmouth when Mrs. Pyatt was only three months. In a 1937 WPA interview with Thelma Dunston, she told of her many experiences as a slave in Portsmouth and recalled the use of the cellar at Emanuel AME Church to help slaves escape through the Underground Railroad. According to Pyatt, the passage way extended to the ferry on the Elizabeth River. And because boats were always present, security was difficult to maintain making escape possible. (Courtesy Portsmouth Public Library.)

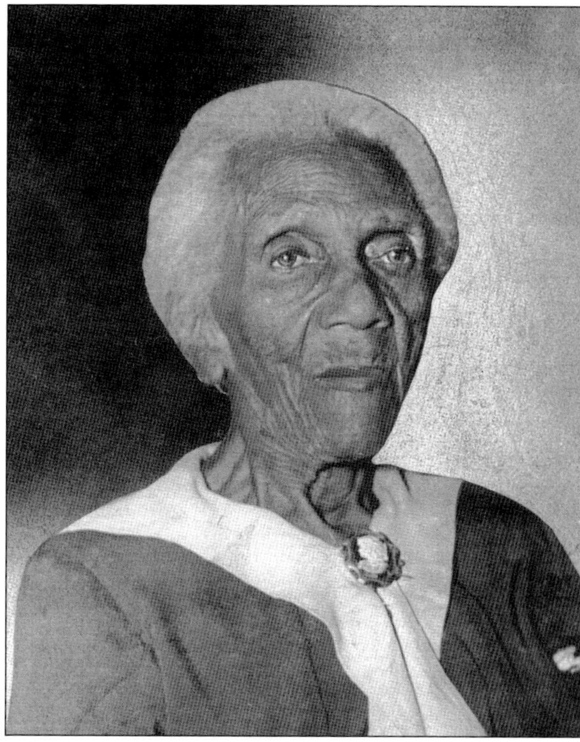

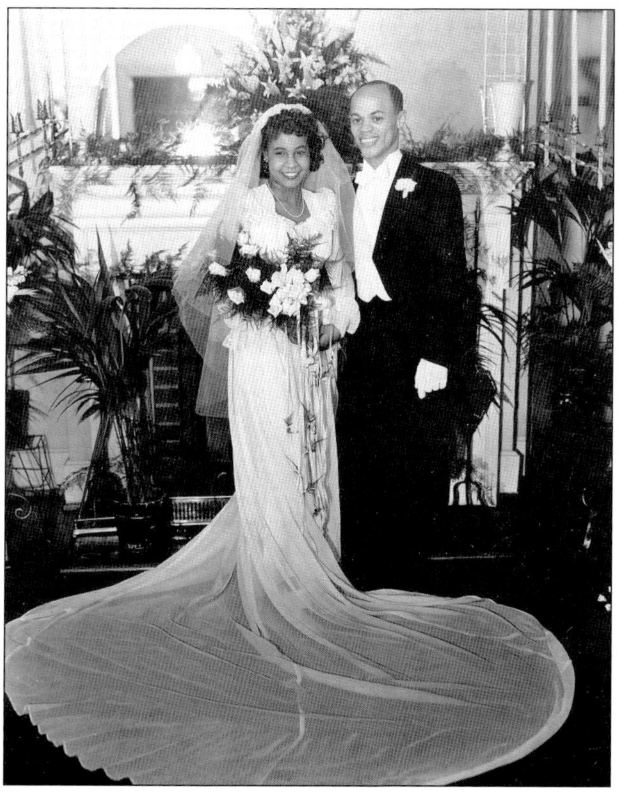

This photograph captures the Deloris Scott and Howard V. Plummer wedding. The couple is posing before a flower-covered mantel, *c.* 1940. (Lee Rodgers Collection, Courtesy Portsmouth Public Library.)

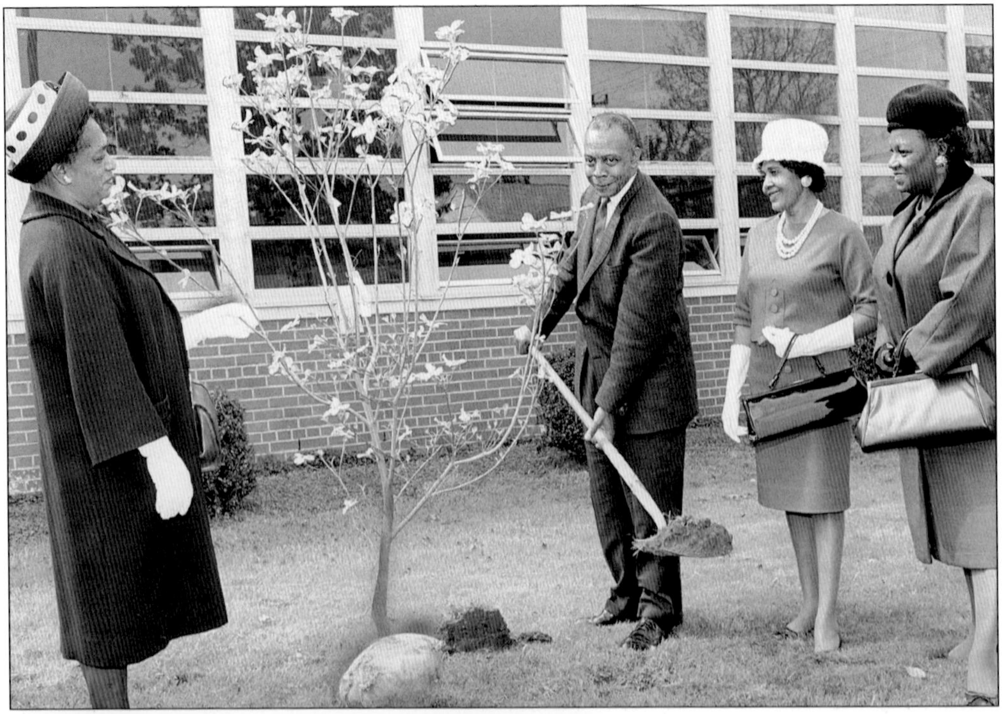

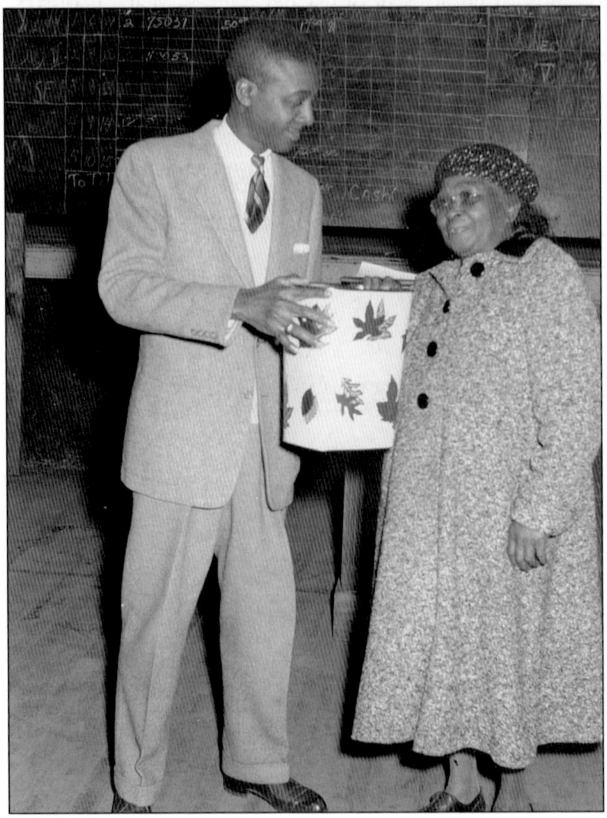

West Mt. Hermon Garden Club donated and planted a tree on the grounds of Mt. Hermon School. The ceremony took place April 22, 1964, with Ralph W. Gholson, the principal, doing the spade work. The ladies, watching approvingly the young tree, from left to right, are Mrs. Mabel B. Allen, president of the Garden Club; Mrs. Arlethia A. Campbell, and Mrs. Eliza L. Saunders. (Lee Rodgers Collection, Courtesy Portsmouth Public Library.)

Dr. Hugo A. Owens is shown presenting an award to Mrs Elinor Wise, the highest fund-raiser of Section "A" at the third report meeting of the Chestnut Street Branch YMCA's membership campaign, *c.* 1950. (Lee Rodgers Collection, Courtesy Portsmouth Public Library.)

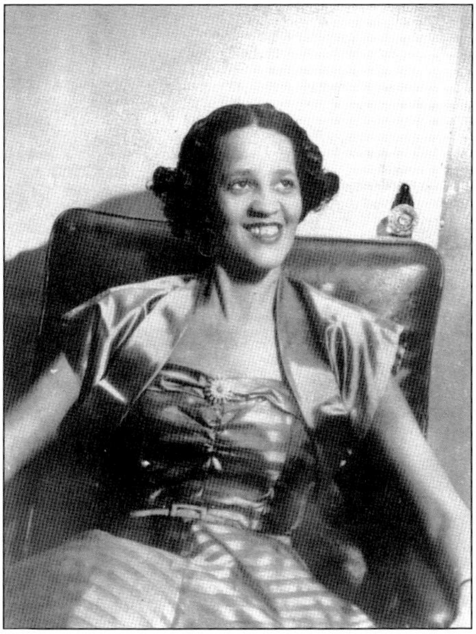
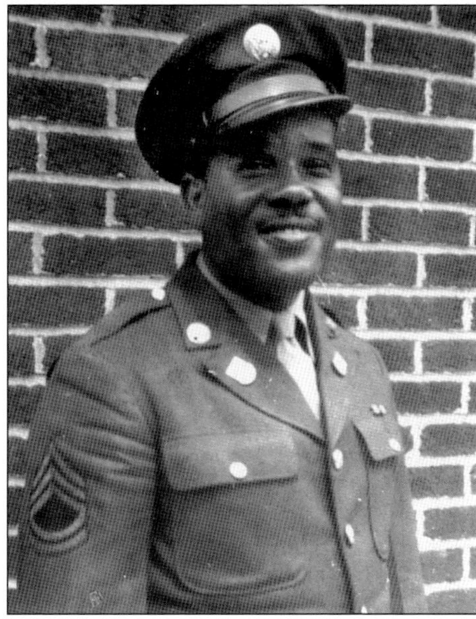

(left) Mrs. Thelma Dunston Wood was a graduate of the class of 1932, I.C. Norcom. She was 87 years old when she died on February 26, 2003. Wood was the widow of Gilbert Wood. Active in social and religious organizations, Wood was a long-time member of St. James Episcopal Church and their Alter Guild and vestry. She was also a member of the Delta Sigma Theta sorority. Virginia Dunston Wood retired as a Portsmouth Public School teacher after 40 years. (Courtesy Mae Breckenridge-Haywood.) *(Right)* Sgt. Gilbert Wood, husband of Thelma Dunston, served in World War II. (Courtesy Lee Rodgers Collection, Portsmouth Public Library.)

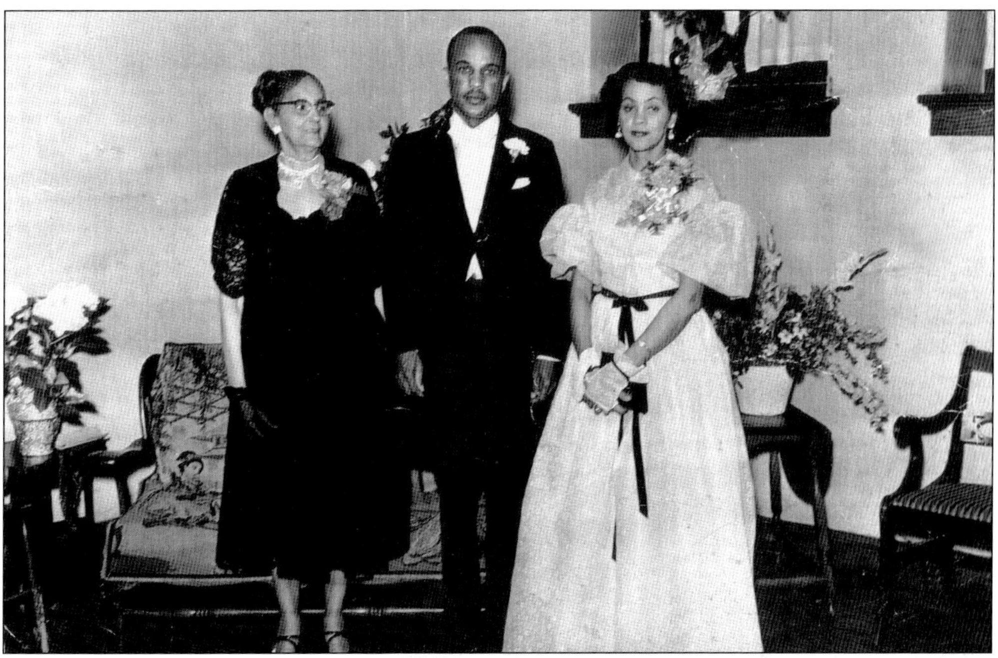

Pictured is the wedding day for Gilbert and Thelma Dunston Wood. (Courtesy Mae Breckenridge-Haywood.)

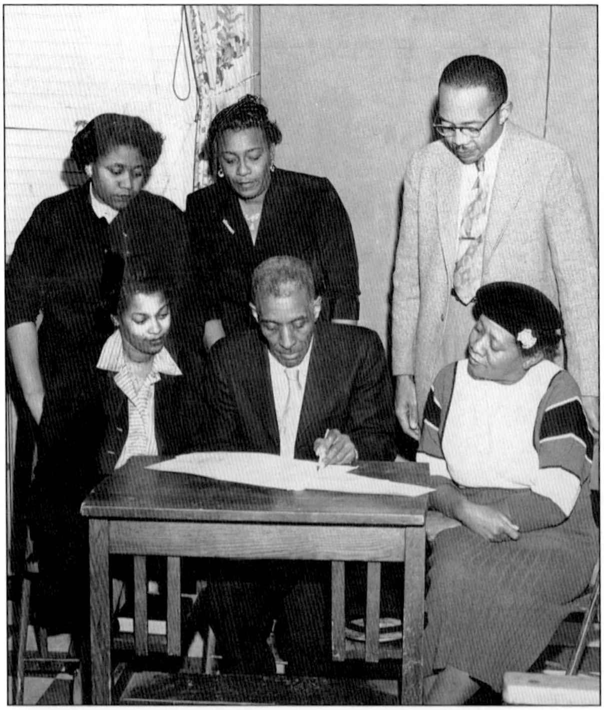

This photograph was taken at the Chestnut Street USO/YMCA on Friday night, February 3, 1956. Sitting, from left to right, are (front row) Mrs. Ethelyn Strong, associate chairman; David Muckle, general chairman; and Mrs. Virginia Taylor, section leader; (back row) Mrs. Essie Bogues, division manager; Mrs. Amy E. King, division manager; and T.J. Lawrence, section leader. (Courtesy Lee Rodgers Collection, Portsmouth Public Library.)

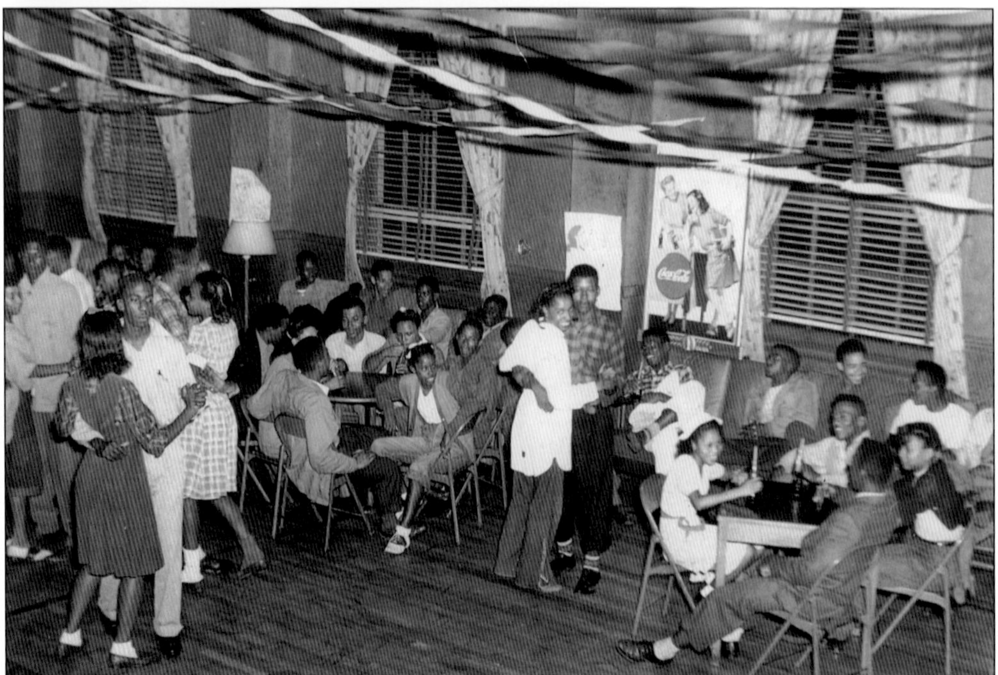

The Chestnut Street USO/YMCA was built with federal funds at the same time that the white YMCA building was constructed. (Courtesy Bertha Edwards Collection, Portsmouth Public Library.)

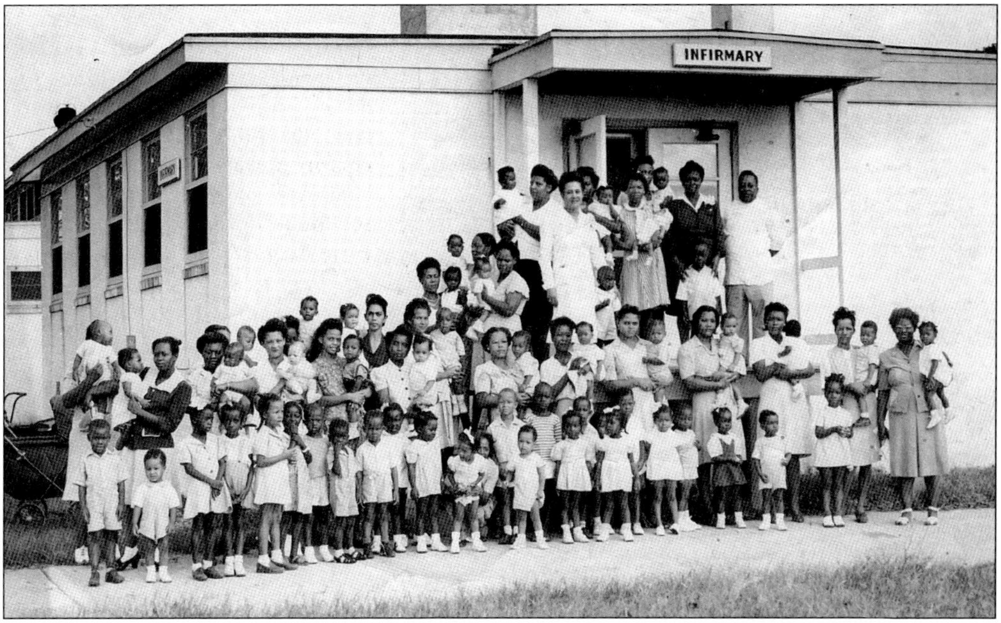

Women and children are pictured outside an infirmary, *c.* 1940. This facility was probably used for the dispersal of inoculations and to treat minor injuries (Courtesy Lee Rodgers Collection, Portsmouth Public Library.)

This is an early 1910s photograph of Ida Barbour, founder of the Miller Day Care Nursery. Barbour was born around 1878 in Portsmouth, Virginia. She lived with her family in the first black section of the city, Lincolnsville. After attending the Institute for Colored Youth in Philadelphia, she returned home and worked as a teacher in the Portsmouth Public School system from 1898 to1909. After initially taking in five orphans, Barbour and 20 other women—known as the Women's League—established the Miller Day Nursery and Home for them and other neighborhood children in 1911. The Miller Day Nursery, the area's first daycare to take in infants, continues today. The Day Care Nursery was similar to the William T. Hall Convalescent Home, because while the nursery provided a needed service to the community, thus allowing both parents to work, it was owned and operated by and was an important source of employment for African Americans. (Courtesy Mae Breckenridge-Haywood.)

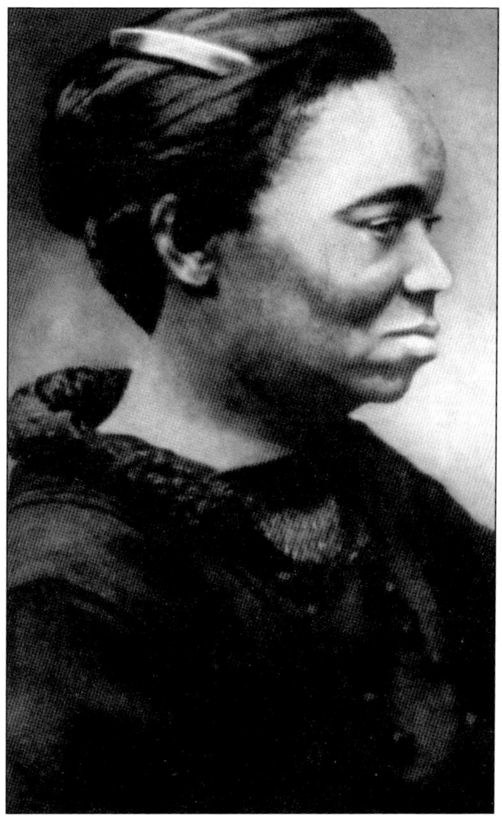

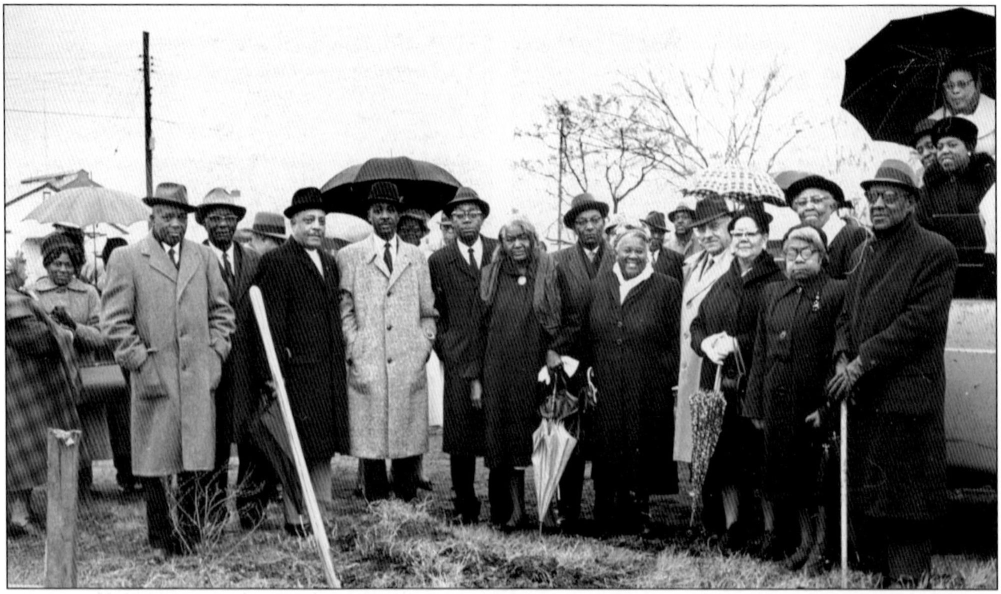

The groundbreaking at the Old Folks Home (William T. Hall Convalescence Home) is shown here. Although the original Old Folks Home facility was listed as a hospital, it did not provide emergency, preventive, or general medical care for its patients or for the community at-large. (Courtesy Portsmouth Public Library.)

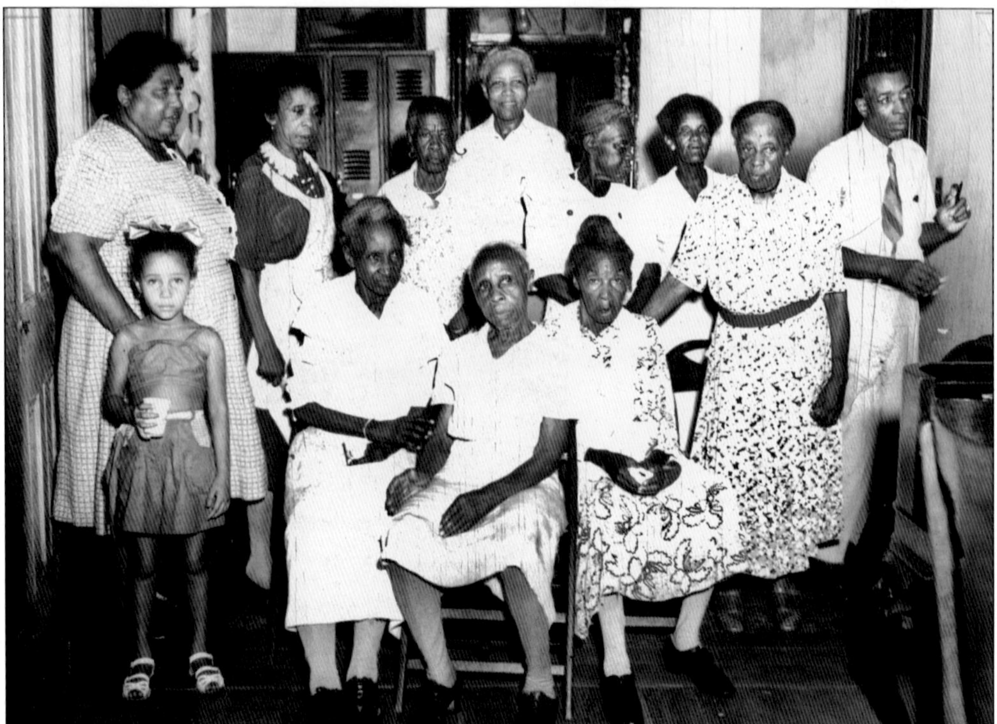

Pictured are patients and employees at the William T. Hall Convalescent Home. (Courtesy Bertha Edwards Collection, Portsmouth Public Library.)

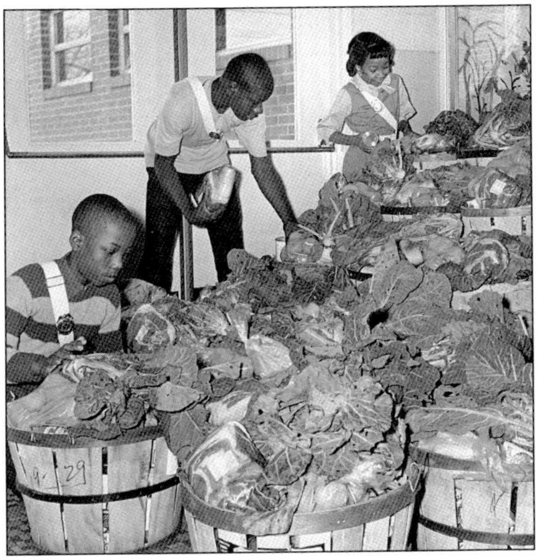

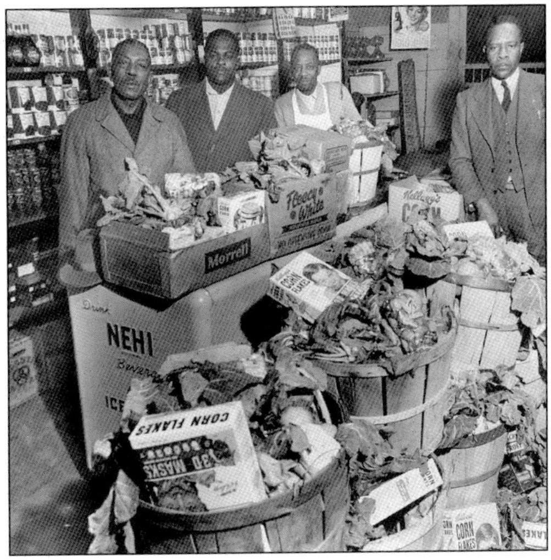

(left) Caring for one another was a crucial element in the survival of Portsmouth's African Americans. Teaching young people to continue that legacy was also important, as this photograph illustrates with the distribution of food to the needy by these children. (Lee Rodgers Collection, Courtesy Portsmouth Public Library.) *(right)* Mr Hendricks (far left), Hodges, and J.E. Knight (far right), and an unidentified man pose in this photograph as they prepare the food for distribution to the needy. The Beacon Light Lodge No. 34 of Elks' Relief Committee typically distributed baskets of food to the Portsmouth Welfare Department in the 1950s and 1960s. (Lee Rodgers Collection, Courtesy Portsmouth Public Library.)

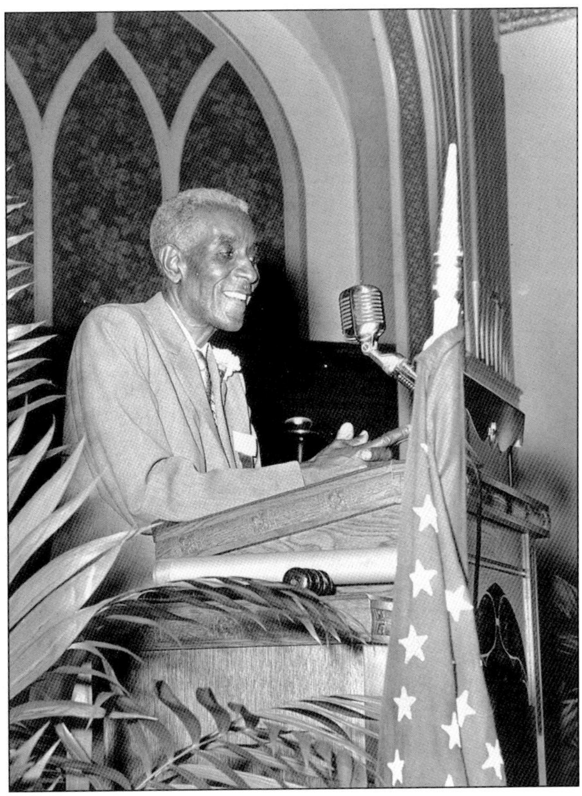

David Muckle, Grand Patron at the Order of the Eastern Star Convention, is shown on July 28, 1964. (Lee Rodgers Collection, Courtesy Portsmouth Public Library.)

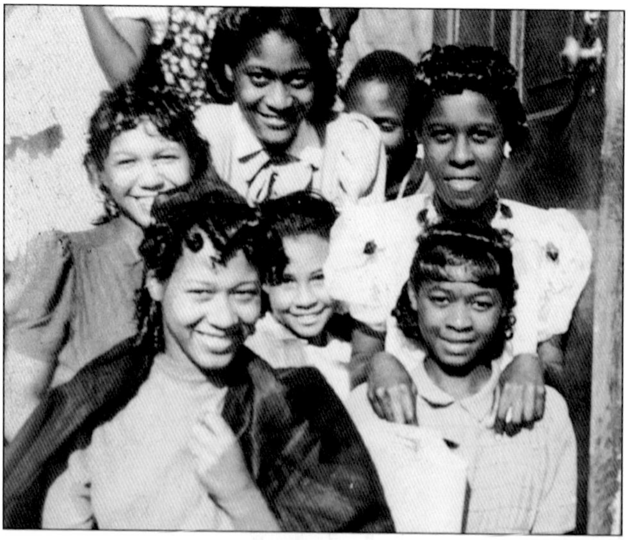

The Virginia State Federation of the Colored Women's Club at Zion Church is shown with the following members: Emma Amos, Mattie Amos, Little Delores Scott, Myrtle Watkins, and Thelma Joyner. This photograph was taken during the afternoon session on June 27, 1940. (Courtesy Lee Rodgers Collection, Portsmouth Public Library.)

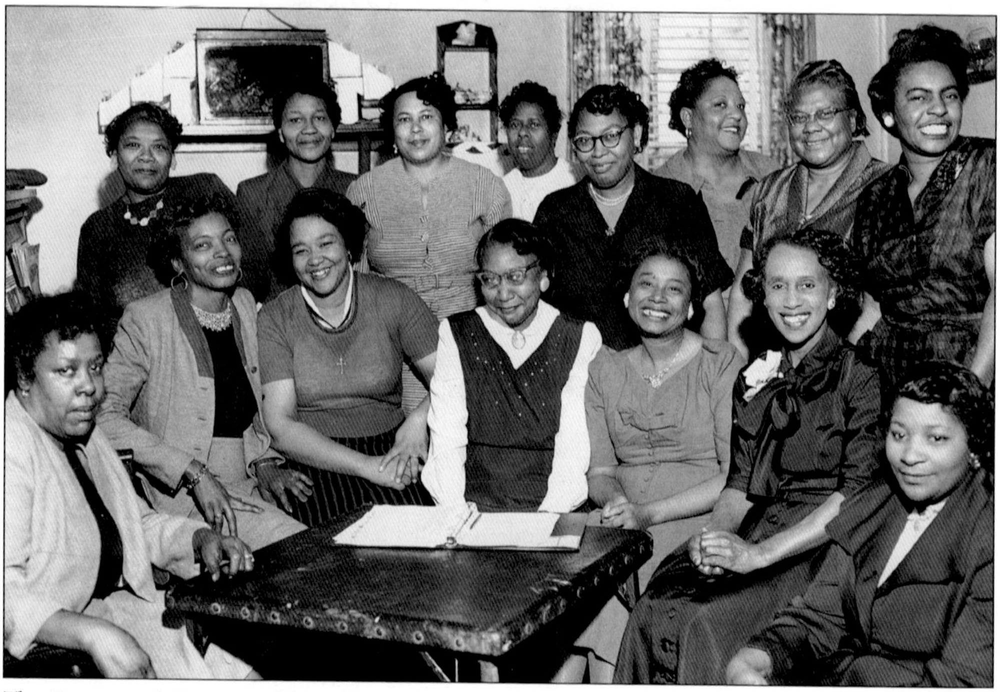

The Portsmouth Registered Beauticians' Association was making preparations to play hostess to the Virginia State Beauticians Association's Seventh Trade Show and Annual Convention at the Chestnut Street Branch YMCA from April 28 to May 1, 1957. Members of the local association, from left to right, are (front row) Mrs. Mae Tazzell; Mrs. Louise Dillard; Mrs. Mary Buffalo, assistant treasurer; Mrs. Mabel D. Jackson, treasurer; Mrs. Mable S. Jackson, vice president; Mrs. Otelia Griffin, president; and Mrs. Mary Johnson; (back row) Mrs. Katie C. Perry, chaplain; Mrs. Rebecca Brown; Mrs. Mamie P. Stalling; Mrs. Helen Davis; Mrs. Etta Roberts; Mrs. Arnetta Champlin; Mrs. Mamie V. Dixon; and Miss Margie Steadman. Not present for the photo were Mrs. Annie Frink, secretary, and Mrs. Blanche Jackson, reporter. (Courtesy Lee Rodgers Collection, Portsmouth Public Library.)

Five

Politics and the Fight for Freedom and Equality

The transformation of the African–American community from slavery to freedom and from freedom to equality has been a long and arduous trek filled with obstacles and setbacks. The participation of African Americans in obtaining their rights has been ignored by most accounts of Portsmouth's history. Although recent local histories have emphasized the importance of the labor of blacks in building Portsmouth, few have even hinted at the active participation and direct influence many blacks had on the development of the city politically, economically, and socially.

The economic development of Portsmouth brought an increase in its African-American population, free and bond. In 1649, there were an estimated 300 blacks (or two percent) among Virginia's population of 15,000. Little evidence exists as to how black Virginians were treated prior to 1640. What historians uncovered was that during the 40-odd year interim, 1620 to 1660, between their arrival and the institutionalization of slavery, blacks experienced a fluid racial environment ranging from acceptance to blatant racial animosity. After 1660, African Americans were increasingly treated as slaves. Consequently, all blacks—free and bond—were denied automatic membership in the community and the same personal and civil liberties as whites.[46]

With the outbreak of the American Revolution at Lexington and Concord in April 1775, Portsmouth and Norfolk immediately felt the effects of the war due to the actions taken by Virginia's Royal Governor, John Dunmore. In October Dunmore sent patrolling warships down the Elizabeth River and established headquarters at Gosport making it the virtual "royal capital" of Virginia. On November 7, 1775, Dunmore issued a proclamation promising freedom to all who joined him in bearing arms against the rebels. Historian Benjamin Quarles estimated that approximately 300 enslaved African Americans from Tidewater joined Lord Dunmore in Norfolk one week after the November proclamation, while a total of 800 enlisted as part of Lord Dunmore's Ethiopian Regiment. But after Dunmore's defeat at the Battle of Great Bridge, he regrouped back in Portsmouth in January 1776 in the area of the Naval Hospital. Although the influence of merchants made Portsmouth a predominant supporter of the British, the majority of blacks remained loyal to the colonies. Perhaps it was because the enslaved African Americans, who worked primarily in the shipping and related industries, were acquainted more with those who aligned themselves with the British, seeing them as the source of their oppression. For example, James Lafayette worked as a spy for the American forces during Gen. Charles Cornwallis's occupation of Portsmouth. Headquartered in a building on North and County Streets, Lafayette, who took his name from the famous French commander, the Marquis de Lafayette, posed as a servant in the office. One day he smuggled crucial plans for the attack of Yorktown from the headquarters and took them to Gen. George Washington, who was camped just outside the city. These papers provided crucial information for Washington's counteroffensive that resulted in Yorktown being the final battle of the American Revolution. Lafayette was rewarded with 30 acres of land and a mule.[47]

The effects of the American War for Independence on Portsmouth's blacks continued for many years. By 1782, Portsmouth was completely disrupted by the war. Its buildings were laid waste in ashes and ruin, its populace was scattered, part of its slave population was dispersed or carried away, and its economy was devastated because large numbers of its ships were destroyed or carried off. The second major result was the passage of an important statute by Virginia's General Assembly that affected the social, political, and economic strata of society. On May 6, 1782, a Virginia statute was passed authorizing the manumission of slaves by their owners. The precedent-setting manumission statute was the result of a revolutionary and evangelical spirit that was sweeping the nation. This statute gave the black community the opportunity, for the first time since the early 17th century, to take advantage of the law by working together to raise the money to buy the freedom of their friends and relatives. In Portsmouth, the appearance of larger numbers of free blacks allowed the rapid growth and stabilization of its free black community.[48]

Little in the way of statistical information is known about the black community that, in 1790, made up approximately 25 percent of the total population in the town of Portsmouth. In 1840, there were 6,387 residents in Portsmouth: 1,890 were slaves and 423 were free blacks. By 1850, one-third of the 8,626 residents in Portsmouth were black.[49]

Since Portsmouth, like its sister town Norfolk, provided an urban environment for enslaved Africans and African Americans, many moved about freely, relatively speaking, with many living apart from their masters. This mobility allowed African Americans, especially those who were enslaved and hired out, to segue into a variety of port-related occupations, albeit at a lower pay rate than whites. Throughout the 1840s and 1850s reports came in from newspapers creating the perception that a clandestine organization was making considerable headway in undermining slavery. This was particularly disturbing for those in port areas such as Portsmouth. Rumors circulated that ship captains were secreting them out aboard their vessels and that a very active Underground Railroad was in operation in their area. The reality was not far from perception. The Underground Railroad was indeed active in Portsmouth. *The Negro in Virginia* noted that the Portsmouth and Norfolk docks were meccas for runaways headed for freedom in New England and Canada. Jane Pyatt, a former slave in Portsmouth, recounted to a WPA interviewer that Emanuel AME church's involvement in the Underground Railroad was extensive. She noted that runaways sought sanctuary inside the church, hidden behind the organ or inside the tunnel that ran from the church to the Elizabeth River. So threatening were the efforts of abolitionists that the *Beacon* sarcastically noted the apprehension of three runaway slaves in 1855 claiming that their capture resulted from the Underground Railroad being "out of order."[50]

What the Underground Railroad's presence illustrated was the intent of African Americans to fight, even covertly, for their freedom. Many knew by the late 1850s that secession by many of the southern states was likely to occur, but most were not interested in a preemptive move. Like Norfolk, Portsmouth delegates demonstrated strong opposition to secession during the February 1861 state convention. But with the firing on Fort Sumter, public opinion changed in April 1861 primarily because Virginia refused to send troops to support the Union Army against southern states. After the Confederate flag was raised over Craney Island in April and troops were sent to organize and command the military and naval forces in the area, Portsmouth's role in the Civil War was set on an immovable course. The situation worsened when the federal government decided to consolidate its forces and abandon the Naval Yard after burning it to the ground along with 11 warships. Ten Confederate companies were eventually organized in Portsmouth with hundreds joining, including the Portsmouth Rifles, the Old Dominion Guard, the National Greys, the Marion Rifles, and the Portsmouth Light Artillery. African Americans, however, took a very different approach in the early months of the war in part because most were enslaved. In Portsmouth, the Confederacy also engaged African Americans as civilians in naval shipyards, ordinance yards, and depots to haul supplies on waterways, to work in naval stores, to fire boilers, and to make naval materials.[51]

Between 1863 and 1865, 200,000 African Americans fought in the Civil War, and 69,000 of them died. In Portsmouth, hundreds of African Americans, ranging in age from 18 to 45, enlisted in the Union Army and served faithfully in the 10th U.S. Colored Volunteers, the 1st and 2nd Colored Cavalry, the 2nd Light Artillery, and the 36th–38th Regiment Colored Infantries. These regiments distinguished themselves by securing Princess Anne and Norfolk Counties from rebel infiltration, freed thousands of slaves, and fought in the battles at Wilson's Landing, Cabin Point, Fort Pocahontas, Bermuda Hundreds, Smithfield, Powhatan, New Market Heights, Chaffin's Farm, Appomattox, and Petersburg. Unlike the army that did not utilize blacks as soldiers until 1863, the navy enlisted blacks as sailors as early as September 1861. Six African Americans received the Navy Medal of Honor. Many others received lesser decorations.[52]

The end of the Civil War in 1865 brought with it significant changes in the attitudes of African Americans and in the legal structure of this nation. In the following decades, Portsmouth and Norfolk, sister cities whose development paralleled each other until the mid-20th century, seemed on the threshold of a new era reflected in population increases from the surrounding rural counties and eastern North Carolina. However, the pull to retain the social and racial hierarchy was greater than the push to industrialize and modernize. Public service expansion occurred slowly, despite a lack of true commitment by its leadership. Efforts to perpetuate white hegemony guided 20th-century urban planning, which ironically resulted in white flight to the suburbs by the late 1950s and 1960s. Efforts were made by white southern leaders to regulate the black community's development by negating its political power while at the same encouraging social and economic growth. As ratios of black to white increased, barriers to participation in local politics crumbled resulting in planning as an important vehicle through which whites curbed black political power. Thus the dominant elements of black politics emerged in the interaction with the larger political culture of white America. One aspect of black politics was the manifestation of strong race pride that led to a politics of self-determination. A second element was the development of pressure tactics using massive protest demonstrations. A third was the effort to participate in the formal political system. Using the vote and membership in the major political parties, blacks sought both elective and appointive office.[53]

The presence of a small but well-established free black community also had a tremendous impact. By the late 19th century, the cultural self-containment that had been the world of many southern slaves for centuries was transformed even further as many blacks in Portsmouth unsuccessfully fought segregation and its accompanying discrimination. Community leaders strove to build bridges between the black and white communities by inviting whites to black community and political functions and by doing everything short of giving up their political rights to conciliate whites. The first step toward politicizing was the involvement of men in civic affairs and law. William M. Reid became Portsmouth's first black lawyer. Reid and other professional and educated blacks encouraged the community's participation in politics through voting. And while women would not receive that right until 1920, that did not bar them from encouraging men to get out and vote. On June 21, 1867, at 9:00 a.m., the Board of Registration began voter registration in their office in the Jefferson Ward, which adjoined the Stokes' Hotel located on High Street between Water and Crawford Streets. Daniel Collins, the former mayor of Portsmouth, and a corps of registrars registered blacks and whites over a six-day period. Although a detachment of city police guarded the polls in case of disorder, the crowd was enthusiastic but orderly. A black music band with drum and fife, mounted on an express wagon, paraded through the ward during most of the morning getting other blacks out to register. At the close of the polls, 868 blacks and 1,377 whites had registered.[54]

In 1868, blacks organized a Republican Convention at Snead's blacksmith shop at South and Effingham Streets. Convention officers Rev. Edinboro Corprew (chair) and Isaac Mullen (secretary) coordinated the nomination of a council composed of black and white men. However, attacks on black enfranchisement began with an 1876 law that deprived delinquent taxpayers of the franchise. Prior to that, African Americans had achieved relative success entering politics. Samuel Davis was elected the first black city councilman while John Wilson served as the first black chief of police and Thomas Davis was Portsmouth's first black justice of the peace. Shortly afterwards throughout Virginia, but especially in Portsmouth and Norfolk, whites removed all blacks from the city councils, gerrymandered black districts out of existence, and disfranchised the majority of black Virginians in the 1902 state constitutional convention. This newly adopted 1902 state constitution insured white economic and political domination by denying the majority of African–American men the right to vote in Virginia. The state leaders believed that the destiny of black Virginians was to serve the white community, doing the menial labor upon which the commonwealth depended, without having a voice in their ultimate destiny. Met with obstinate resistance to any form of integration, blacks reluctantly accepted segregation and turned to building a strong black community. Responding to the growing restrictions of the late 19th century, African Americans provided even more services to their communities. Leaders concentrated on building pride through churches and schools, establishing health care services, constructing rudimentary economic infrastructures in the neighborhoods, encouraging the growth of a middle class, and solidifying their political power.[55]

The Spanish-American War was the first opportunity many local young men had after the Civil War to participate in an armed conflict. Some local African Americans, who had re-enlisted after the Civil War, fought against the Native Americans in the western states from 1867 until 1877. Afterwards, soldiers were needed to enforce the peace agreement. Local African Americans who served in the Spanish American War did so primarily aboard naval vessels. The irony of this period in which President Theodore Roosevelt hailed the newly built American fleet as the "Great White Fleet," was that African Americans were key fighting units in Cuba and the Philippines. Those who served aboard the ships would later recall that this was the last war for 50 years in which African Americans served on ships that were not segregated. Perhaps that explains why many monuments dedicated to the black Civil War veterans also include those who fought during the Spanish American War. In 1912, President Woodrow Wilson closed the chapter on racial advances by issuing an order that segregated all federal offices and agencies. It would be in this environment that World War I would erupt, eventually involving the United States.[56]

The First World War rudely awakened Portsmouth and ended its provincial world with unprecedented activity resulting in the establishment of a naval base in Norfolk. This development would spill over into Portsmouth's shipyard and shipbuilding industries. The yard expanded with three new dry docks and plenty of contracts to build battleships and destroyers that would be invaluable in America's war effort. For those who did not enlist during the war, wartime employment boomed as navy yard workers reached an all-time high of 11,234. This meant that African Americans, although limited to low-paying, unskilled positions, would at least be hired in the yard.[57]

In World War I, black combat troops were organized into two divisions (the 92nd and 93rd), each composed of four regiments. The 92nd consisted of the 365th to 368th regiments while the 93rd consisted of the 369th to 372nd regiments. The most famous of these regiments was the "Fighting 369th." Needless to say, black soldiers met the same kind of racism when they returned home to America as existed before they left for Europe. The only thing that was different was the black soldier. With each war and new experience came a hunger and desire for change and dissatisfaction with life in segregated America.

The war also contributed markedly to rising black aspirations, because 360,000 blacks fought to make the world safe for democracy. Once the war concluded, many wondered whether they might begin to enjoy democracy's benefits. In the 1920s, Portsmouth's blacks fought against discrimination in education. Efforts to provide a single voice against the most virulent forms of racism resulted in the founding of the NAACP. In Norfolk-Portsmouth, that organization found an unsteady place for itself among blacks who were accustomed to maintaining an uneasy balance between accommodation and self-actualization. Becoming more insulated by focusing on the building of their community and acquiring more tax dollars, which would give them access to the same facilities as whites, was the route many blacks chose. They would have a modicum of success until the reports of a civil rights movement reached even the most steadfast accommodationists.

In World War II, although black combat troops continued to fight in segregated units, they were given more technical tasks and opportunities than in any previous war. This change in policy resulted in the registration of three million blacks for service: 700,000 served in the army, 165,000 in the navy, 900 in the coast guard, 17,000 in the marines, 24,000 in the merchant marines, and 4,000 in the WAVES and WACS. Blacks assigned to the 93rd Division were sent to Bougainville, the Treasury Islands, and later to the Philippines participating with MacArthur as he led the troops in a triumphant return in 1944. The 92nd Division was sent overseas to fight in Africa and later in Italy. The all-black 761st Tank Battalion, who fought under the command of Gen. George S. Patton, was on hand for the German capitulation in Austria. And finally, the 99th Pursuit Squadron, the most glamorous black unit associated with World War II, was commanded by Col. Benjamin O. Davis, who later became the first black general in the army, and distinguished themselves in over 1,600 combat missions.[58]

The resources required to fight World War II were more extensive than in any previous war, with the exception of the Civil War. Many who in 1942 had been previously rejected by the military as physically inadequate for duty were drafted by 1944. Fighting a war on two fronts drained America unfamiliar with conflict of this nature or degree, forcing it to loosen some of its social and racial constraints. Black men, who previously were barred from skilled jobs in the Norfolk Naval shipyard, the railroads, and other national defense positions, now had opportunities previously denied them. Of all the services that provided opportunities, it was the navy that changed the most during this period, in stark contrast to its record in World War I. While the Navy maintained restrictions on supervisory positions—the majority were still relegated to serving as messmen—Camp Robert Smalls, a separate training facility, was established for African Americans at the Great Lakes Naval Training Station. By 1944, 500 black seamen, primarily in the Pacific, served aboard auxiliary vessels in a wide variety of positions barred to them on the regular naval vessels. Moreover, African American women gained admission to the WACS and WAVES, opening doors for advancement in the military infrastructure.[59]

In the aftermath of the war, the NAACP took steps to insure that the wartime advances would not be withdrawn in the years following. Even before the war's end, NAACP leaders and the black press vigorously pressed the President and Congress for full equality. Fortunately, President Harry Truman showed himself a friend to African Americans. In 1948, he established a civil rights commission and issued a presidential proclamation requiring fair employment in federal service and integration in the armed forces. Portsmouth was directly affected because of the naval shipyard. While discrimination continued, it did not do so without challenges, most of which emanated from numerous former soldiers who took advantage of Truman's program that funded college education for military personnel. These young, highly trained individuals would later become the professionals who would fill the ranks of the upper middle classes in Portsmouth, many of whom were the advocates for change. Not until the Korean Conflict (1950–1953), did integration become a reality. Civil rights advocates also hit the civilian sector hard. Many of President Franklin D. Roosevelt's New Deal agencies, such as the Federal Housing and Home Finance Agency, forbade discrimination in housing. While many of these new policies would not be vigorously enforced, they set the tone for what would follow by the mid-1950s.[60]

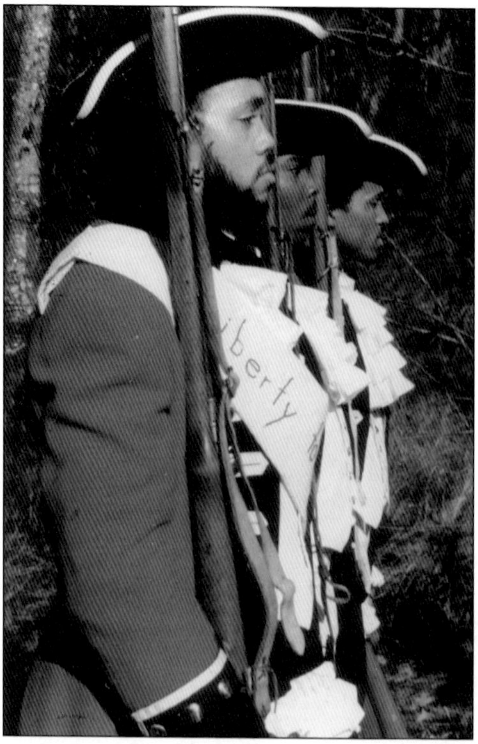

This is a reenactment of Battle of Great Bridge in which William Flora distinguished himself as a war hero. Flora (1755–1820) was a free black born in Portsmouth who stood his ground at the Battle of Great Bridge, defending it against the British attack in December 1776. His bravery was credited with sparking an American victory that eventually forced the British to withdraw from Norfolk. At the end of the war, as a reward for his meritorious service, Flora received the standard 100-acre land bounty, which allowed him to become a successful livery stable operator. So successful was Flora's livery stable with blacks and whites that he became one of the first free blacks to buy town property. When he died, Flora owned two homes and numerous horses and carriages. (Courtesy Portsmouth Public Library and Mae Breckenridge-Haywood.)

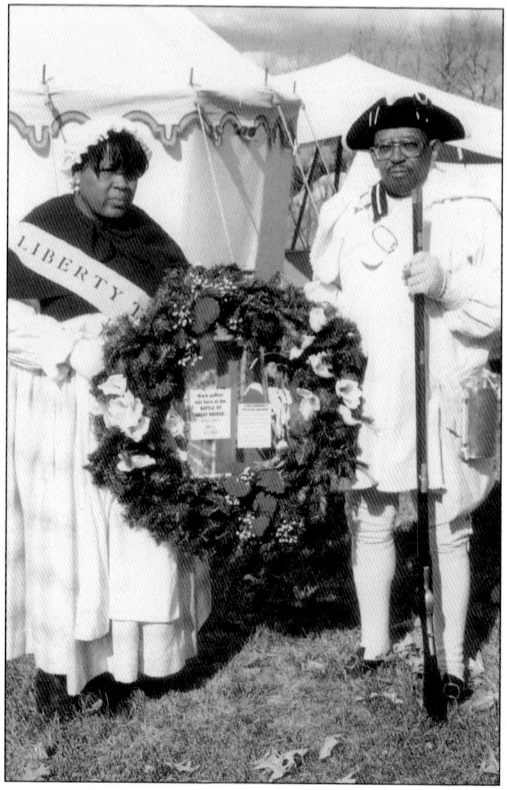

Thomas Sledge, social studies teacher in Chesapeake, is dressed as William Flora. Edna Hendrix is dressed as a woman of that period. (Courtesy Portsmouth Public Library and Mae Breckenridge-Haywood.)

The Emanuel AME Church attic was used as a lookout for the Underground Railroad. Whenever the church was harboring runaways, lookouts were posted in case city officials invaded the church. (Courtesy Sarah Choate Brown.)

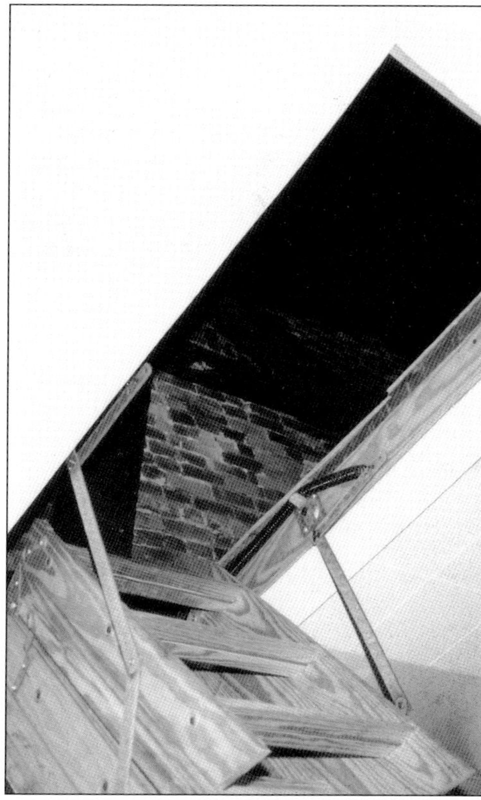

The area behind the organ was where members hid escaped slaves in Emanuel AME Church. Visitors to the church can see these historic hiding places and access to the tunnel that has been bricked in since the 1860s. Although the church grounds have not been excavated, it is probable that archeologists would find numerous artifacts related to the Underground Railroad in Portsmouth. (Courtesy Sarah Choate Brown.)

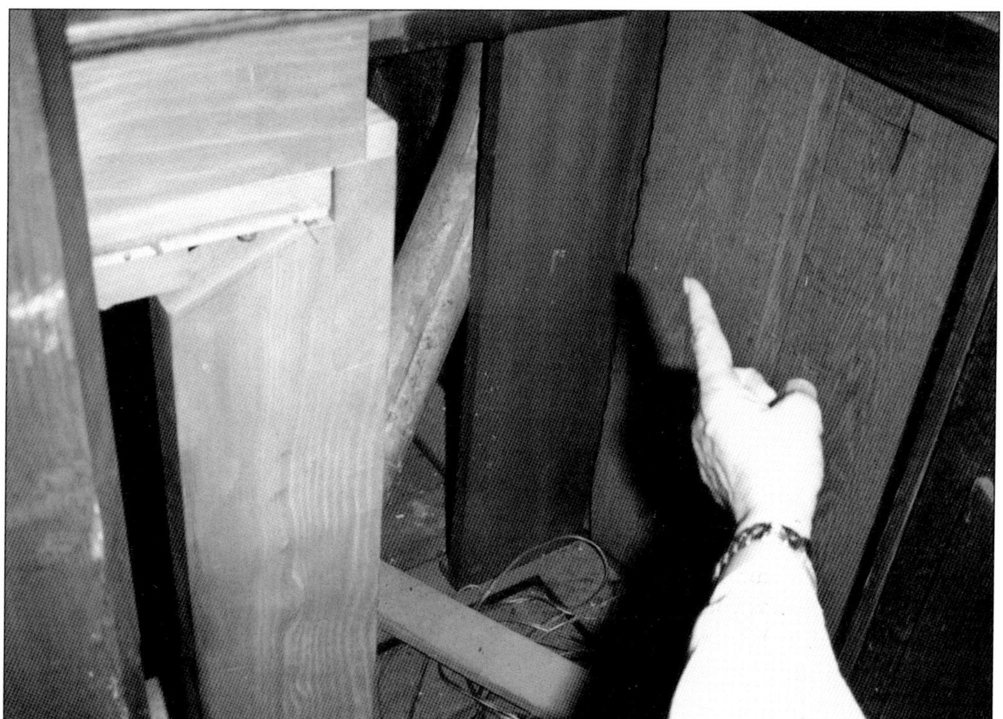

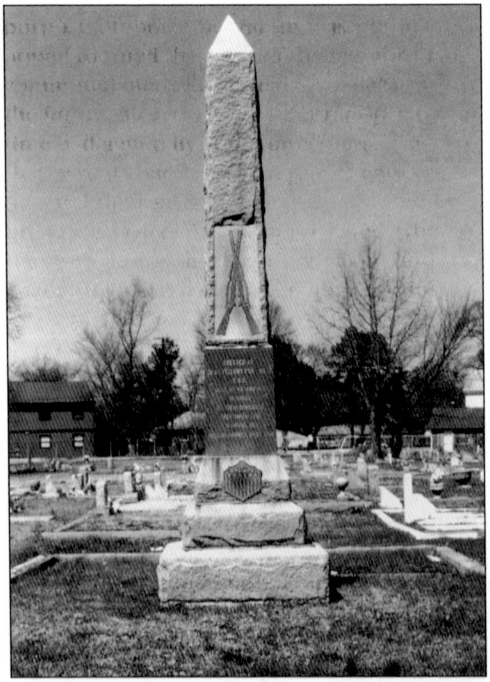

The Civil War Monument, located in Lincoln Memorial Cemetery on Deep Creek Boulevard, was dedicated to the African-American Civil War veterans. The Silas Fellows Lodge honored Nelson Carney and others who fought in the Civil War with this huge obelisk monument. (Courtesy Mae Breckenridge-Haywood.)

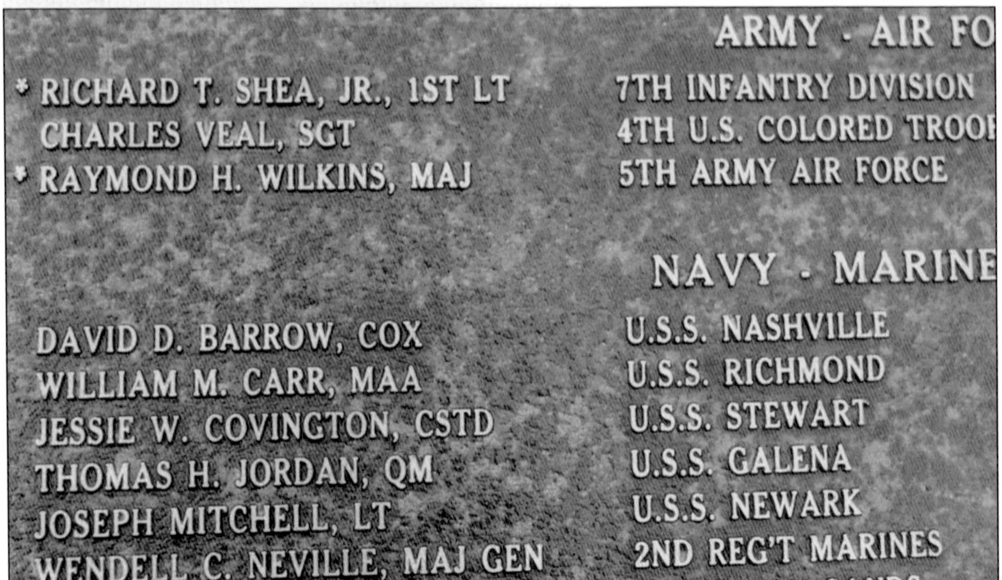

Charles Veal was born in Portsmouth, Virginia in 1835 and worked as a fireman until his enlistment in the army at Baltimore, Maryland, in July 1863. He served with Company D in the 4th U.S. Colored Infantry when cited for heroism at the Battle of New Market Heights, Virginia, (also known as Chaffin's Farm) on September 29, 1864. Veal was awarded the medal on April 6, 1865, because he "seized the national colors, after two color bearers had been shot down close to the enemy's works, and bore them through the remainder of the battle." He was eventually promoted to the rank of sergeant in November 1864. Pictured is a plaque on High Street Landing regarding Charles Veal. (Courtesy Mae Breckenridge-Haywood.)

George Teamoh was a Portsmouth native and former slave who used the Underground Railroad while in New York working aboard the schooner *Currituck* in 1853 to escape. When the Union Army occupied Portsmouth in 1862, he returned and began working in the shipyard after it was rebuilt. It was while advocating for fair wages of shipyard workers that his taste for politics began. In 1867, Teamoh was elected to the state constitutional convention. Afterward, he became a state senator and a property owner. He owned a house at the corner of Green and Queen Streets. Teamoh was a trained ship carpenter who worked in the Gosport shipyard prior to escaping. Like Frederick Douglass, he taught himself to read and write. (Courtesy Harrison B. Wilson Archives, Norfolk State University.)

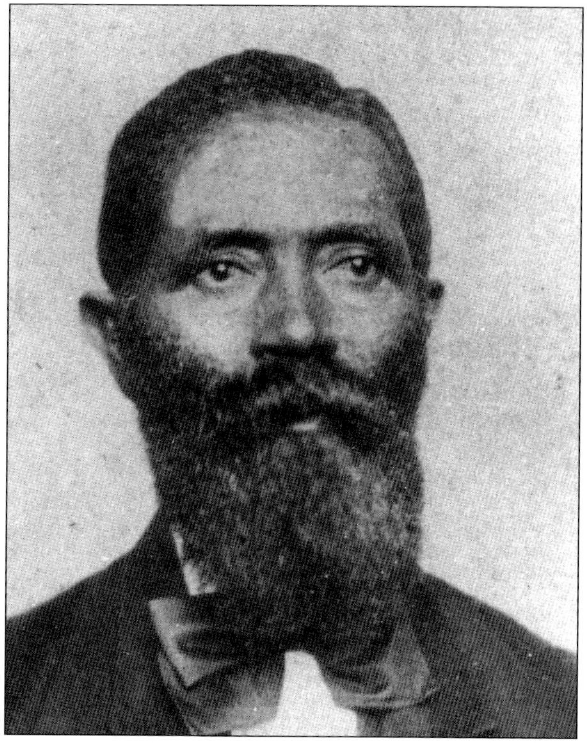

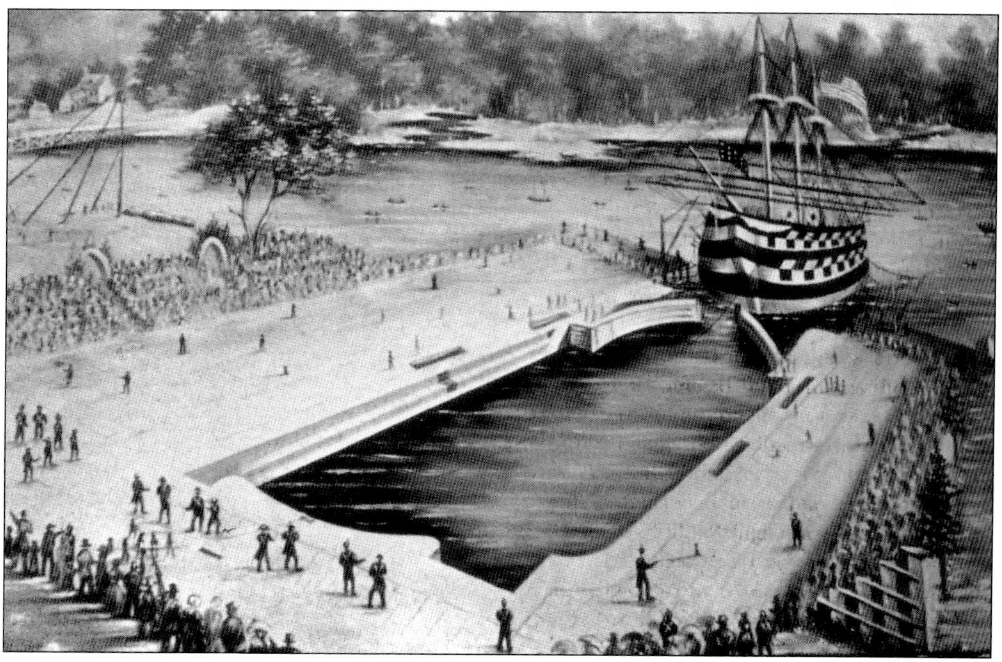

Dry Dock No. 1, built by black stonecutters, was the first dry-docking in America. This engraving depicts the entrance of the USS *Delaware* at the Gosport Navy Yard on June 17, 1833, heralding Portsmouth's commercial and military importance to the shipping industry. (Courtesy Portsmouth Public Library.)

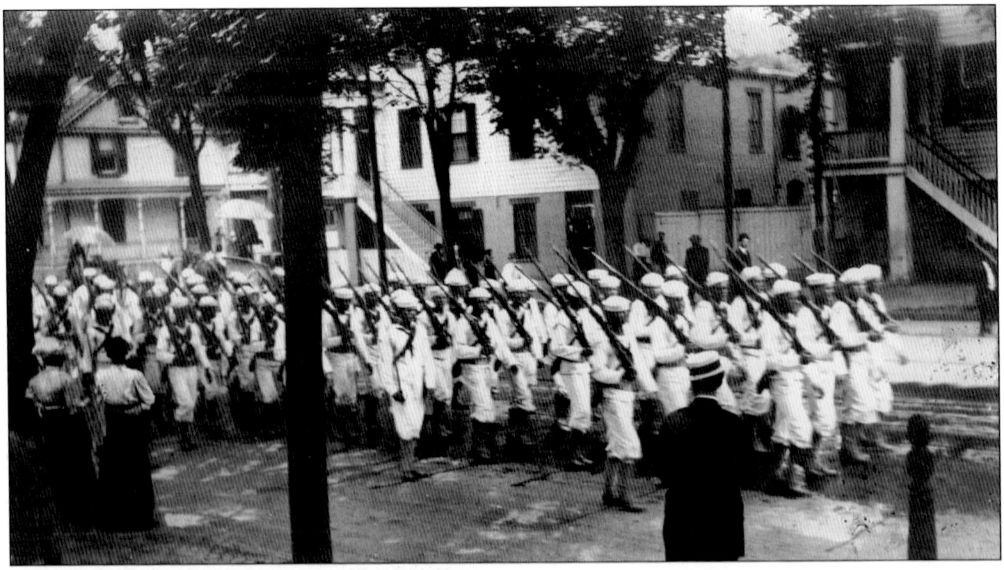

This was a parade of African-American soldiers on the north side of High Street at Dinwiddie, *c.* 1911. (Courtesy Olde Towne Collection, Portsmouth Public Library.)

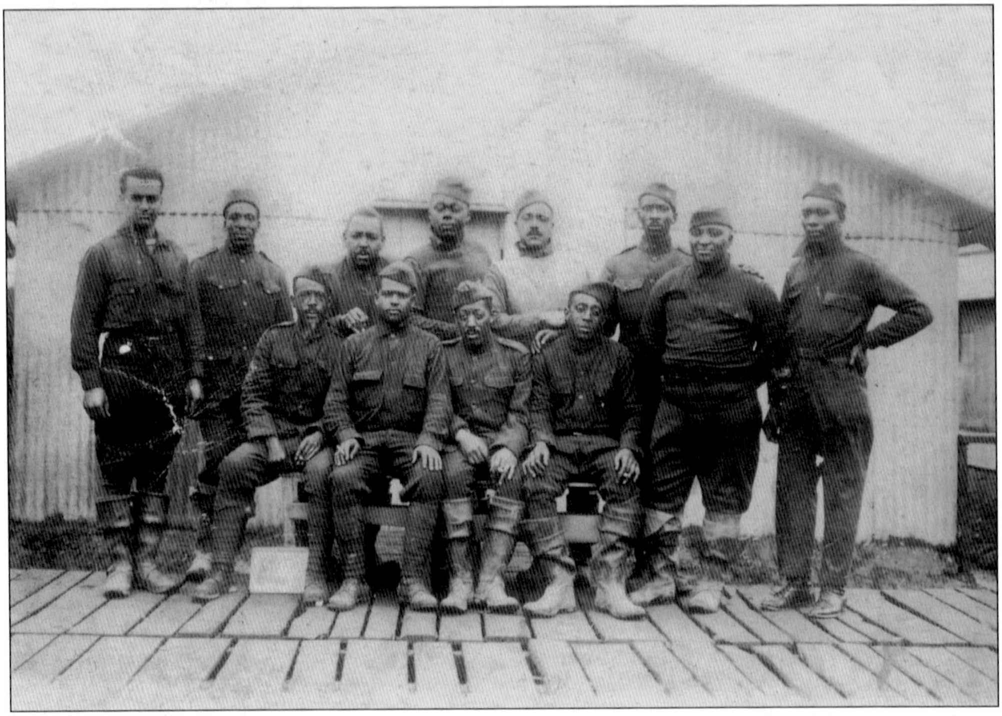

Portsmouth African American soldiers who served during the period of the Spanish American War are depicted here. Although this is an undated photograph, the granddaughter of I.C. Norcom, Rachel Norcom-Smith, believes it to have been during this era. James G. Norcom Sr., Rachel's father, was seated at the far left front of the photograph. Like his father, James Norcom was an educator who taught at I.C. Norcom High School and sang with the Hampton University Glee Club. (Courtesy Rachel Norcom-Smith.)

This May 30, 1939 photograph is of J.H. Green who served in the Spanish American War as a seaman. After the war, Green founded the American Legion in Portsmouth and served as its first president. He was also a merchant, who owned a general store on Green Street, and a hardworking member of Ebenezer Baptist Church. (Lee Rodgers Collection, Portsmouth Public Library.)

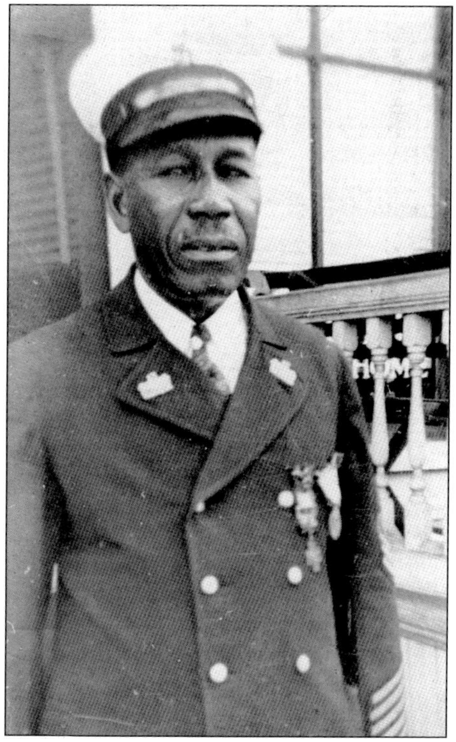

Chaplain Robert W. Odell of the Portsmouth Naval Hospital installed the newly chosen officers of the Lillie B. Chamberlain Navy Wives Club No. 35 on January 19, 1961. The ceremonies were held at the Fleet Reserve Building at the Naval Shipyard, with guests present from other Navy Wives Clubs. Shown below with Chaplain Odell are Mrs. Mildred Johnson (left), the outgoing president; and Mrs. Helen Lassiter, the new president. (Lee Rodgers Collection, Portsmouth Public Library.)

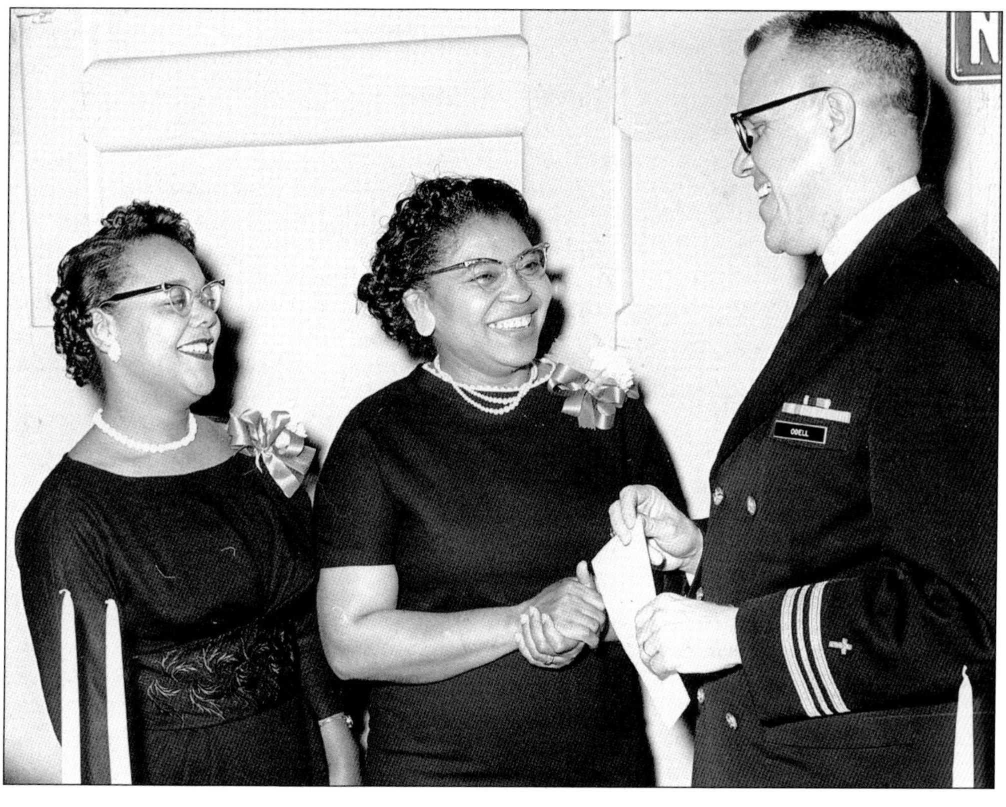

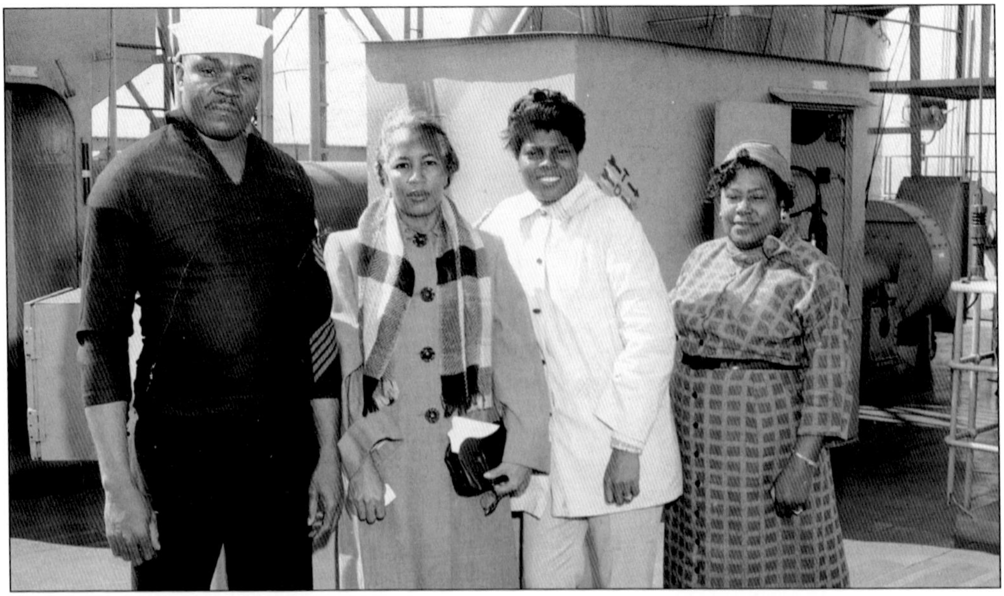

Navy Steward Elijah Turner and his wife Troy lived at 1307 Washington Street in Portsmouth. They are pictured along with guests Marilyn Maultsby, of 1312 Effingham Street, and Mary Griffin, of 1202 Effingham Street. On October 9, 1957, Turner and his guests were taking time out to relax while on board the Service Force attack cargo ship USS *Wyandot* for a one-day dependents cruise off the Virginia Capes. This photograph appeared in the "Colored News" in the *Norfolk Ledger-Dispatch* and the *Portsmouth Star* newspaper, October 16, 1957. (Lee Rodgers Collection, Portsmouth Public Library.)

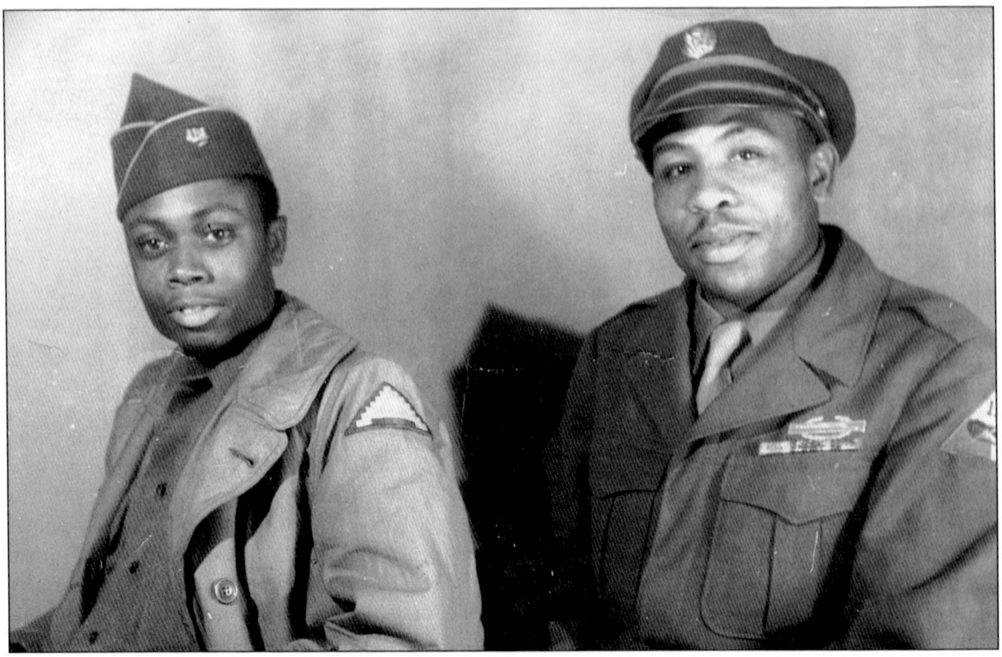

Two World War II African-American soldiers, Moses Gibson of Portsmouth (left) and J. Miller (right), are shown in this undated photograph. (Courtesy Portsmouth Public Library.)

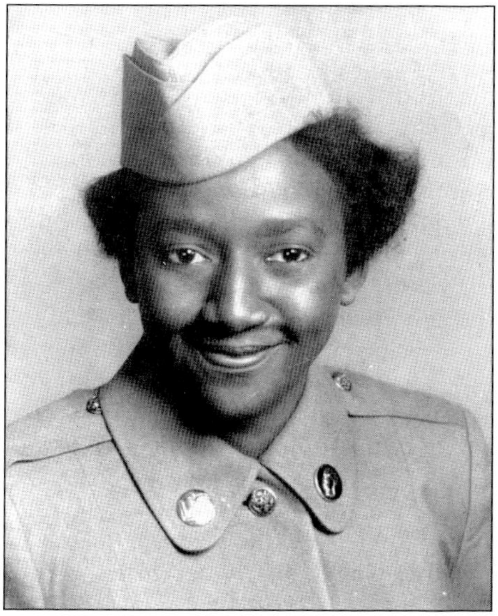

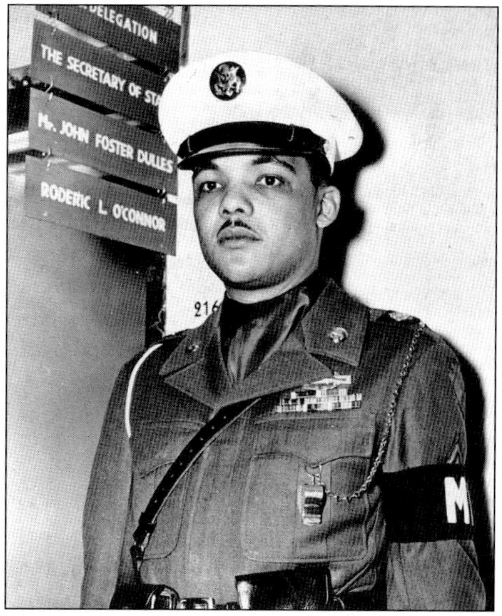

(left) This is a 1955 photograph of Pvt. Katie E. Robinson, taken by the Georjen photography studio in Anniston, Alabama. Robinson, a 1954 graduate of I.C. Norcom High School in Portsmouth, was typical of the men and women from the Portsmouth area who joined the military, especially the navy, as a career option. (Lee Rodgers Collection, Portsmouth Public Library.) *(right)* Sgt. Harvey F. Morgan Jr. was photographed standing guard outside the office of John Foster Dulles, Secretary of State, *c.* 1954. The photograph appeared in the column "Colored Notes" in the *Portsmouth Star* newspaper on February 16, 1954. (Lee Rodgers Collection, Portsmouth Public Library.)

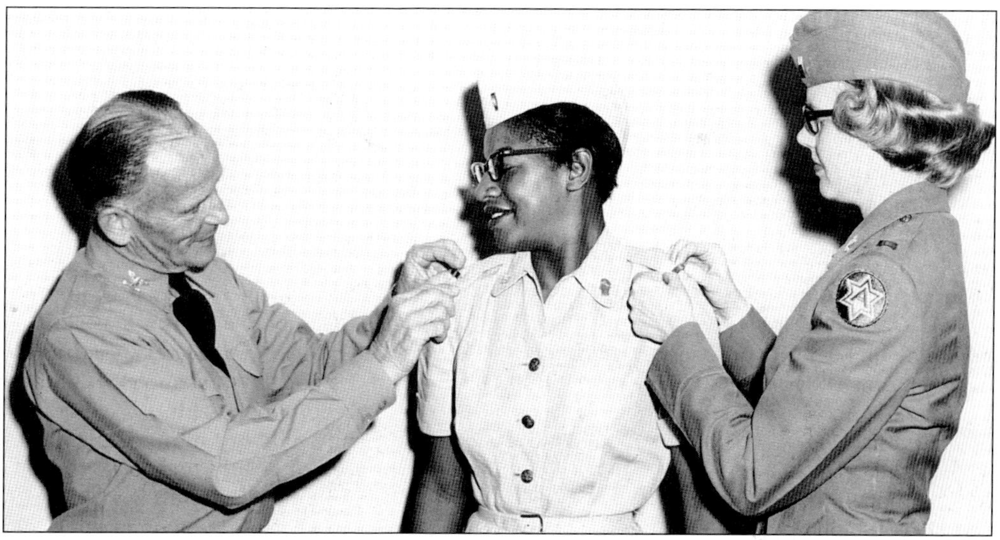

Second Lt. Mary E. Williams, Assistant Special Service Officer at Fort Lawton, Washington, is shown receiving her first lieutenant's bars in the Women's Army Corps from Col. Hal Randall, Executive Officer of the U.S. Army Military District, State of Washington, and from First Lt. Jo Anne Pauley of the WAC, on August 1957. Lieutenant Williams is the daughter of Mr. and Mrs. Augustus Williams of 923 Mt. Vernon Avenue. (Lee Rodgers Collection, Portsmouth Public Library.)

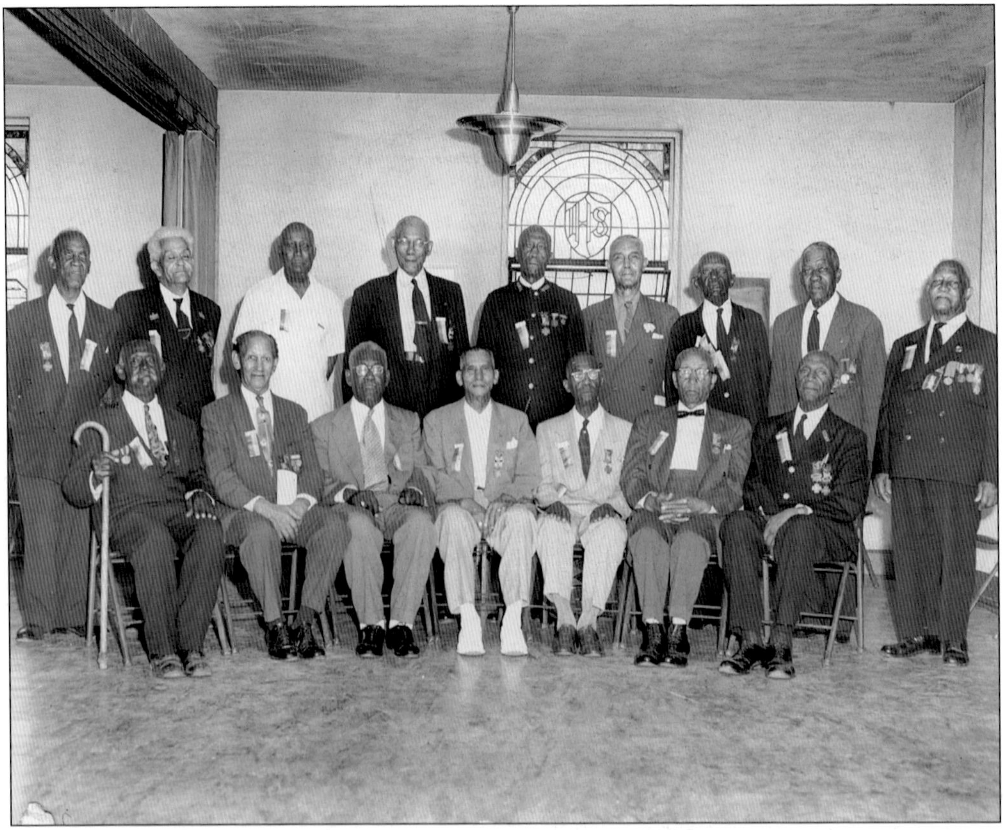

In 1898, "Fifty-eight years ago these men and others of their comrades were in the Army and Navy of the United States in the war with Spain—the short but decisive conflict that lost Spain the last remnants of her once vast colonial empire in the New World and in the Pacific. The Department of the Potomac, United Spanish War Veterans, and Ladies' Auxiliary, met in the 46th annual encampment Thursday, June 28, at the Ebenezer Baptist Church. In the face of thinning ranks, the 'boys' always have a great time in their annual get-togethers. Pictured above are members of the department staff (left to right) are as follows: W. Perry, bugler; Fred L. Landers of High Point, North Carolina; Jeremiah Green of Portsmouth, quartermaster; Joseph Carter of Baltimore, Maryland, newly elected department commander; David P. Porter of Norfolk, past department commander, just succeeded by Carter; George T. Walker of Richmond, chaplain; Edward Harris of Washington, D.C.; (back row) Rev. Edward T. Johnson of Washington, chief of staff; Bruce of Washington, junior vice commander; William R. Giles of Washington, adjutant; J.E. Jordan of Washington; T.J. Jackson of Baltimore, senior vice commander; George West and James D. Blair of Washington; George Williams of Portsmouth, department inspector, and William H. Minor of Washington, color bearer." The photograph and accompanying article appeared in the "Colored News" column in the *Norfolk Ledger-Dispatch* and the *Portsmouth Star* newspapers on July 3, 1956. (Lee Rodgers Collection, Portsmouth Public Library.)

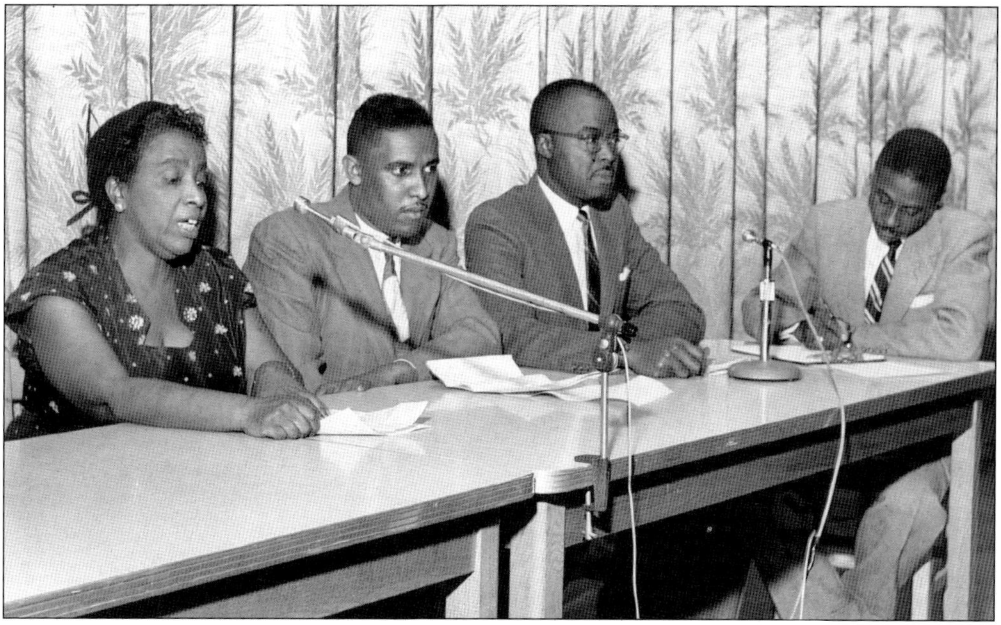

Black leaders in Portsmouth often held press conferences, such as the one depicted of Mrs. Meyers, Thomas B. Hargrove, James A. Overton, and Hugo A. Owens in January 1956, at the USO/YMCA building. Dr. Owens was most known for a lawsuit against the city of Portsmouth seeking equal services and opportunities for blacks. Judge Overton and Dr. James Holley often joined Owens in these legal challenges. (Courtesy Lee Rodgers Collection, Portsmouth Public Library.)

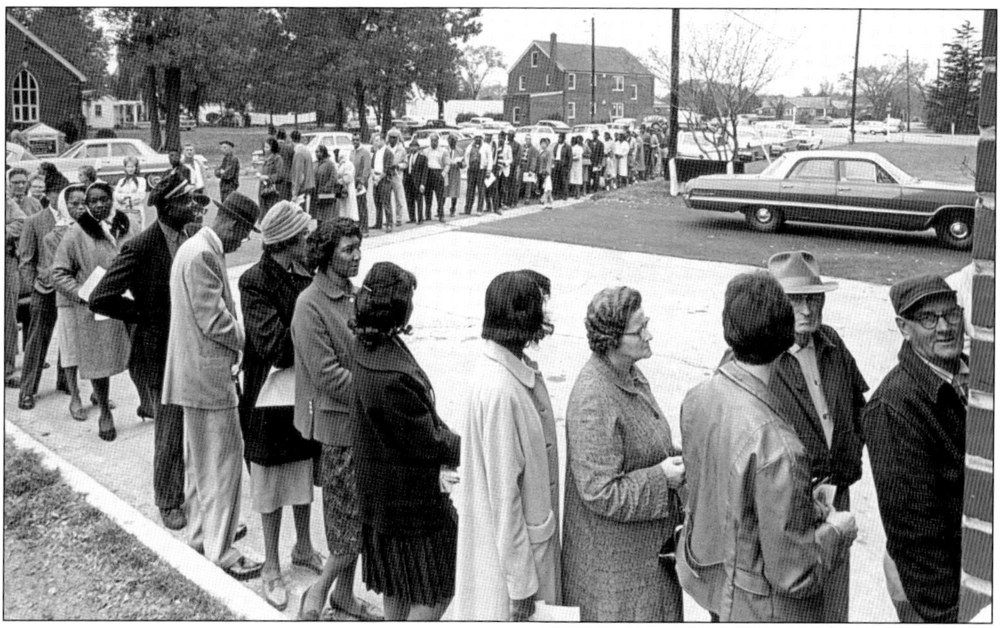

Westhaven Fire Station voting is shown here on November 3, 1964. This was one of the earliest periods during which blacks in Portsmouth were allowed to vote since Reconstruction. (Courtesy Portsmouth Public Library.)

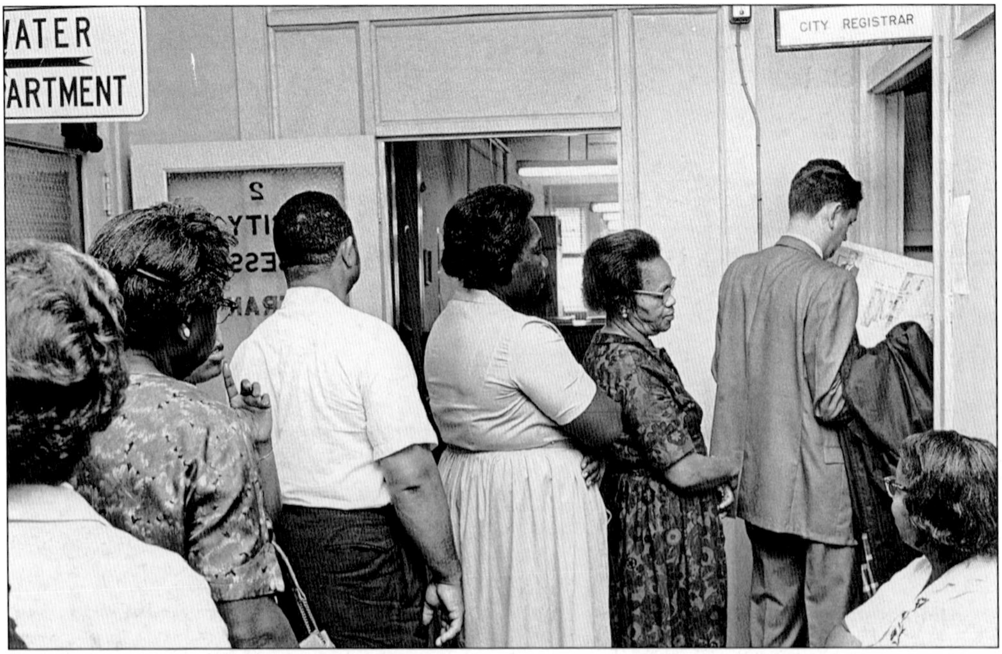

Several people, mostly African American, line up at the City Registrar's office to register to vote on September 29, 1964. (Courtesy Lee Rodgers Collection, Portsmouth Public Library.)

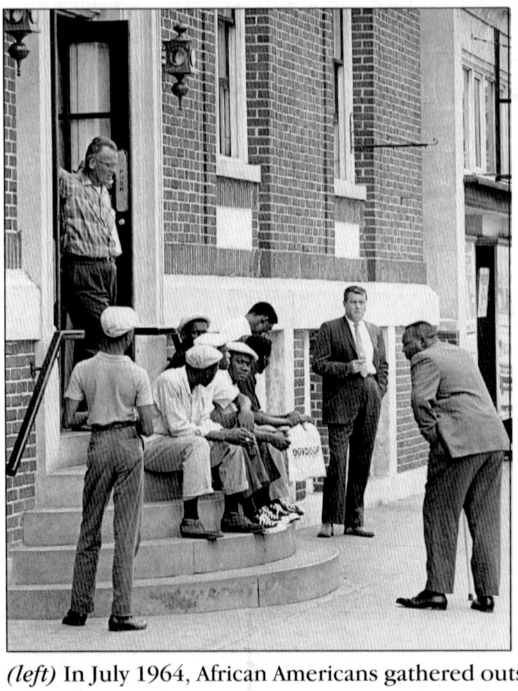

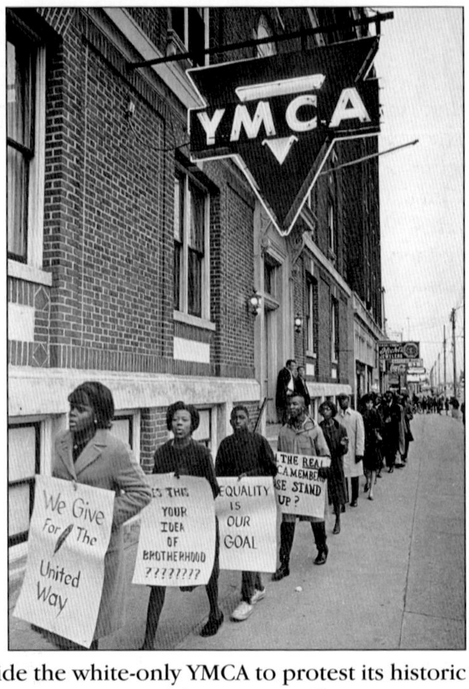

(left) In July 1964, African Americans gathered outside the white-only YMCA to protest its historic all-white policy that excluded blacks. James Horne was the leader of this protest effort. (Courtesy Lee Rodgers Collection, Portsmouth Public Library.) *(right)* Some of the protesters marched, as seen above, while others conducted a sit-in to protest the all-white policy of the local YMCA. (Courtesy Lee Rodgers Collection, Portsmouth Public Library.)

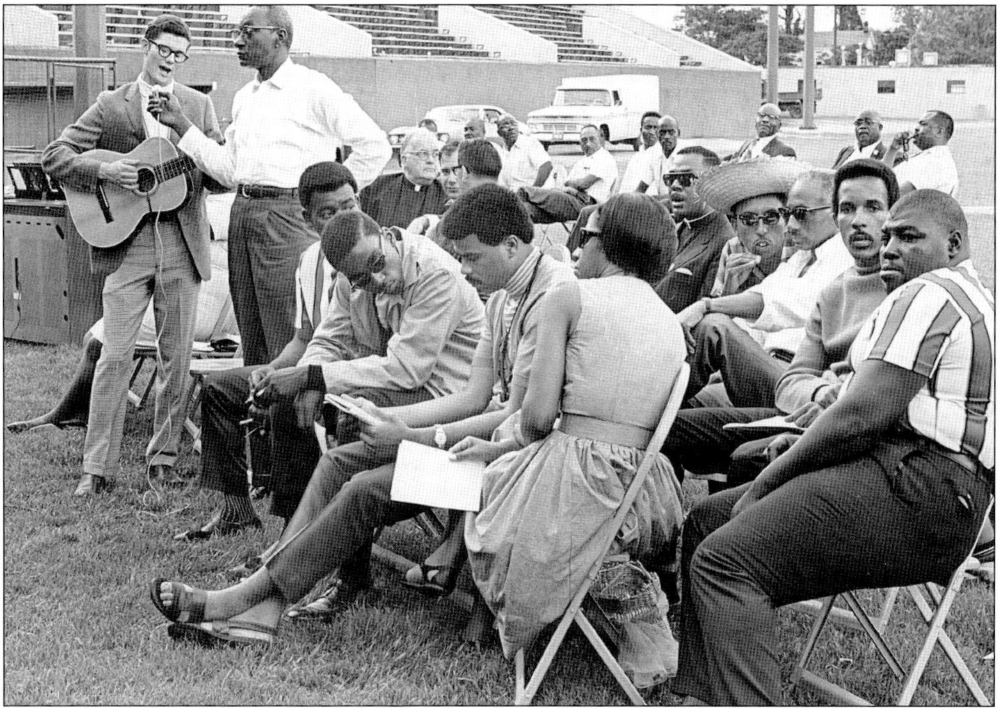

Pictured in this May 12, 1968 photograph of a rally for the Poor People's Campaign at the Frank D. Lawrence Stadium are mostly clergymen, including Charles Bowens, Melvin Boone, Harvey Johnson, James Pointer, Edward Whitaker, and Reverends Trotter and Wilkerson. (Courtesy Lee Rodgers Collection, Portsmouth Public Library.)

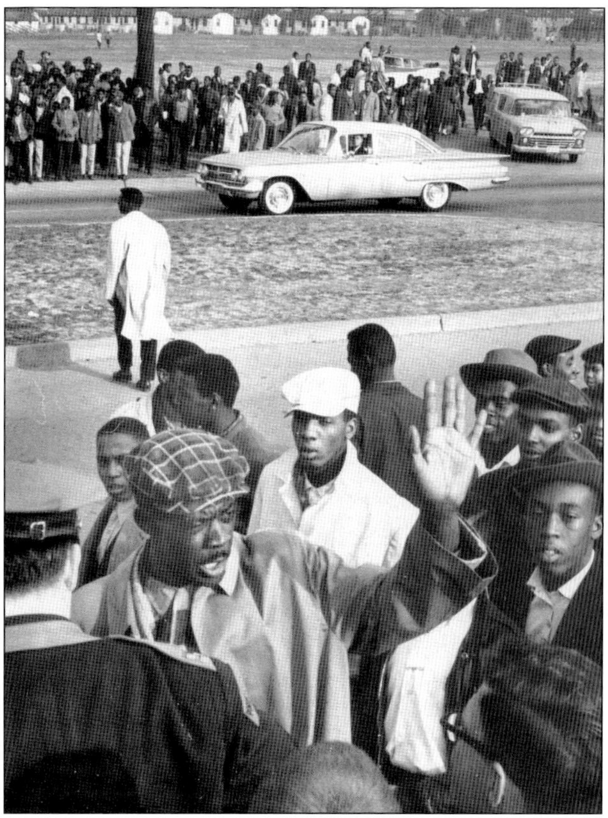

Students protest in 1972 at I.C. Norcom High School. Howard Park can be seen in the background. The students were protesting the closure of I.C. Norcom as a comprehensive high school. The school board wanted to change the school into a vocation training school. While the board's decision prevailed, the vocational program adopted was highly technical and was finally accepted by the students and neighborhood. (Courtesy Portsmouth Public Library.)

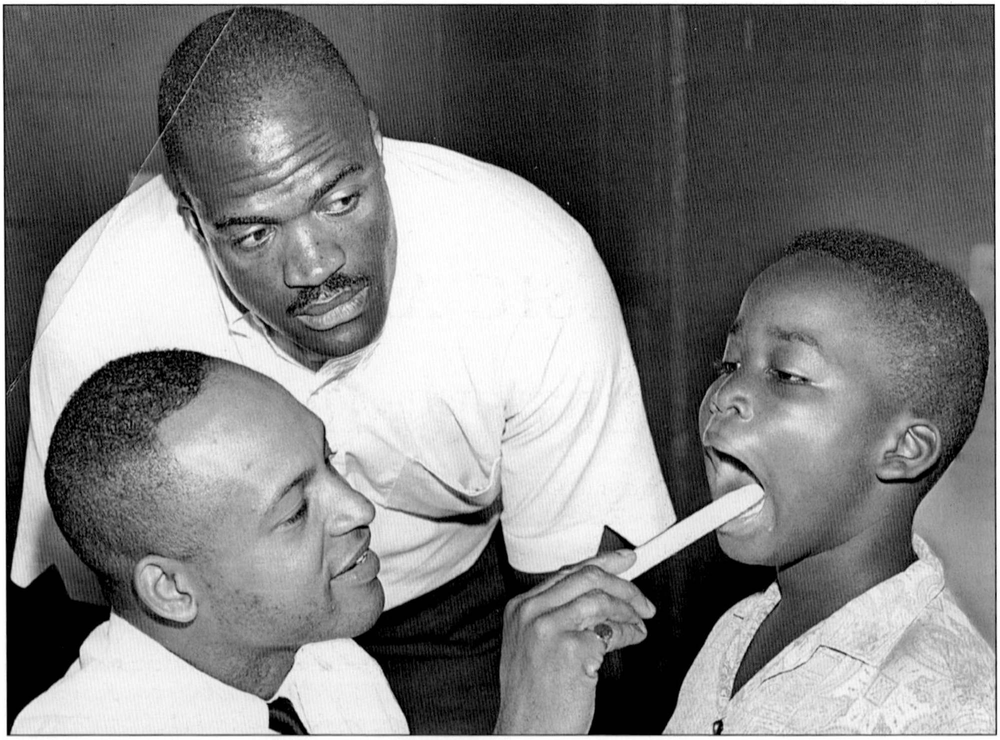

Dr. James Holley examines a young patient in his office. (Courtesy Lee Rodgers Collection, Portsmouth Public Library.)

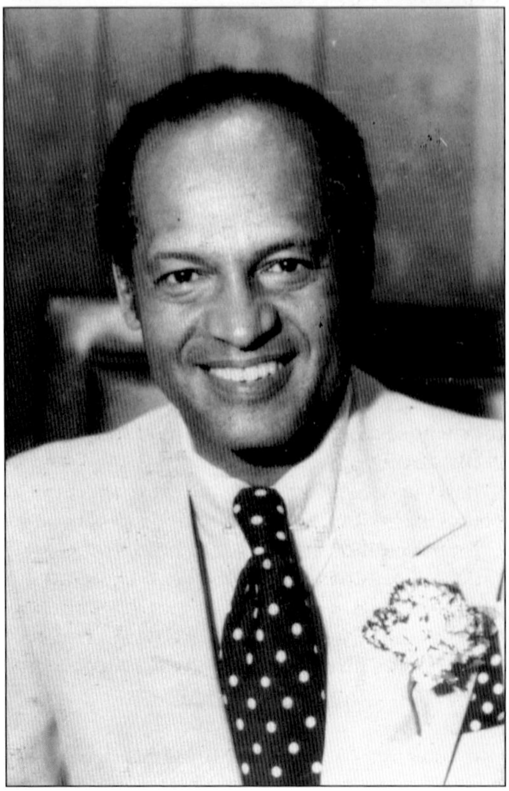

Dr. James W. (Jim) Holley III was elected as the first black mayor of Portsmouth, serving from 1984 to 1987 and then again from 1996 to the present. (Courtesy Portsmouth Public Library.)

Six

Music and Entertainment

Little of the pre–Civil War African-American music traditions survived in printed form that could have been preservation. Instead, only a few musical pieces surviving through the oral traditions remain, especially in the form of the quartet. These a cappella groups would appear in the neighborhood churches, often in support of institutional and organizational fund-raisers. The majority of the quartets in Portsmouth thrived from the 1800s through the early 1960s, performing before primarily church audiences with a music repertoire seeped in the spiritual and hymn folk culture of the Tidewater area. Those who sought national recognition, performing blues, minstrel, and pop music, venturing to vaudeville, record, and radio left the area for a more expansive arena. Northeast migrations by Hampton Roads residents, especially from Norfolk, assisted the national success of some of these groups who sought fame and fortune in New York. So plentiful were these transplants to the "Big Apple" that some referred to a section of Harlem as the "second Norfolk." Audience familiarity with these Tidewater music groups provided needed popularity and subsequent success in the New York venues. Most of these quartets were composed of men, although some had female members with a few made up exclusively of women. Because music was integral to black church services, choirs, choruses, and quartets were crucial. Additionally, this a cappella tradition was a natural result of the scant existence of pianos or organs in most churches until the 20th century. Many of these groups were musical extensions of social organizations within the community landscape. In 1924, the Elks Quartet marketed their organization with one of their songs, "Why not be an Elk." They used this composition in newspaper and concert ads. While many of these groups were not trained to read music, their harmonizing strength and ear for music enabled them to create arrangements quickly for the frequent community concerts and appearances.[61]

The most noted singing groups were the Roland Hayes, Glee Club, Treble Club, Mu-So-Lit Club, Music Makers Glee Club, the Hiram Simmons Glee Club, and the Elks Quartet. In Portsmouth, Hiram Simmons was the most influential composer whose work shaped the choral traditions in the black Hampton Roads churches from the 1920s through the 1950s. Simmons was born in Princess Anne County, now Virginia Beach, in 1874. A latecomer to Portsmouth, moving there at the age of 41, Simmons quickly established himself as an organist, music teacher, and composer at Ebenezer Baptist and Emanuel AME churches. What solidified his and other black composers' musical reputations was the work of Simmons' Church Music Publishing House. This printing company allowed composers to disseminate their works to larger audiences. In fact, Simmons' own compositions, "Heavenly Father Bless Us Today," and "Around the Great White Throne," garnered national recognition from the National Association of Negro Musicians and inclusion in the *Baptist Standard Hymn Book*.[62]

From 1915 until his death in 1938, the musical works of Hiram Simmons continued to influence Hampton Roads not only because of his established compositions, but also through the choirs he founded. Simmons' Merry Music Makers and the Hiram Simmons Glee Club performed traditional spirituals and church hymns, classical religious music, and the founder's own intricate compositions in local churches throughout Hampton Roads. This practice of performing at numerous local churches helped to break down denominational barriers throughout the area and blend the musical traditions. Other singers trained by Hampton Institute's professor Nathaniel Dett formed choirs that were typically called quartets. James G. Norcom Sr. (the Roland Hayes Glee Club), Mandonia P. Owens (the Voices by the Sea), Essie Joyner (the Naomi Jubilee Chorus), and Laura Elliott (the Treble Clef Glee Club) founded quartets and choral groups that enjoyed fame throughout Hampton Roads. By the 1940s, this quartet and choral tradition would begin to be supplanted by the gospel singers whose influence emerged from the Holiness and Pentecostal churches in America. In Portsmouth, the Soul Stirrers and the Starlight Four would incorporate the previous musical forms into the newer gospel music. Like their predecessors, this music would not just be contained in their native denominations; instead, they would enlarge their audience base through performances in a wide variety of churches throughout Tidewater. Concurrent with the quartet tradition was the emergence of individuals who attained prominence in the musical world. The names of Graham Washington Jackson and Sissieretta Jones may be unfamiliar to today's society, but they were widely known during their respective eras. Like the quartets, these individual musicians left the Portsmouth area to attain fame and to make their mark nationally.[63]

Graham Washington Jackson was born February 22, 1903. on Canal Street in the Lincolnsville section of Portsmouth to Graham and Pauline Hinton Jackson. It was on Canal Street and in that close-knit neighborhood that Jackson grew up and thrived. Born with an extraordinary musical gift, accounts noted that beginning at the age of three Jackson would play hymns on the church organ after hearing them just hours before. He continued to develop as a promising pianist, accordion player, and orchestra leader, such that at the time of graduation from I.C. Norcom High School in February 1923, Jackson formed his own band, the Seminole Syncopators, and traveled throughout the country in search of fame. Within a few months after leaving Portsmouth, the Seminole Syncopators performed in Atlanta and soon became the hit of the season. Afterwards, Jackson relocated permanently in Atlanta, performing at prominent social and political functions, including the Democratic National Convention in 1932. The following year Jackson was invited to play the piano in a personal performance for President Franklin D. Roosevelt, who was so impressed that he took him to the Little White House in Warm Springs, Georgia. He became an overnight celebrity and a familiar guest at the Little White House. With the outbreak of World War II, Jackson took his talents to the troops, enlisting in the navy and entertaining the public at bond rallies that raised money for the war effort. However, Roosevelt did not forget Jackson and continued to have him perform at various functions. Despite these achievements, Jackson would be remembered more for the *Life* magazine photograph taken as he and thousands of other mourners waited for the presidential hearse as Roosevelt's body was being transported from Warm Springs to its place of rest in April 1945. "While looking at the long line of mourners, Jackson lifted up his accordion and began playing 'Goin' Home,' Jackson's face . . . was the embodiment of sorrow—a black sailor with an accordion, eyes cast upward, and tears streaming down his cheeks—became a symbol of national grief."[64]

Ironically, it was this photo that catapulted Jackson to national fame. Afterwards he appeared in everything from commercial ads with his accordion in one hand and a bottle of coke in the other, to motion pictures and books about Roosevelt. His prominence would continue, especially among the presidents, performing before Harry S Truman, Dwight D. Eisenhower, John F. Kennedy, Lyndon B. Johnson, and Jimmy Carter. Graham Washington Jackson, Portsmouth's most renowned celebrity, would die on January 16, 1982, at the age of 79 in Atlanta, survived by his wife Helen Jackson and two sons, Graham Jr. and Gerald.[65]

Sissieretta Jones was born Matilda Sissieretta Joyner in Portsmouth, Virginia. She was brought up in the church musical tradition. Her father, who was a minister, and mother sang in the church choirs throughout Portsmouth, including the one at Ebenezer Baptist Church. Early in life, her family moved to Providence, Rhode Island, and she studied voice at the Providence Academy of Music and the New England Conservatory. Jones had many successes in her career: several of them were breakthroughs that paved the way for later artists. She sang at the Chicago World Fair in 1893 and Madison Square Garden and for several Presidents of the United States. Abroad, she sang for royalty. Her experiences were not all positive, despite the acclaim. Early in her career, Jones was dubbed the "Black Patti" by the white press. This was a dismissive (although intended as complimentary) comparison to Adelina Patti (1843–1919), a successful Italian soprano at that time. And while the name stuck, it did not guarantee fame. The late 19th century was not kind to African Americans who chose to perform in the world of serious musicians. Despite her talent and training, she was not able to perform at the Metropolitan Opera in New York because of her race. In fact, the Met would continue this exclusive policy until 1955 when contralto Marian Anderson made her national concert stage debut. Undaunted by these setbacks, Jones turned to the black theatrical circuit, performing in 1896 for the vaudeville act *Black Patti's Troubadours*, which initially performed popular minstrel acts with arias from operas. Later *Patti's Troubadours* would perform musical comedies that centered on unified themes. She retired in 1916. In her final years, Jones took in homeless children while sinking into poverty. She died in 1933.[66]

Sissieretta Jones may not be remembered by most in the 21st century, but her musical legacy will. During the latter part of her career, she combined elements of European classical music with the folk song traditions of southern African Americans. Since that period, this hybrid creation would be a common practice within the spiritual, rhythm and blues, and rap musical forms. Black composers would be instrumental in bridging this late 19th century pioneering effort and making it a tradition in the 20th and 21st centuries. Throughout the region composers began to surface with works that became popular standards, especially within the religious culture.[67]

Parades and picnics were common recreational activities for the masses in the nation, black and white, in part because they were cheap and could be arranged with little effort or money. During the first half of the 20th century, the July 4th celebration planned by blacks were described as the most commendable demonstration seen in Portsmouth's history, mirroring the rich old national jubilees of the pre–Civil War era. Various religious fraternities, Masons, Union Sons of Freedmen, and civic societies, arrayed in ornate regalia and carrying banners, flanked by marshals, paraded in a procession through the streets of Portsmouth until midday. Afterwards, they enjoyed refreshments and at 3:00 p.m. formed a procession with Frederick Douglass who marched with them to the courthouse where he made a speech. The Rev. Edward G. Corprew had the honor of introducing Frederick Douglas who "arose with much dignity and composure to address the multitude."[68]

African Americans in Portsmouth enjoyed their picnics on the grounds of the Naval Hospital that was adjacent to Lincolnsville. Stannard's Hall was the dance hall used by blacks at the corner of Queen and Water Streets. Moreover, throughout the nation the emergence of a growing middle class brought about the creation of numerous recreational facilities, including beach resorts, performance and music theaters, and amusement parks. Because most of these facilities excluded African Americans, the small black middle class banded together to create their own facilities. The Brights, owners of Little Bay Beach in Norfolk, worked with numerous churches, fraternal, sororal, and social organizations in Portsmouth, Norfolk, Berkley, Hampton, Princess Anne, and Norfolk Counties to provide recreation for their community members. Miller Day Care Nursery, the Skull and Bones Club, the Eureka Club, Minute Club, and St. Thomas Church in Portsmouth were frequent seasonal visitors to Little Bay Beach.[69]

A key component in encouraging and facilitating the expansion of recreational activities for blacks was the establishment of a black YMCA on August 15, 1946 in the 1300 block of Chestnut Street. It was at the YMCA that dances, social gatherings, and meetings were held. But African Americans did not own all the recreational facilities they patronized in Portsmouth. Many whites owned businesses that specifically catered to and were a source of employment for blacks. The Bland, Capitol, and Lyric, for example, were Jewish-owned theaters located in the heart of the black business district in Portsmouth. From the 1920s to the 1940s, Portsmouth was inundated with skilled artisans and laborers seeking employment as sailors, longshoremen, and shipyard workers who migrated to the region primarily from rural Virginia and eastern North Carolina. As housing developed to accommodate these workers and their families, so did the recreational facilities. Moreover, the creation of I.C. Norcom High School provided a focal point for teenagers whose common experiences also resulted in similar after school activities. Those who owned the Bland, Capitol, and Lyric theaters recognized this economic opportunity that other white theater owners ignored. To insure patronage from these groups, theater owners advertised their movies in local yearbooks, flyers, and posters around town, and newspapers such as the Norfolk *Journal and Guide*.[70]

During the 1920s, 1930s, and 1940s local theaters showed a myriad of films ranging from silent films in the 1920s, to the "talkies," Technicolor, and "serial" films of the 1930s and 1940s. Serial films were western cowboy, war, adventure, and science fiction films designed as an inexpensive diversion for people unfamiliar with movie-going. The Bland Theater, with a 500 seat capacity, was located at 831 High Street. The theater shared space with Sutton's Furniture store before a separate movie house was built in 1942. Along with the Capitol Theater, it was part of the Jewish Lichtman movie franchise that was headquartered in Washington, D.C. The Bland was noted for showing mostly westerns during its heyday. Interestingly the Bland shared a split shift with employees from the Capitol Theater. Opened in December 1925, the Capitol, located at 608 Effingham Street, was considered the first, the classiest, and most popular of the black theaters in Portsmouth. The Capitol, an oddly constructed building with its back wrapped around the King Street pool hall, seated between 800 and 900 people with an interior designed to mimic an opera house. What also distinguished the Capitol was the talent night and stage show that featured local singers and bands. Ruth Brown, a famous singer and Portsmouth native, began her career during one of the Friday night amateur performances.[71]

The Lyric Theater, the smallest of the three, opened at the corner of Chestnut and Queen Streets in 1939. Like the Capitol, the Lyric was Jewish owned and showed "B" class movies. A fire gutted the original building. Saul Soroko, who also owned a grocery store, owned the second Lyric located at 907 High Street. The managers of the Lyric wore business suits and the doormen wore black capes, military-style hats, and white gloves. Journalist Edgar Rouzeau wrote that the Jews, who owned most of the theaters in New York City—including the Apollo Theatre—"also owned or controlled the film production options of individual owners by circulating better pictures only to their own establishments." Thus, even if a black man purchased his own theater, he would not have the money to buy directly major films for his theater resulting in the ultimate failure of the theater.[72]

The Bland, Capitol, and Lyric Theaters contributed much to the economy of Portsmouth from 1925 to 1945. Like most black institutions, or those that catered to the black community, the theaters sponsored community events including an annual movie and candy Christmas party for children aged 12 and under. Moreover, these theaters allowed churches and social organizations to utilize their buildings during their sponsored food drives. Schools used the theater for graduation ceremonies and the theaters co-sponsored summer school fund-raising contests that provided free tuition and summer school sessions at the Norfolk Unit, Virginia Union University (currently Norfolk State University) for winners. It was not until integration in the 1960s that Portsmouth's black theaters began declining and eventually closed through loss of business. Blacks began to patronize what were white Portsmouth theaters—Commodore, Colony, State, and Virginia— because of their better location and amenities, and because just-released films were shown in those theaters. The Capitol was demolished in the 1980s, leaving only a memory for those who remember its glory days. The Bland Theater was converted into the Meyers and Tabakin Furniture Store while the Club DePorres, a non-profit charity and social organization, purchased the Lyric hoping to historically restore the building.[73]

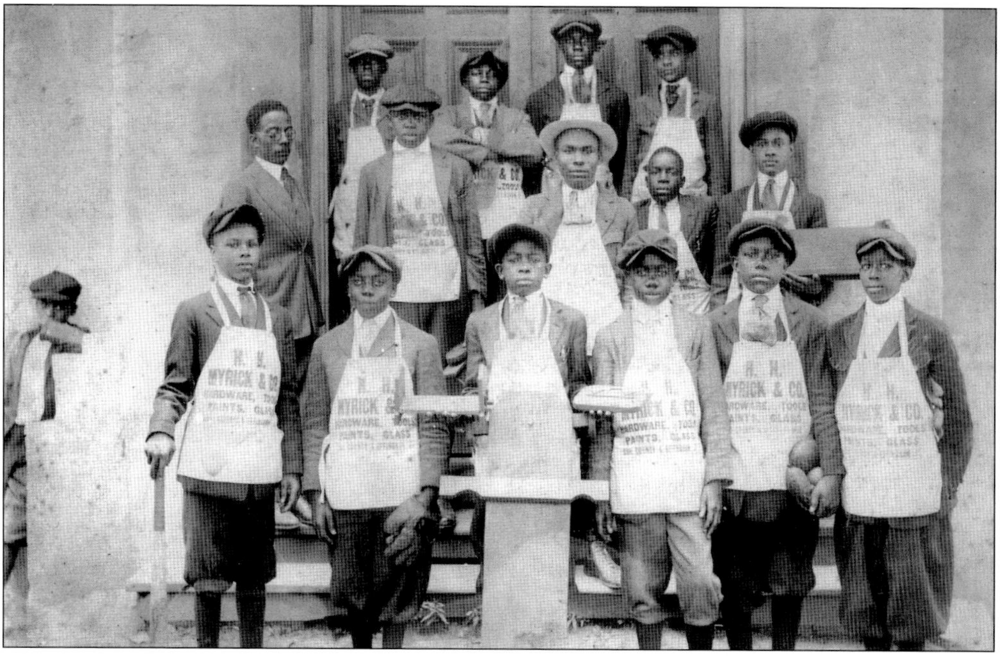

The baseball team, "No Holiday Tomorrow," was coached by Prof. S.H. Clarke (with glasses in the far left corner). The team was sponsored by H.H. Myrick and Company who sold tools and hardware. The business was listed at 608 County and Effingham Streets, *c.* 1912. (Courtesy Mae Breckenridge-Haywood.)

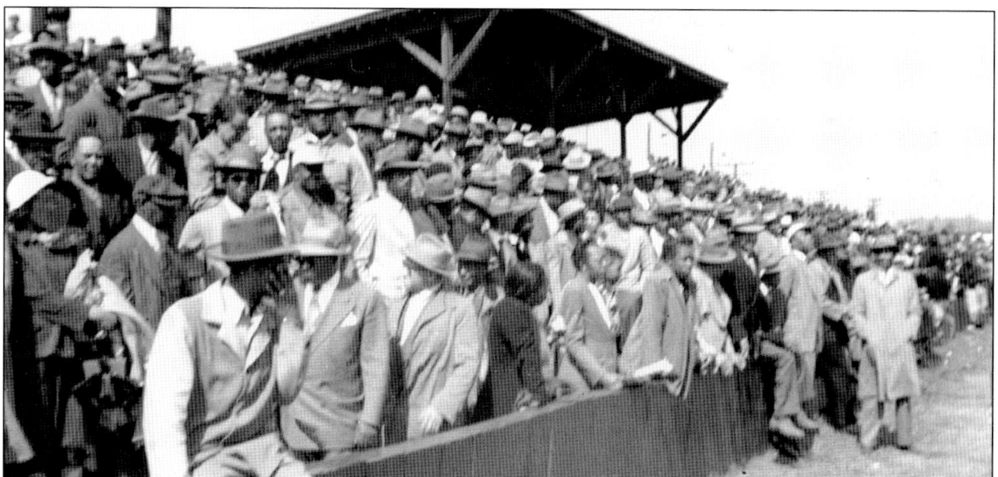

The Green Street Park, also called Swanehee Stadium, was a popular arena for all sporting events including professional Negro Baseball League games, Norcom High School games, and May Day activities. So popular were these events, including May Day during which all school children participated, that the local cook shops sold pies and other foods immediately outside the arena. Ann Stancil, a long-time Portsmouth residence, remembered that the park extended into the Brighton section, along Fayette, Maupin, Jefferson, and Lincoln Streets. This photograph of a crowd observing an event at the Green Street Park was taken sometime around 1939–1940. (Courtesy Lee Rodgers Collection, Portsmouth Public Library.)

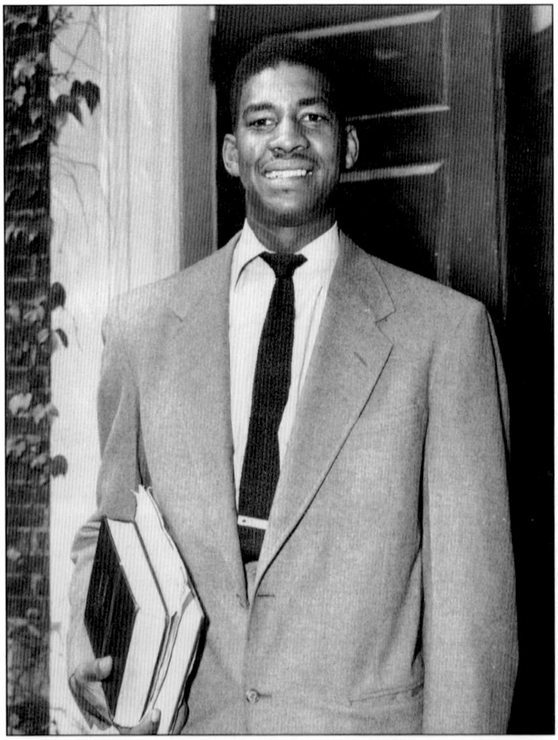

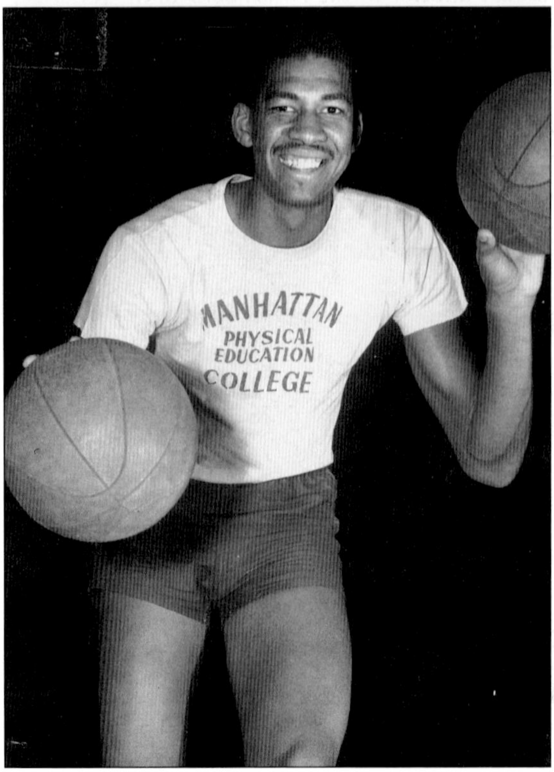

Junius Kellogg was a football, track, and basketball athlete who, after serving in the army for over three years, won a scholarship to Manhattan College, renowned as a basketball powerhouse. After graduation, he joined the Harlem Globetrotters but tragedy was soon to find Kellogg. On April 2, 1954, an automobile accident would render him a paraplegic. Undaunted, he became Deputy Assistant Commissioner of the New York Community Development Agency. The following is taken from a November 13, 1951 newspaper article: "Basketball Star Returns to College. New York. Junius Kellogg, Manhattan College basketball star who exposed an attempted bribe and helped clear the path for authorities to deal with persons guilty of the crime, has returned to Manhattan College after being released from the army. He was called back for a short time as a reservist, but was let out after five months because he was too tall. He is six feet, eight inches in height . . . Shot from this odd angle, the long, muscled limbs of Kellogg are a study in essential basketball equipment. Those legs can travel at amazing speed and with hairline accuracy when Junius wants to collect two points for the team on a rebound shot." (Courtesy Bertha Edwards Collection, Portsmouth Public Library.)

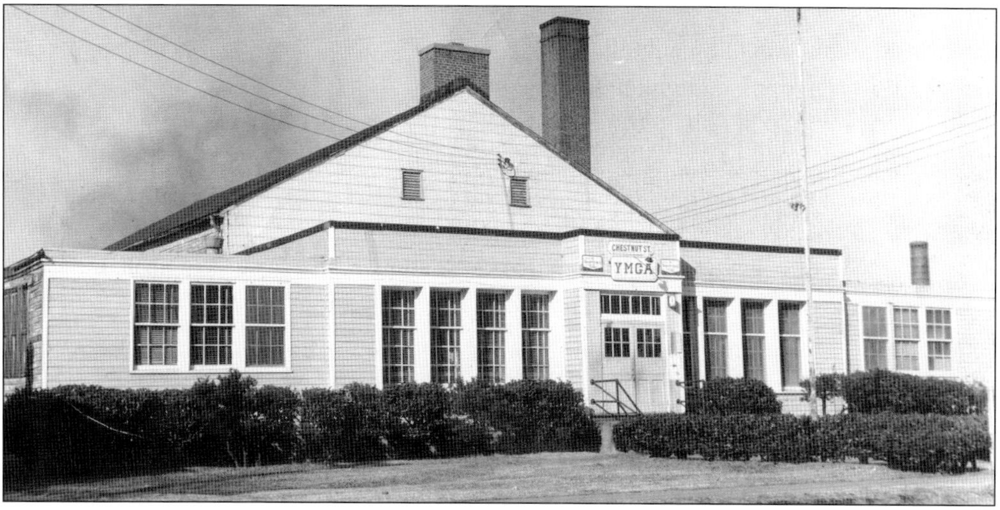

The USO Club, which also serviced the community as the Chestnut Street branch YMCA, was located by the railroad tracks at 1300 Chestnut Street. The photograph was taken on March 19, 1942. "Colored USO Club at 1300 Chestnut Street—Unusually active is this club's famous musical revue and band, developed and directed by La Vozier La Mar, the club's director. The musical show will be presented Monday night at Norfolk's Palais Royal. On Tuesday night, the show will be offered at the Newport News USO Club. The musical revue and band will perform Wednesday night in the Carver Homes auditorium. On the last Saturday night in this month, the show will go to Alexandria for a performance in the USO Club there. The director of the USO at Alexandria is W.L.D. Johnson, former assistant director of the Portsmouth USO." (Courtesy Portsmouth Public Library.)

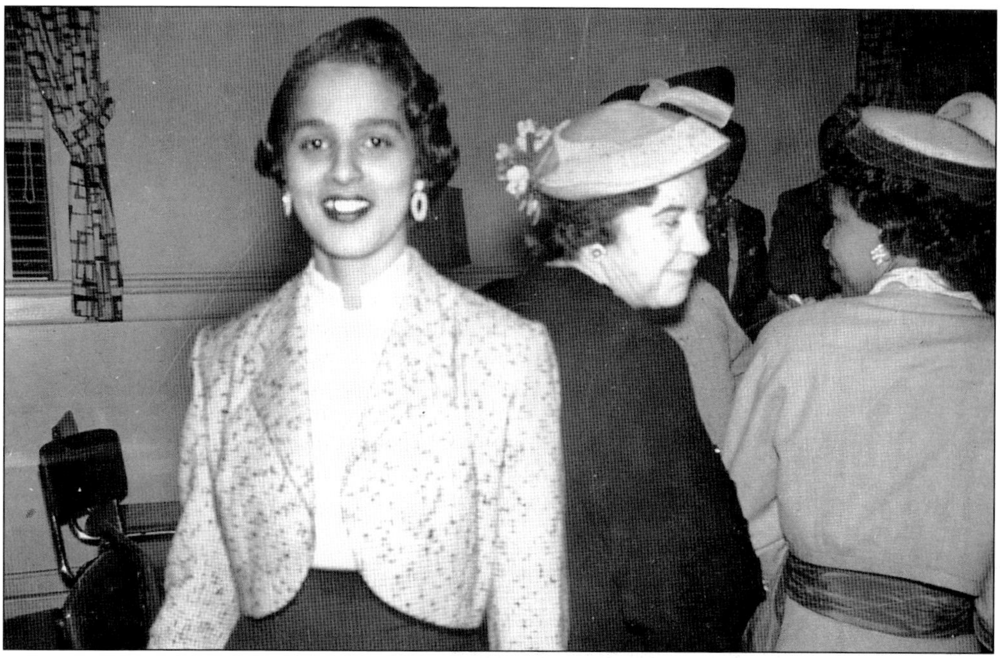

This is Miss Sarah Choate at the USO Club dedication on March 1, 1942. (Courtesy Lee Rodgers Collection, Portsmouth Public Library.)

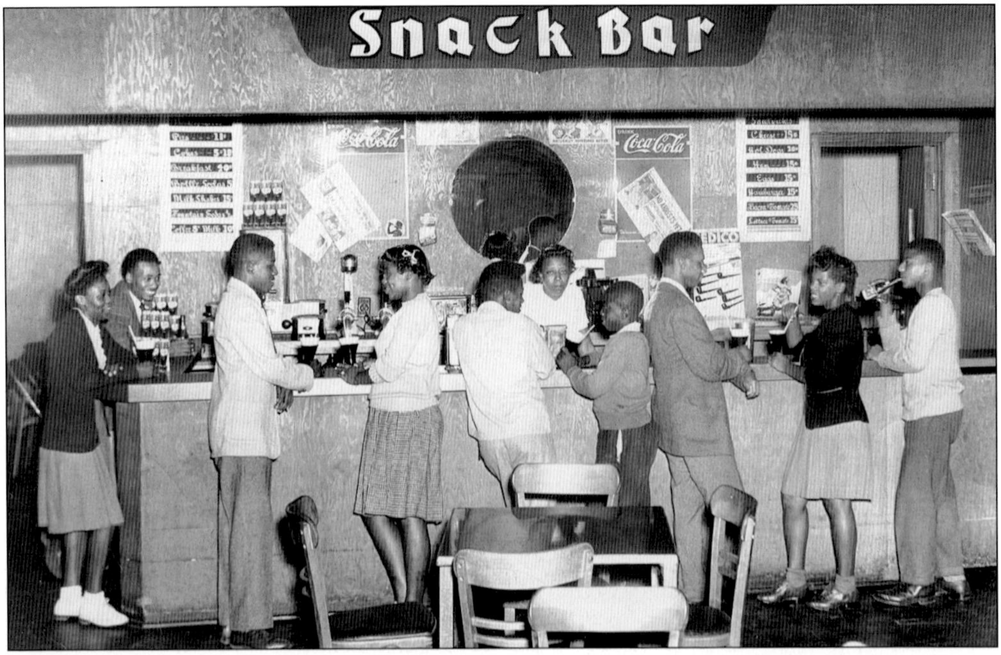

This was the snack bar inside the Chestnut Street USO Club/YMCA building where Ruth Brown actually sang, *c.* 1950. (Courtesy Lee Rodgers Collection, Portsmouth Public Library.)

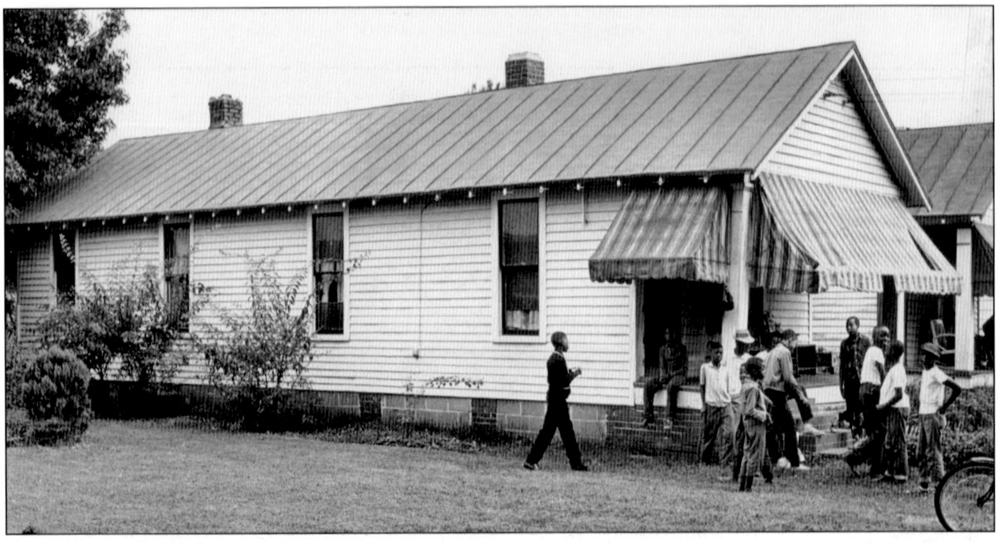

The house in this photograph was the site of what was called "The Mt. Hermon Poltergeist." A bizarre incident in September 1962 left the Daughtry home at 949 Florida Avenue abandoned. Charles Daughtry, 90, his approximately 100-year old wife and his 13-year old great grandson, Cleveland Harmon, left the house and "encamped with relatives" until the disturbances abated. "Explanations were lacking. Of those near the house today, only one person, a neighboring housewife, thought she had inkling of what happened. 'You take a black cat,' she said, 'and boil it down to the bones, and eat the bones. That'll bring 'em around every time.' 'Ain't nobody in that house see no black cat,' a man said. 'No I reckon not,' the housewife admitted. With that, leas(?) all fled." (Courtesy Bertha Edwards Collection, Portsmouth Public Library.)

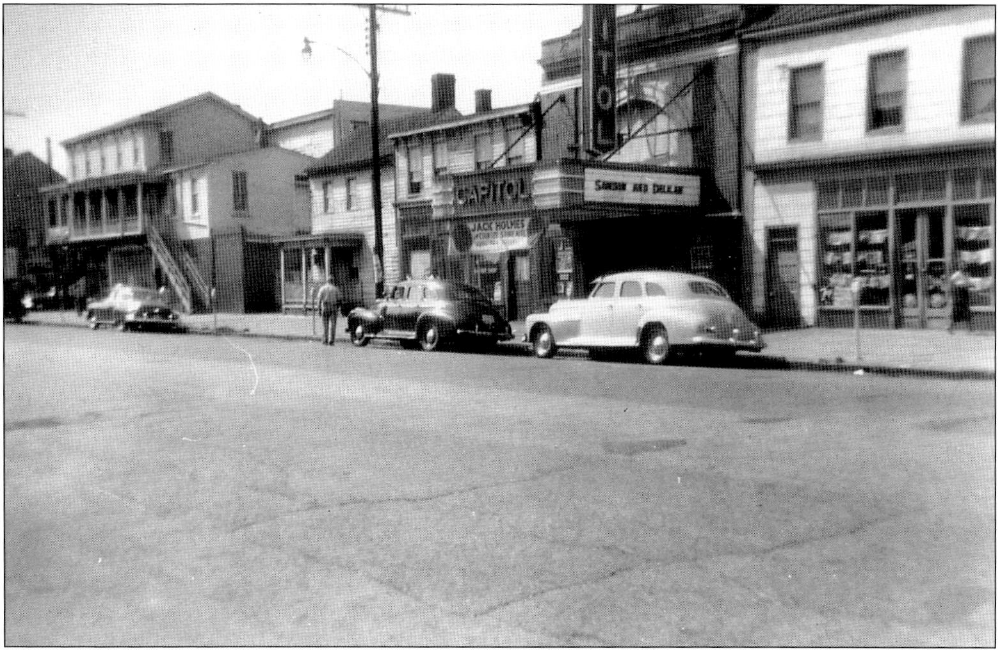

Capitol Theater is pictured in the 600 block of Effingham Street in Portsmouth. (Courtesy Bertha Edwards Collection, Portsmouth Public Library.)

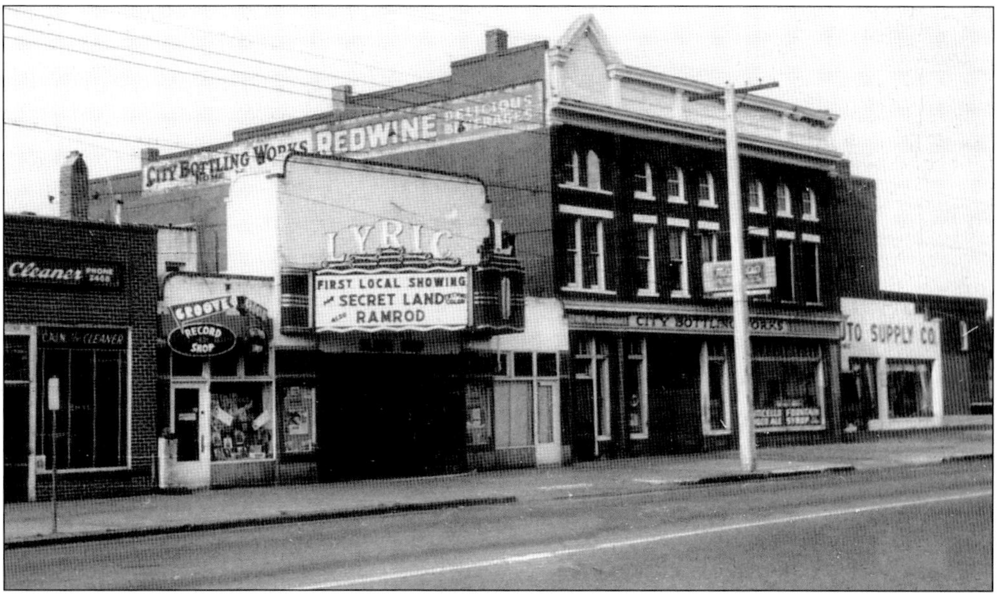

The Lyric Theater, which was originally named the Queen Theater, was owned by Solomon Soroko and began operation at 401 Chestnut Street in 1939. The seats cascaded around the "hot blast stove" that heated the small theater. After a fire destroyed the building, also claiming the life of the reel operator, the Lyric reopened at 907 High Street by 1945. (Courtesy Emmerson Collection, Portsmouth Public Library.)

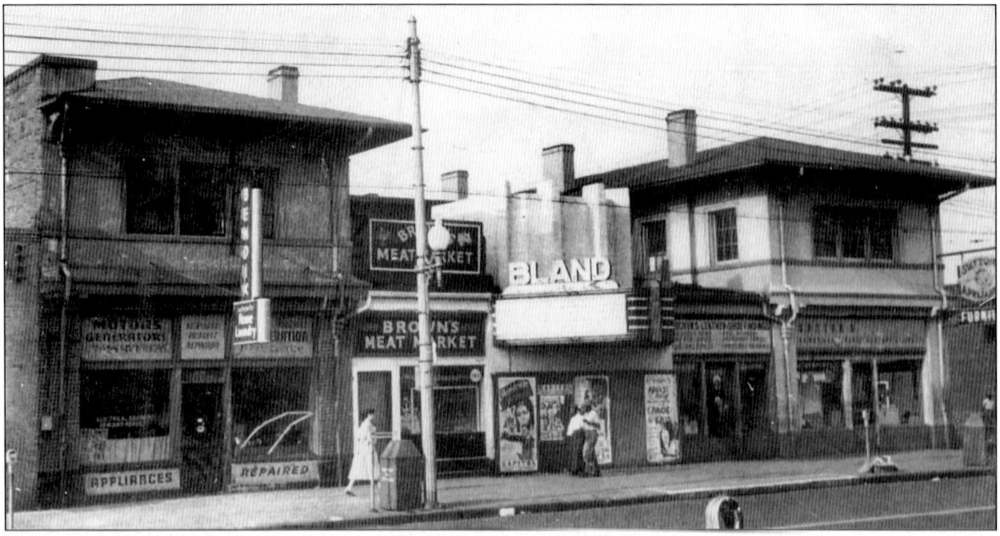

The Bland Theater was located at 831 High Street near Chestnut Street, formerly part of Sutton's Furniture storage warehouse before it was turned into a movie house in late 1942. It was part of the Jewish Lichtman movie chain out of Washington, D.C.; Solomon Soroko ran the theater during the early 1940s. The Bland and Capitol were owned by the same movie chain and shared workers. These "split shift" employees would work mornings to afternoons at the Capitol, take a one or two-hour break, then go back to work at the Bland to finish out the night. The Bland showed "B" class movies, mostly westerns at 25 cents. It was not as large as the Capitol and not as well patronized, but it managed to fill its 500 or so seats from time to time. This picture was probably taken in May 1948. (Courtesy Emmerson Collection, Portsmouth Public Library.)

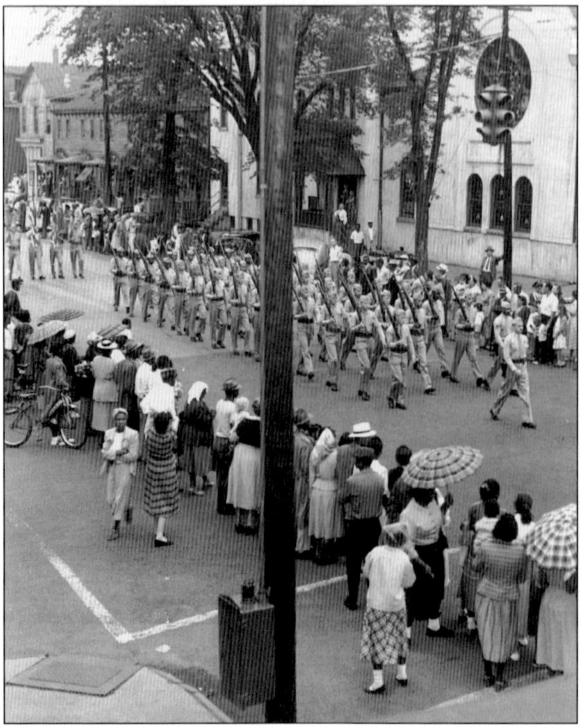

This undated photograph taken at the intersection of Effingham and South Streets, illustrates the popularity parades had in the African-American community. (Old Towne Collection, Courtesy Portsmouth Public Library.)

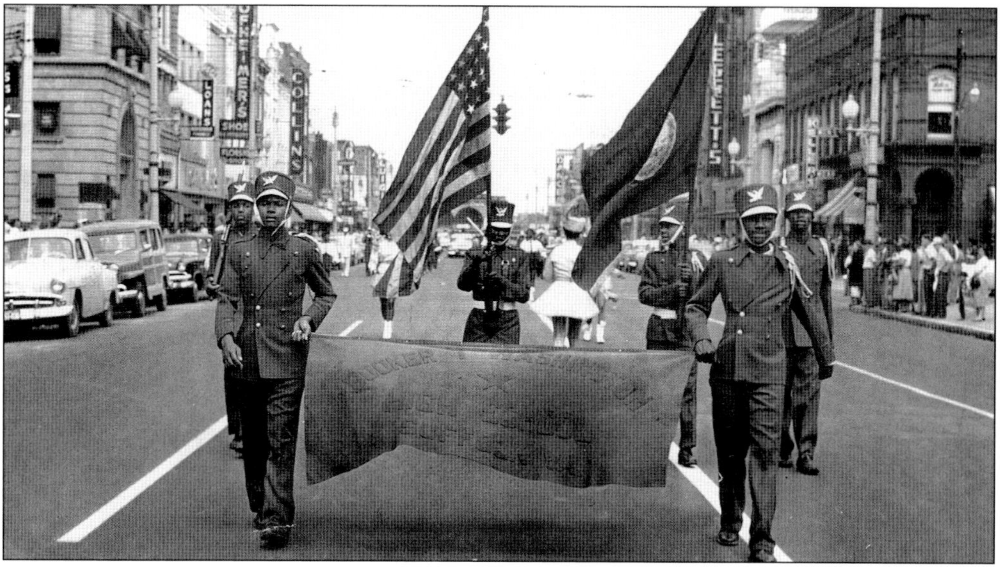

This was a typical Memorial Day parade scene. In Portsmouth, there was a black and a white Memorial Day Celebration. Many of the prominent black organizations, such as the Elks as depicted in this May 1954 photograph, marched. Shown here are the colors and color guard and banner, ahead of Booker T. Washington High School Band of Suffolk. The Peanut Capital musicians made a good showing in the parade, along with bands of other Virginia cities that furnished music in the procession. This was a colorful feature of the annual session of the Virginia State Association of Elks that convened in Portsmouth May 15–19. The above scene is downtown High street. The parade route for African Americans went down County to Crawford and then High Streets, and then to the Portsmouth Municipal Stadium. According to the article that accompanied this photograph in the "Colored Notes" section of the *Portsmouth Star* newspaper, good weather prevailed for the procession, but the events planned for the stadium were rained out. (Courtesy Lee Rodgers Collection, Portsmouth Public Library.)

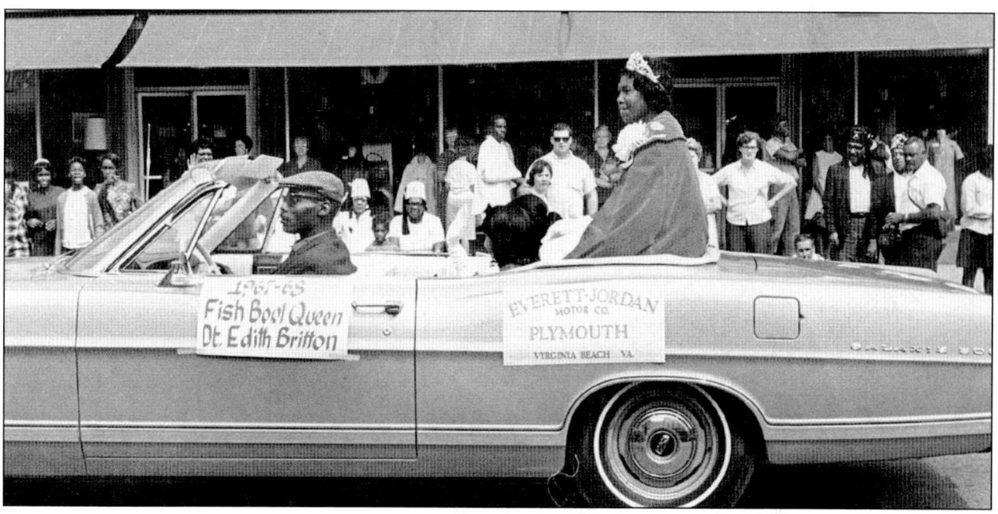

Another popular parade and celebration was the Fish Bowl. The photograph on the left is the "1967–68 Fish Bowl Queen Dt. Edith Britton" on September 21, 1967. (Courtesy Lee Rodgers Collection, Portsmouth Public Library.)

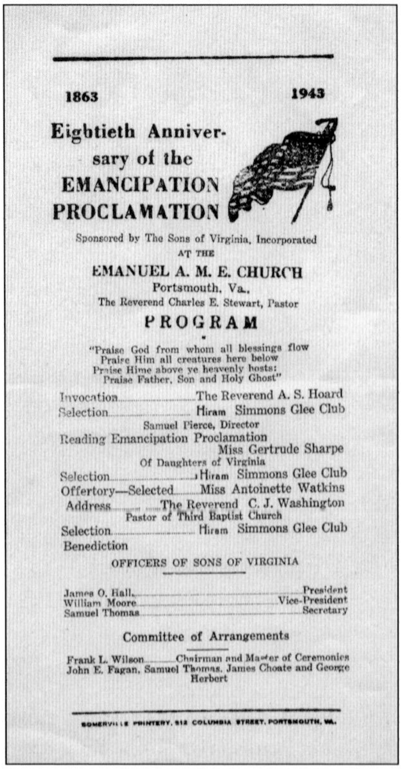

1863 1943

Eightieth Anniversary of the EMANCIPATION PROCLAMATION

Sponsored by The Sons of Virginia, Incorporated
AT THE
EMANUEL A. M. E. CHURCH
Portsmouth, Va.,
The Reverend Charles E. Stewart, Pastor

PROGRAM

"Praise God from whom all blessings flow
Praise Him all creatures here below
Praise Hime above ye heavenly hosts:
Praise Father, Son and Holy Ghost"

Invocation............The Reverend A. S. Hoard
Selection............Hiram Simmons Glee Club
Samuel Pierce, Director
Reading Emancipation Proclamation
Miss Gertrude Sharpe
Of Daughters of Virginia
Selection............Hiram Simmons Glee Club
Offertory—Selected............Miss Antoinette Watkins
Address............The Reverend C. J. Washington
Pastor of Third Baptist Church
Selection............Hiram Simmons Glee Club
Benediction

OFFICERS OF SONS OF VIRGINIA

James O. Hall............President
William Moore............Vice-President
Samuel Thomas............Secretary

Committee of Arrangements

Frank L. Wilson............Chairman and Master of Ceremonies
John E. Fagan, Samuel Thomas, James Choate and George Herbert

SOMERVILLE PRINTERY, 512 COLUMBIA STREET, PORTSMOUTH, VA.

Emancipation Day Program is shown in this photograph. (Courtesy Bertha Edwards Collection, Portsmouth Public Library.)

Members of the Order of the Eastern Star—Martha Chapter #10 are pictured on July 28, 1964. (Courtesy Lee Rodgers Collection, Portsmouth Public Library.)

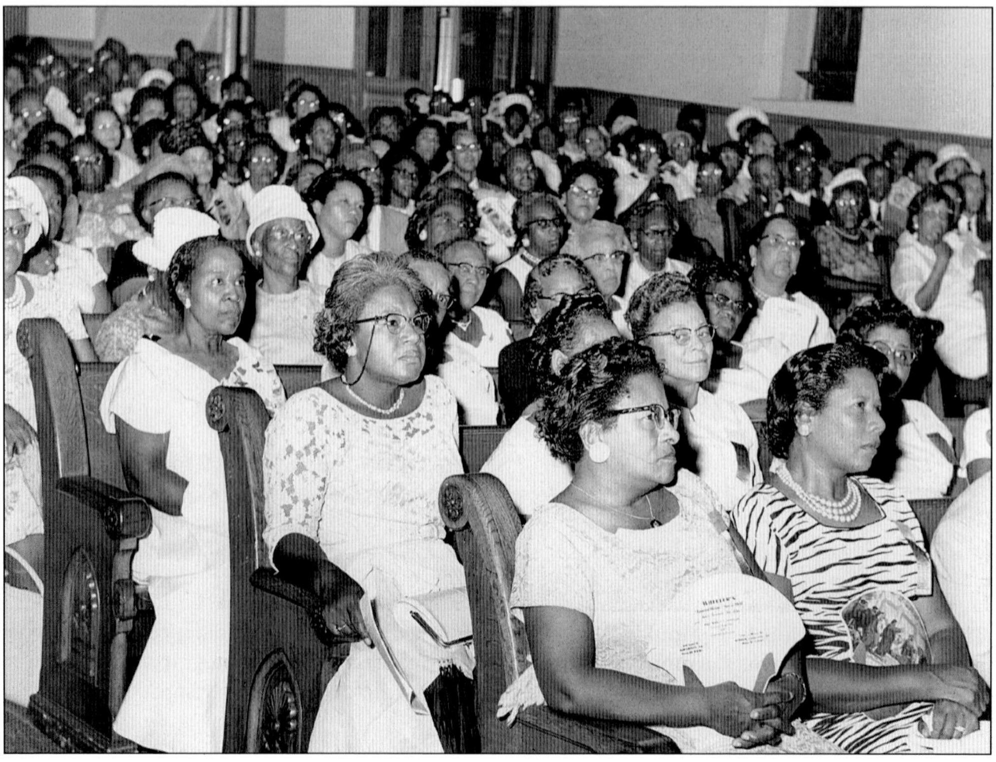

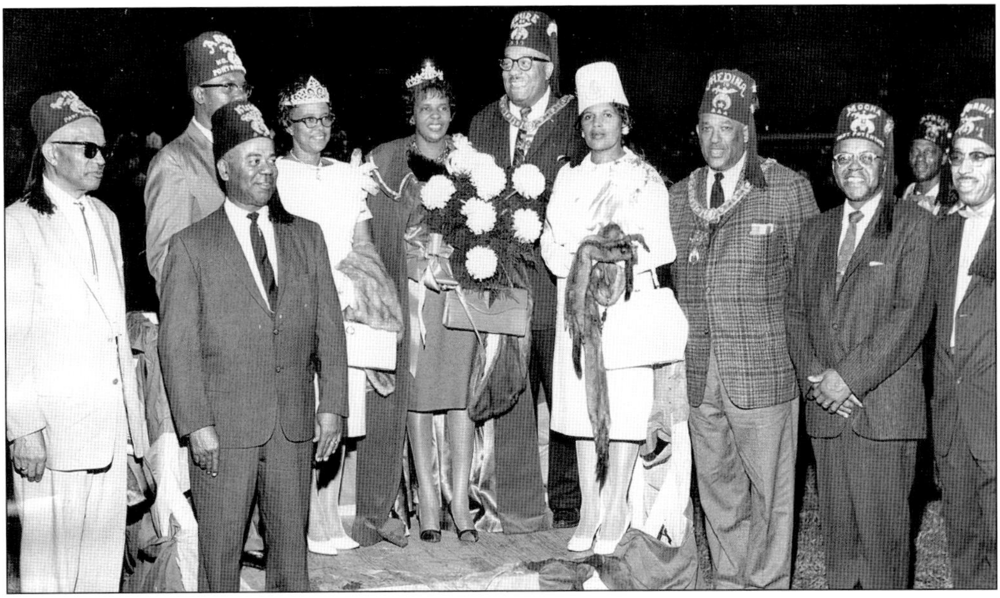

Participating in the Shriners dedication in 1961, from left to right, are Noble Charles H. Harris, Imperial Deputy of the Oasis; Noble M.C. Martin, Imperial Recorder; Noble James H. Turner, Illustrious Potentate—Arabia Temple #13; Daughter Mary Jefferson, Illustrious Commandress, Dt. of Isis, Arabia Court #23; Daughter Carrie Brooks, "Fish Bowl Queen 1961;" Noble John H. Hester, Imperial High Priest & Prophet; Daughter Bernice Whitehurst, Chairman Queen Contest; Noble Charles A. Dorgan, Imperial Oriental Guide; Noble Walter Louis, Post Imp. Potentate; Noble David Ward, Arabic Patrol; and Noble Milton W. Keeling, Director of Fish Bowl Classic. (Courtesy Lee Rodgers Collection, Portsmouth Public Library.)

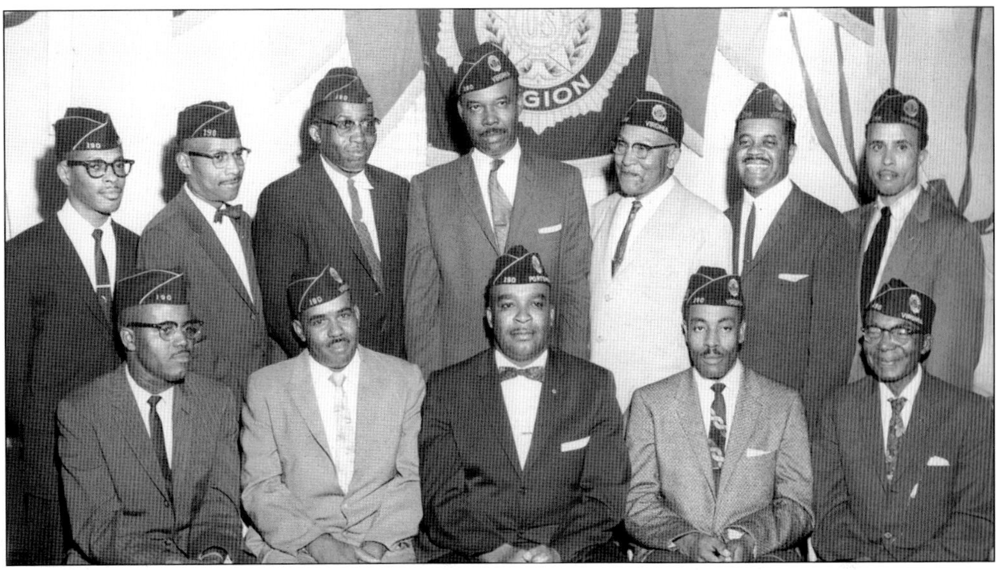

The American Legion is a popular fraternal organization in Portsmouth. Pictured on the front row are Ernest Brown, Raymond Bogues, and Joseph Bryant. The photograph was taken at the Harrison American Legion, Post 190, located on Peach Street in Portsmouth. (Courtesy Portsmouth Public Library.)

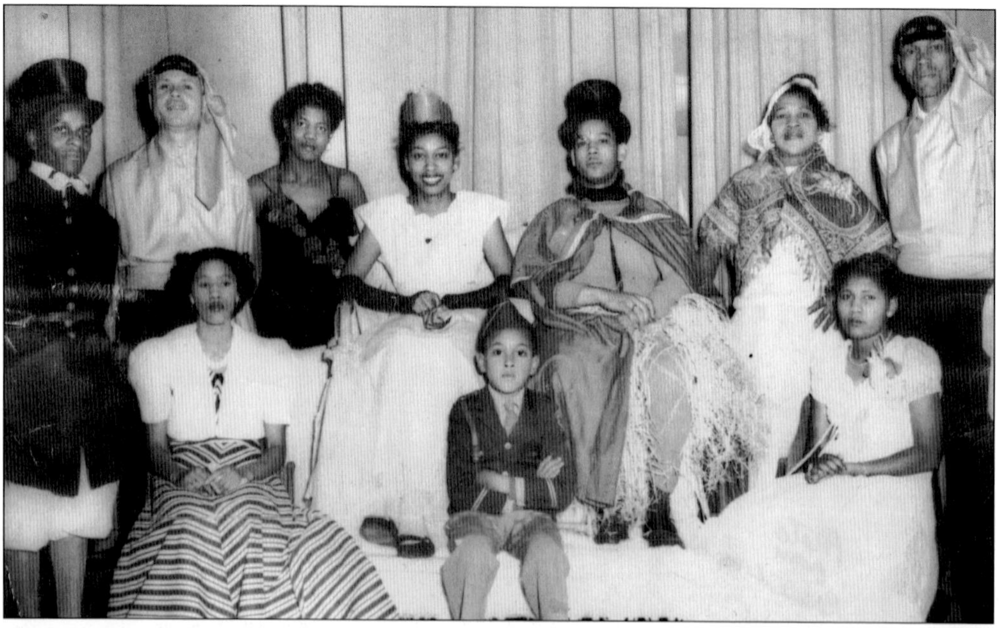

Members of the El Dorado Club, Mardi Gras, 1947 are (front row) Bernice, unidentified, and Betsy McAllen; (back row) "Jimmy" McHarney, Laurence James, Murphy Richardson, Evelyn Palmer (Watkins), Rosamon McCallen, and Frank Raney. (Courtesy of Bessie Liverman.)

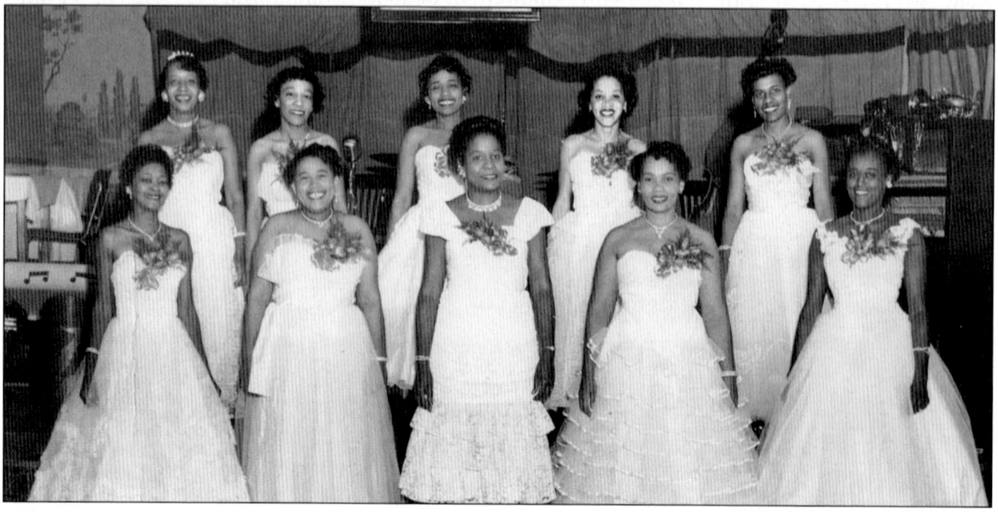

This is a 1955 photograph of the Merrymakers Club. This club was founded in October 1945 by a group of hostesses who worked at the Portsmouth USO Club. Their initial meeting was held in the Lincoln Street home of Clarissa Edwards, and the organization's name came from their work as hostesses. The group of women elected Ethel Harrison and Annie Wise as their president and vice president, respectively. Originally the club's purpose was to foster entertainment and fun for the members. However, civic and community projects were a natural outgrowth because of their dedication to serving the community. Members from left to right are (first row) Thelma Riddick, Cornelia Harrison, Katie Smith, Alice Duke, and Agnes Wilson; (back row) Verna McIntyre,Bertha Edwards, Ethel Robinson, Thomasine Wade, and Charlotte Reid. (Courtesy Bertha Edwards Collection.)

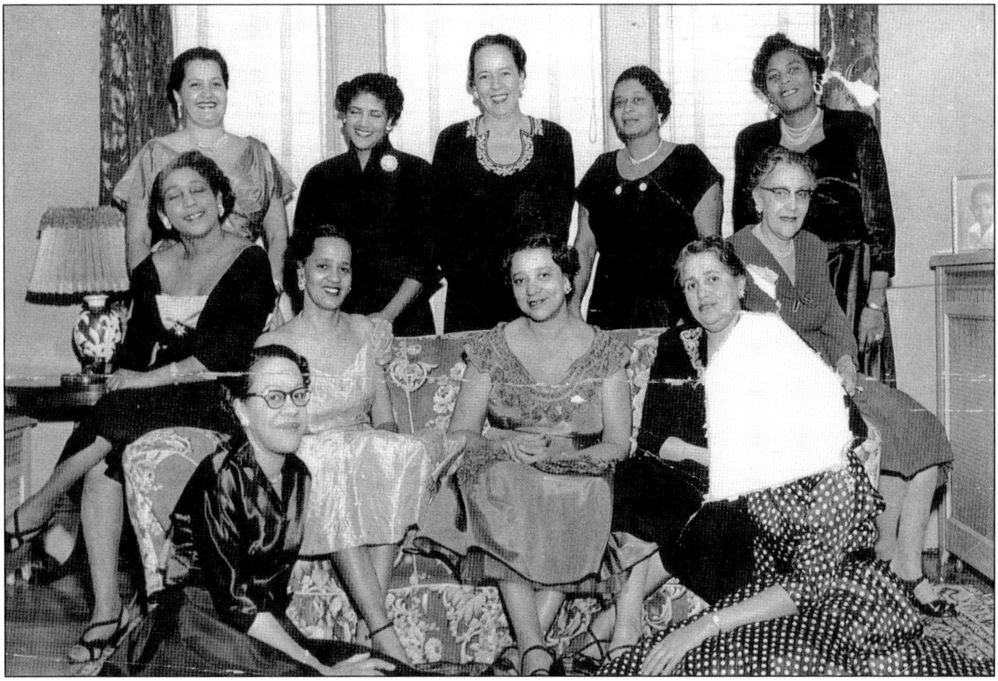

Pictured is the Portsmouth Chapter of the Links, Inc., January 7, 1956. Members, from left to right, are (front row) Louise Elliott and unidentified woman; (middle row) G. Bushell, Virginia Dunston, C. Jackson, H. Reid, and Mrs. Laura Elliott; (back row) Pat Green, Margaret Bond, ? V. Watts, M. Walker, and Mrs. A Carey. (Courtesy Mae Breckenridge-Haywood.)

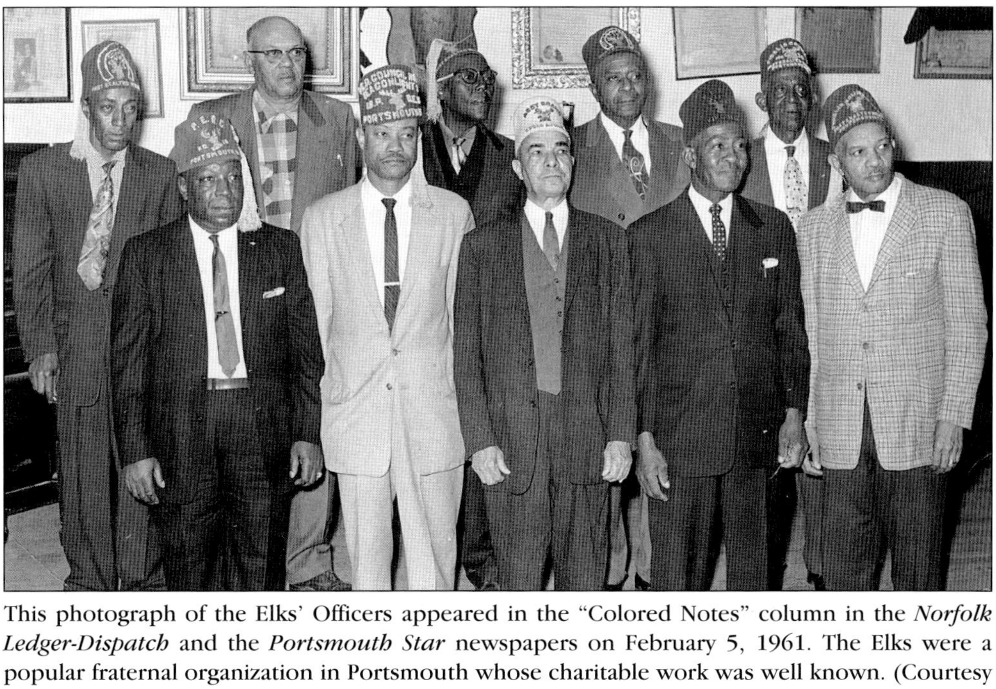

This photograph of the Elks' Officers appeared in the "Colored Notes" column in the *Norfolk Ledger-Dispatch* and the *Portsmouth Star* newspapers on February 5, 1961. The Elks were a popular fraternal organization in Portsmouth whose charitable work was well known. (Courtesy Lee Rodgers Collection, Portsmouth Public Library.)

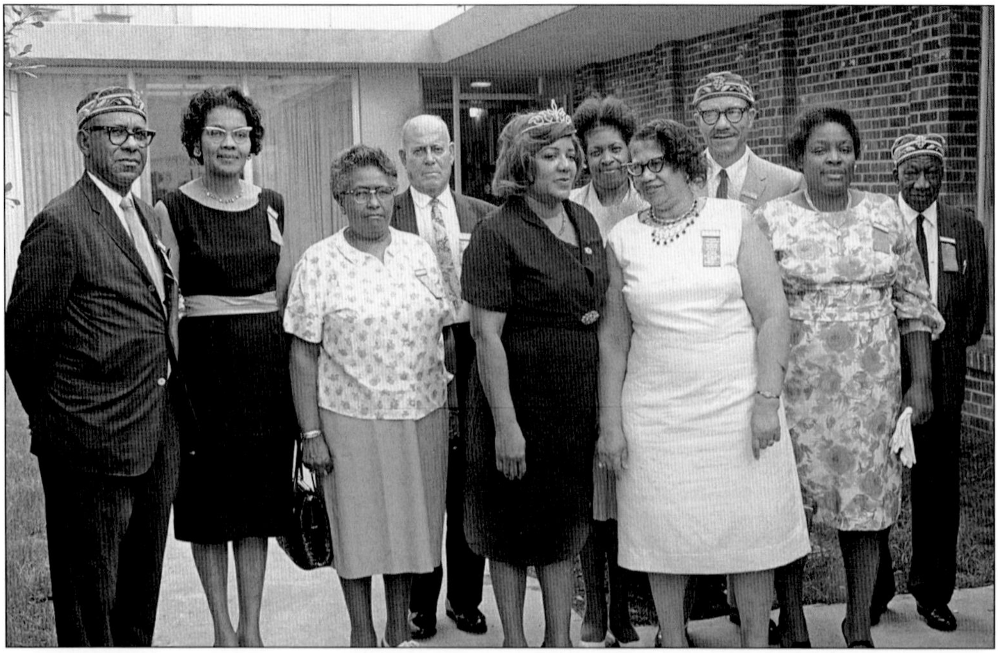

A convention drew some 200 delegates from nine states to Portsmouth this week. Central Jurisdiction principals of the Scottish Rite are, from left to right, W.W. Hoover, grand commander; Mrs. Dorothy Foster, Eastern Star deputy; Mrs. Mary Raper, treasurer; J.W. Wilkins, auditor; Mrs. Daisy M. Long, matron; Mrs. Oaissa Norris, recording secretary; Mrs. Elizabeth Morris, deputy; William Carson, grand prior; and Charles C. Willette, grand treasurer. This photograph appeared in the "Lee F. Rodgers Column" of the *Ledger Star* newspaper on August 12, 1966. (Courtesy Lee Rodgers Collection, Portsmouth Public Library.)

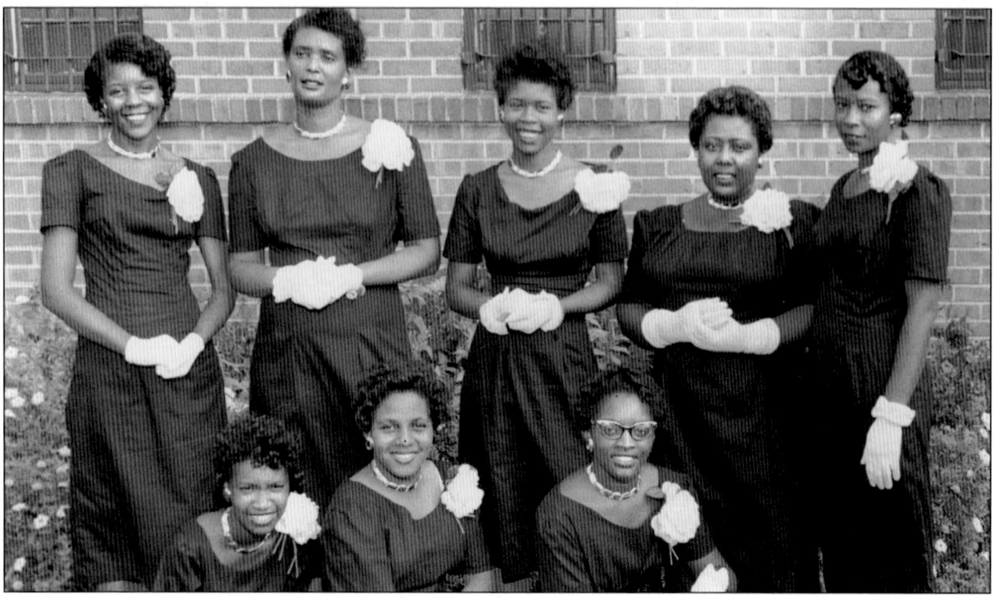

Cherokee Social and Saving Club are shown in an undated photograph. (Courtesy Lee Rodgers Collection, Portsmouth Public Library.)

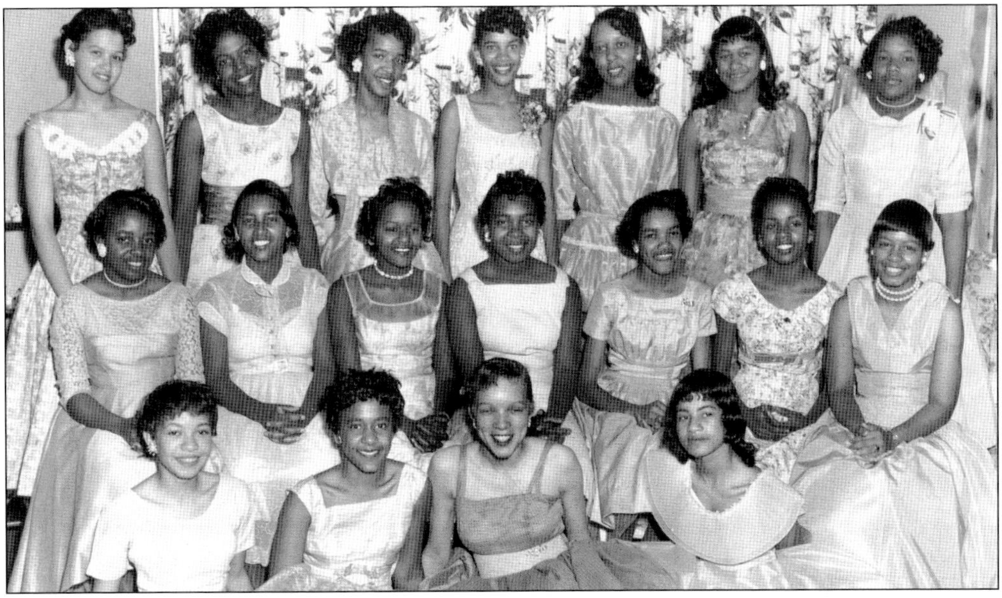

The Eureka Club, Inc. sponsored the fifth Annual Debutant Ball on Friday May 24, 1957, at Our Lady of Victory Auditorium. Twenty young ladies were presented and were chosen from the January and June graduating classes of I.C. Norcom High, Crestwood High, and Our Lady of Victory High schools. The Eureka Club president at this time was David Driver, with Moses Gibson Sr. as the Debutant program chair. The wives of members of the Eureka Club assisted the organization with this event. Pictured from left to right are (front row) Phyllis Moody, Ocie Moore, Wilfreda Gourdine, Carolyn Joyner; (middle row) Delores Pearson, Delores Williams, Delores Stewart, Helen White, Kay Spruill, and Mae Alice Hardy; (back row) Carol Rose Green, Celestine Copeland, Juanita Etheridge, Delia Weston, Jessie Mae Hill, Elsie Elliott, and Florine Chesson. Georgia Daughtry was not pictured. (Courtesy Portsmouth Public Library.)

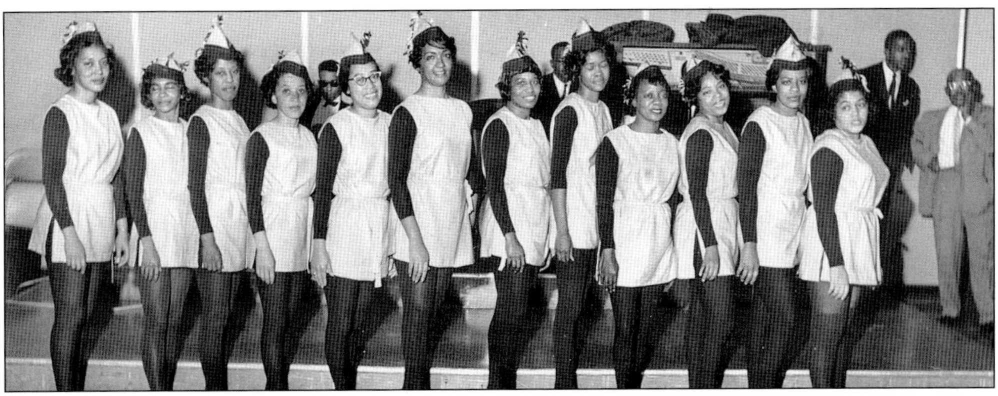

This undated photograph is the annual dance of the Portsmouth Chapter, Pinochle Bugs Social and Civic Club held at the Sahil Club. This group, organized in the early 1960s with Clarine Roberts as president, illustrates the annual costume dance that required all members to dress in the same outfit, which consisted of gold tops, black leotards, and a hat that resembled a "Robin Hood" style. The club sold tickets to this annual fund-raising dance and awarded prizes for the best costume. Members pictured, from left to right, are Sylvia Harrison, Ophelia Blackburn, Jane Boyd, Audrey Walton, Thomasine Wade, Clarine Roberts, Sarah M. Ward, Lucia Windley, Viola Taylor, and Margaret Bogues. (Courtesy Lee Rodgers Collection, Portsmouth Public Library.)

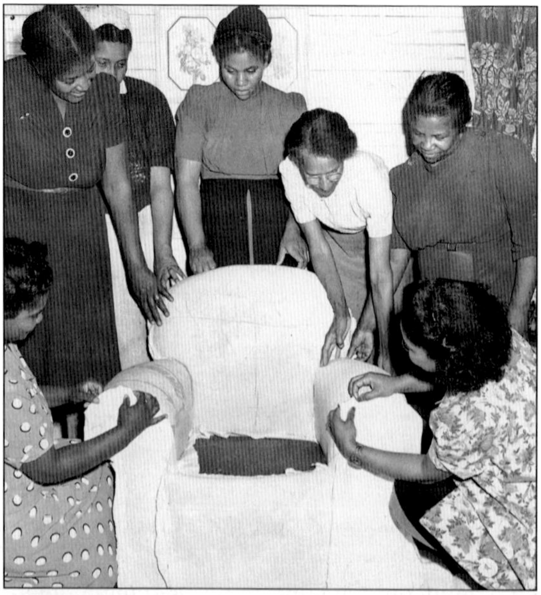

These seven African–American women piecing together a chair slipcover are members of the Fentress Home Club. Miss Cleopatra Williamson, Norfolk Division of the State College, Norfolk County, was the Home Demonstration Agent, *c.* 1950. (Lee Rodgers Collection, Portsmouth Public Library.)

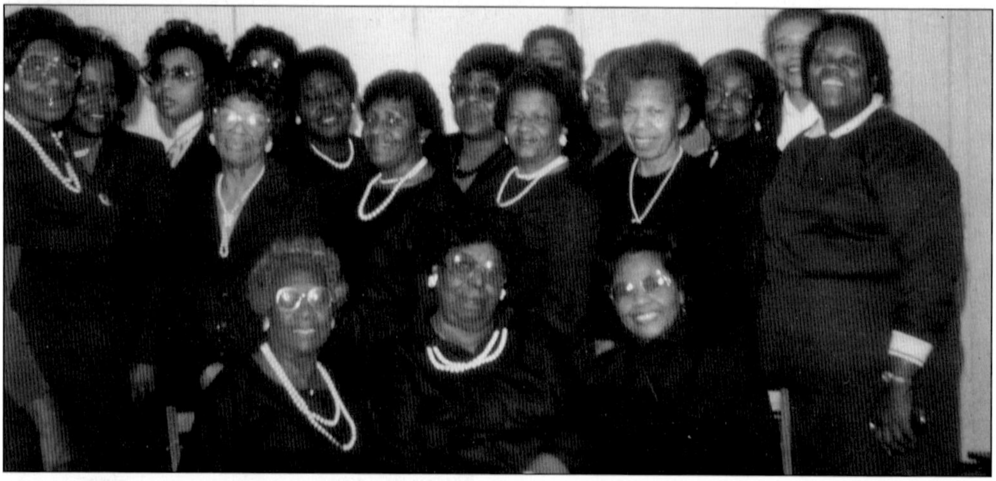

The United Order of Tents is the oldest lodge in Portsmouth and was established to create better living conditions for Christian women. Founded by Mariah Savage of Norfolk and led by the late Jane Jones, the exact date of its establishment is unknown because a fire destroyed its charter. What does remain is that in 1927 the following officers were elected to carry on the spirit of the founders: Grace Fisher (senior matron), Precilla Twine (junior matron), Ellen Rogers (recording secretary, Lottie Reed (finance secretary), Gussie Johnson (mistress of ceremonies), Roberta Morgan (mistress of wardrobe). Sarah Diggs and Mary Bolden (tyleress), Maggie Hawkins and Mary Butler (ushers), Fannie Easter (conductor), and Bessie White (mistress of the key). In this photograph, members of the Cassandra chapter #139, Portsmouth District No. 1, from left to right, are (front row) Helen Battle (leader); unidentified; Margaret Miller; (second row) Elydia Eley; Nancy Sutton; Lois Wiggins; Mary J. Smith; Mrs. Johnson; Vivian H. Yancey (assistant leader); (third row) Cheryl Wilson; Mary L. Pitt; Alice Moody; Elnora Jones; Mary King; Mrs. Patilio. Mrs. Anderson was a long-standing member of the Tents who allowed the organization to hold meetings in her family-owned building. The family also rented its facilities to other lodges. (Courtesy Vivian H. Yancey.)

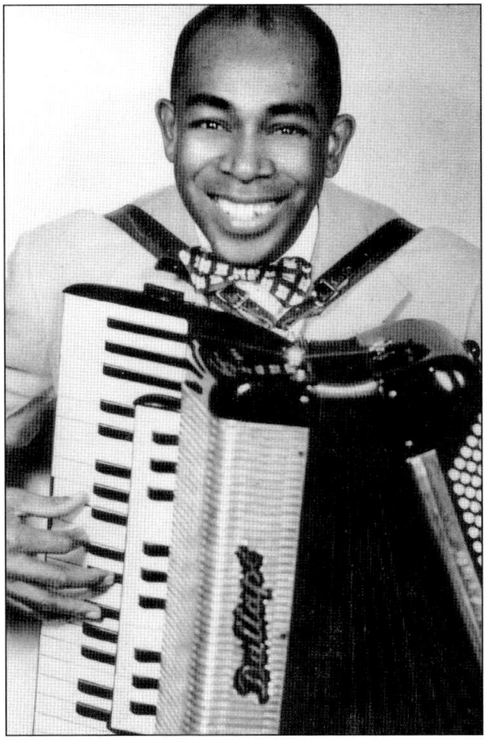

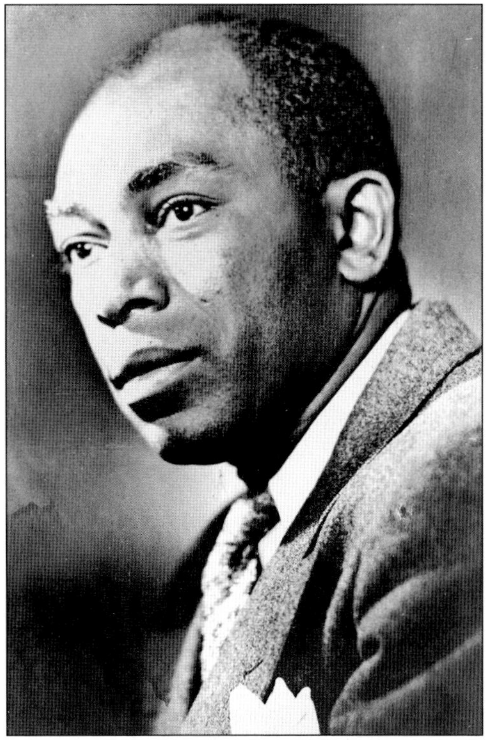

Above: Portsmouth native Graham Jackson played the accordion with tears streaming down his face when President Roosevelt died in 1945. (Courtesy Bertha Edwards Collection, Portsmouth Public Library.) *Above, right:* Graham Jackson, a musician who was proficient with several musical instruments, was a favorite of Franklin D. Roosevelt. (Lee Rodgers Collection, Portsmouth Public Library.) *Right:* Sissieretta Jones (1868–1933) distinguished herself as one of America's leading prima donnas and formed the Black Patti Troubadours. In describing her love of singing, Sissieretta Jones said, "The flowers absorb the sunshine because it is their nature. I give out melody because God filled my soul with it." Jones studied at the Boston Conservatory and in 1888 toured with the Tennessee Jubilee Singers. Racism forced her to begin her own company, the Black Patti Troubadours, which appeared in black-owned theaters around the nation. (Courtesy Portsmouth Public Library.)

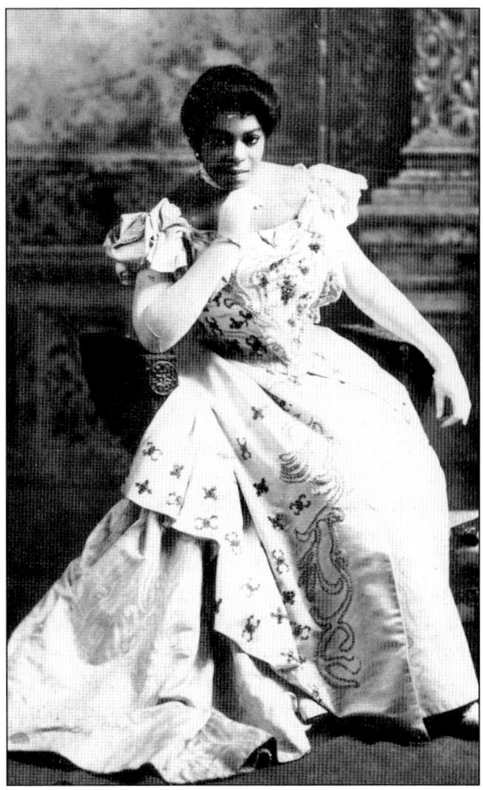

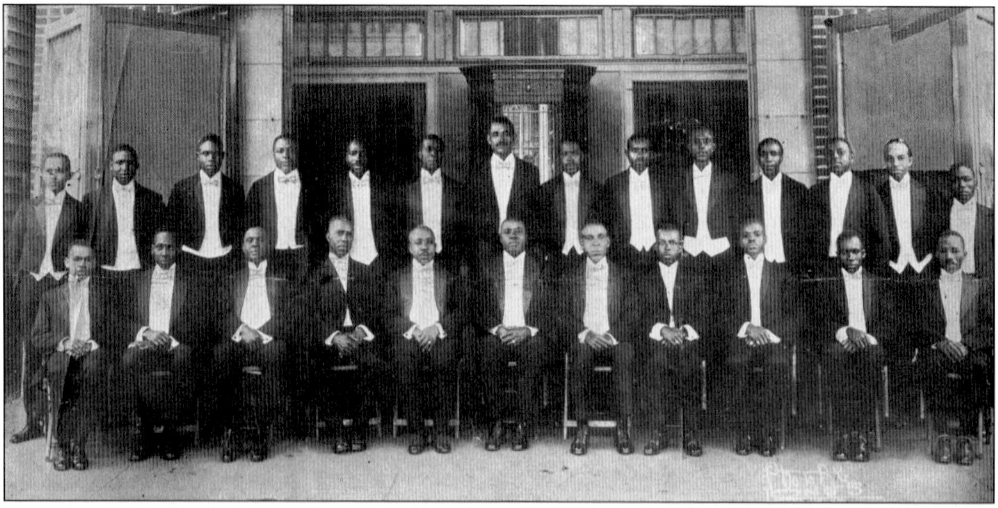

Roland Hayes Glee Club, named in honor of the famous composer and musician, was a popular and well-known singing group composed of local talent. Pictured from left to right are (front row) Lawrence McDaniel, unidentified, Alston, unidentified, William Ewart Riddick, three unidentified men, Charles Butts, unidentified, and Clarence Cannon; (back row) Gilliam Broadnax; two unidentified men, Richard Riddick, unidentified, W.B. Anderson, unidentified, James G. Norcom Sr., R.C. Creekmur, Alexander Davis, two unidentified men; Lee Rodgers; and Sam Pierce. (Courtesy Portsmouth Public Library.)

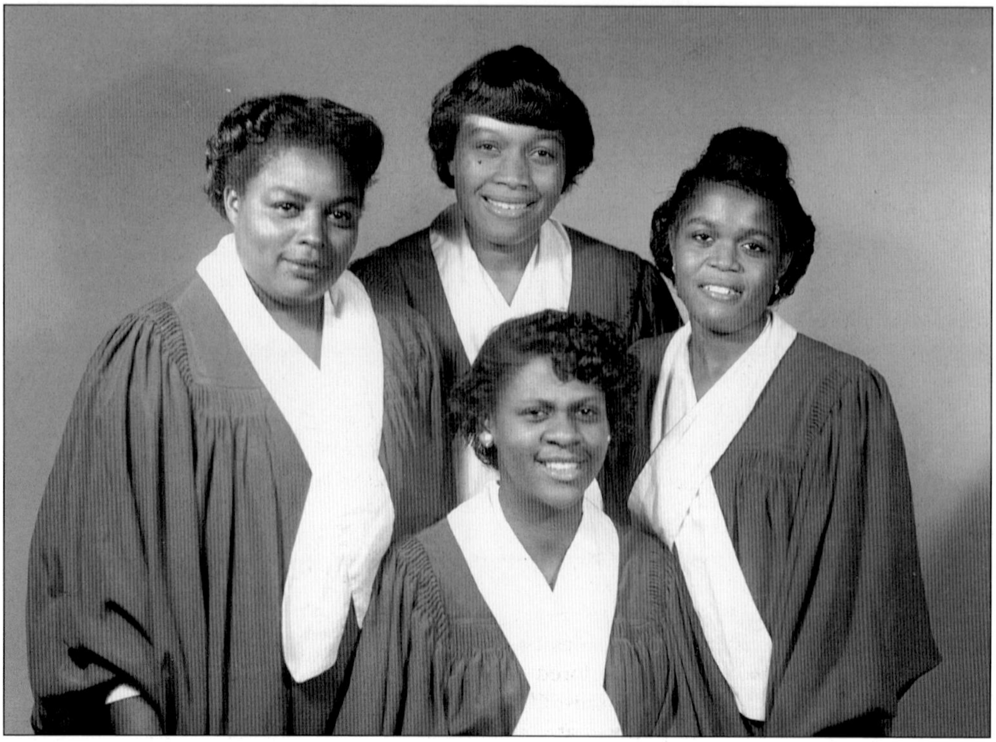

Star Light Gospel Singers Mrs. Mabel Minor (far left) and Dorothy Johnson (back row middle) are shown here. (Courtesy Lee Rodgers Collection, Portsmouth Public Library.)

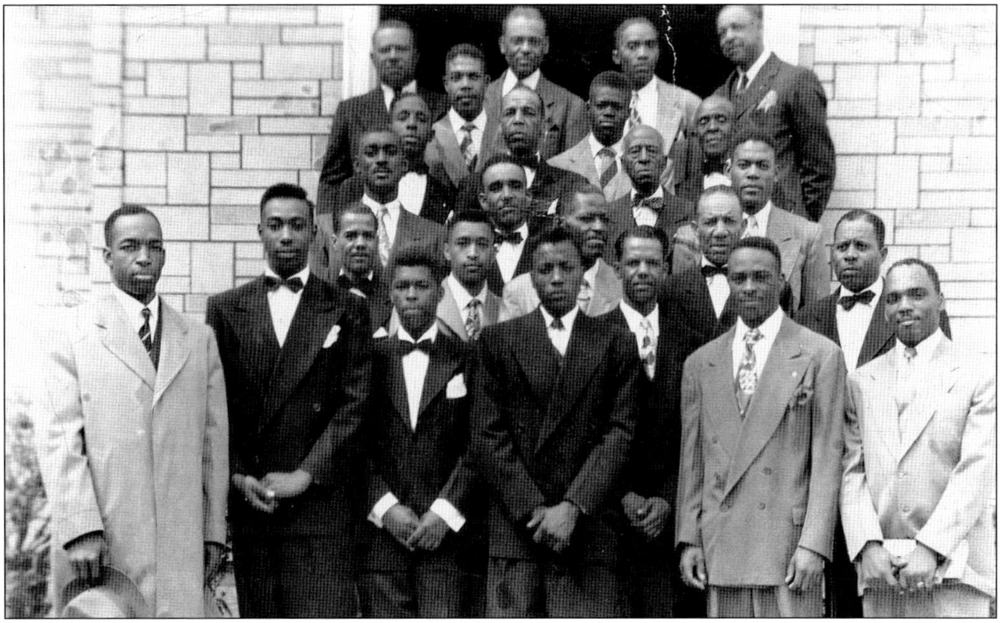

Pictured is the First Baptist Glee Club, *c*. 1950. Many churches had their own singing groups aside from the church choirs. (Courtesy Lee Rodgers Collection, Portsmouth Public Library.)

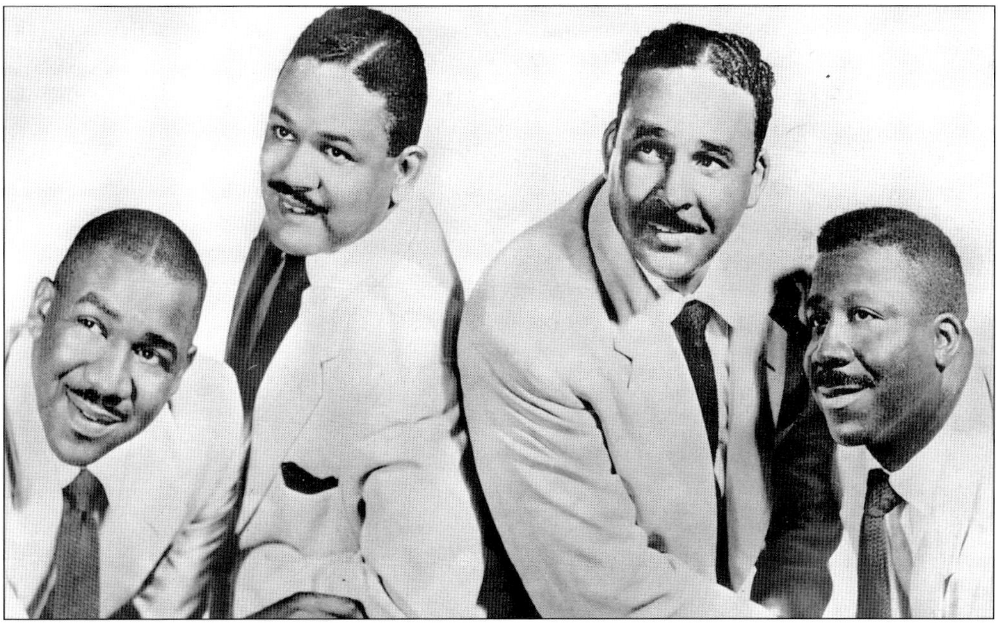

The Vikings was one of America's most promising quartets when this photograph was taken. The members include Walter Scott, James G. Norcom Jr., Harry Turner, and William Harding. An article in the *Portsmouth Star's* "Colored Notes" announced that on September 28, 1954 the Vikings gave a concert at Ebenezer Baptist Church, sponsored by the Church's Willing Workers' Club. The group was slated to perform at a meeting of the Men's Club of Lee Ward at the Elm Avenue Methodist Church on September 28th. (Courtesy Lee Rodgers Collection, Portsmouth Public Library.)

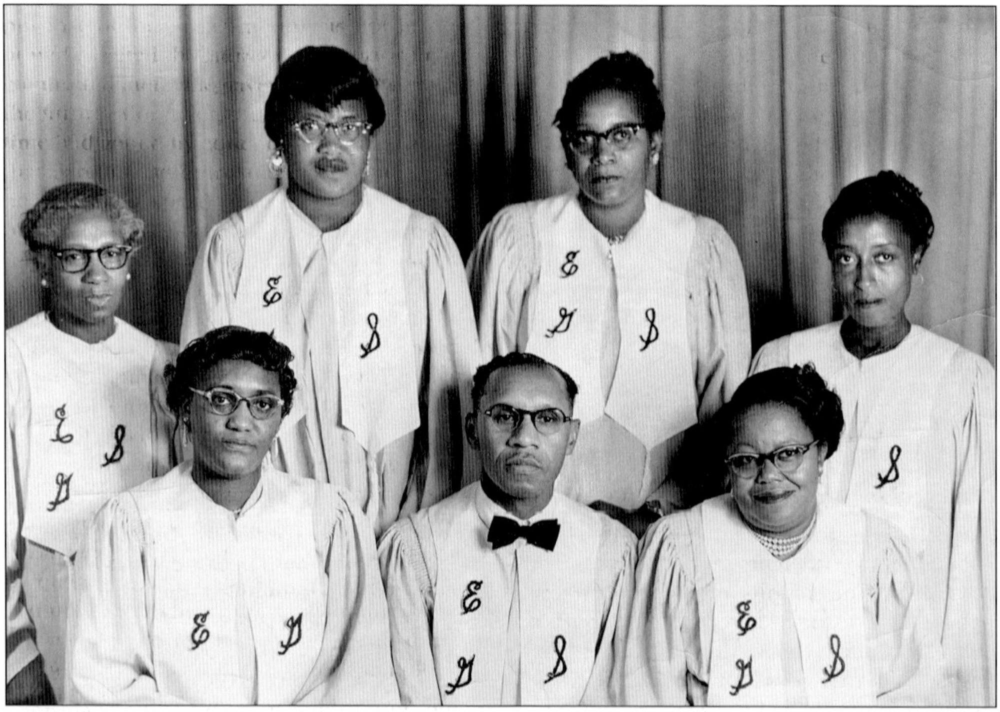

Edler Gospel Singers are shown here on October 25, 1952. (Courtesy Lee Rodgers Collection, Portsmouth Public Library.)

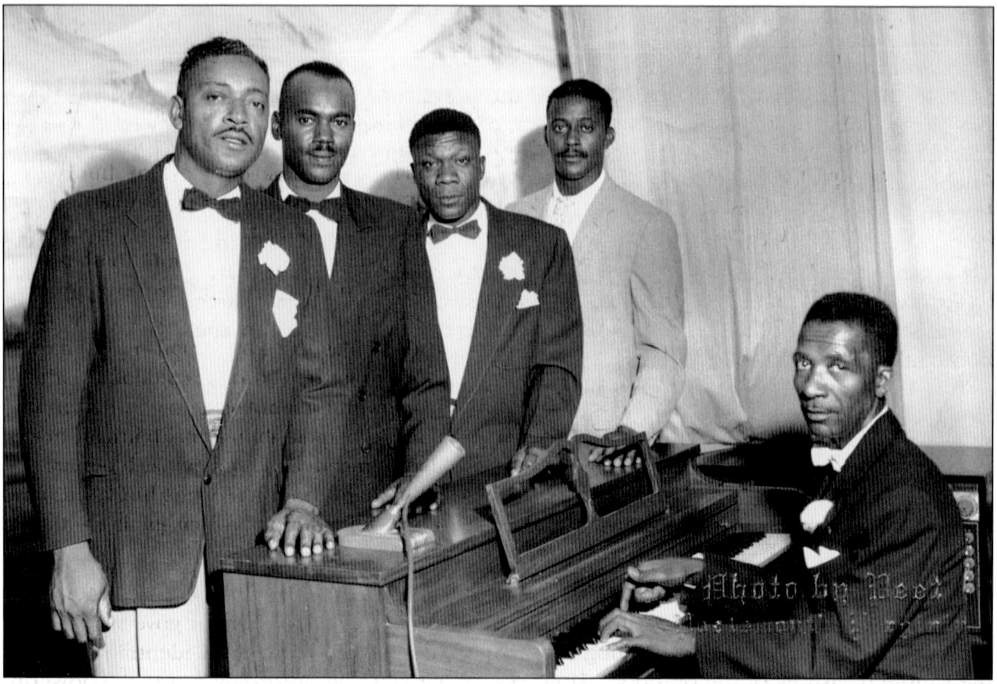

The Millionaires Quartet is shown with Kid Spruill on piano and four men standing. (Courtesy Portsmouth Public Library.)

Seven

The Boy Scouts

In his book, *In Their Own Interests,* Earl Lewis tackled the emergence of a 20th-century African-American middle class elite in the city of Norfolk and suggested that this group sought to empower itself through what he termed the "home sphere" once the white community closed access to political power.[74] This depiction, although specific to Norfolk, can be applied to any other city in the South, but most especially Portsmouth because it was Norfolk's sister city. The actions of the African-American community exemplified the 20th century political landscape changes in Portsmouth and Norfolk, which were reflected not only in their cultural heritage, but also in what occurred throughout America and most especially in the South. This change was best illustrated in the emergence of a new professional elite in the black community, which galvanized its economy and educational structure and transformed the expectations of its members. These leaders were on banks or educational boards, or were involved in initiating institutions such as hospitals, local banks and businesses, branches of the NAACP, schools, and social organizations to help the youth such as the Boy Scouts and the YMCA.

Despair about the state of society was not an uncommon phenomenon, especially in the early years of the 20th century. Society witnessed the prevalence of apocalyptic warnings, the belief that the frontier, so important to American idealism, was vanishing, and the conviction that the character of the American youth was deteriorating. These dire realities impacted blacks even more. The scarcity of organized activities and facilities worsened problems among blacks, especially for the youth who were barred even from enjoying the amenities of the YMCA, the Boys and Girls clubs, and most of the area's parks and beaches. Despite all of the prevailing racial attitudes, the black leaders in Tidewater were determined to make sure all citizens were given a fair chance to succeed, despite abject poverty and the increasing number of male juvenile delinquents. In response, a group of concerned black Norfolk citizens in the late 1920s sought ways by which they could get Boy Scouting started for African-American boys.[75]

The Boy Scouts became an influential organization throughout the western world shortly after its creation, in part because it addressed the fears people had of a changing society that was becoming increasingly urban. In 1908, Lord Baden-Powell of England conceived of the Boy Scouts as a remedy for the community's moral and physical weakness and as a defense from the threats within and without. In the years following the Boer War, Baden-Powell lamented how Britain was filled with men whose physical deficiencies were equaled by their lack of loyalty to British ideals. His vision was for a mass movement that would regenerate a nation. To be successful, Baden-Powell understood that it could not have any barriers to membership, such as a specific church or class affiliation, and that it would need the unofficial support of government. The objective, to be sure, was that scouting would attract the masses through its identification with the simple pleasures of the outdoors. However, underlying the organization was the powerful ideology linking good character and discipline that would produce a certain kind of serviceable citizen. This individual would never question authority and thus be a benefit to the nation and to an employer.[76] In short, the Boy Scout's ideology stressed "unquestioning obedience to properly structured authority; happy acceptance of one's social and economic position in life; and an unwavering, uncritical patriotism, for which one would be willing, if necessary, to die, as the key both to social utility and personal fulfillment."[77]

Despite these altruistic ideals, Baden-Powell's motivations came from a basic imperialistic and racist rhetoric that expressed a fear of the decline of the British Empire and of supposed European racial superiority. Even more, Baden-Powell's ideals mirrored those of other social imperialists whose worries about their empire led them to worry about the usefulness of their nation's populace and the maintenance of social order. This dichotomy of ideals was realized in South Africa when Africans were encouraged to adopt the precepts of the Scouts, but not be admitted into the brotherhood. Baden-Powell's fear was that admittance of blacks would deter whites from joining. So the Boy Scouts' founder rationalized the exclusion of non-Europeans while preaching brotherhood and a commitment to equality, by publicly questioning the intelligence, loyalty, character, and honesty of non-Europeans.[78]

The Boy Scouts of America (BSA) was incorporated on February 8, 1910, and chartered by Congress in 1916. It provided an educational program for European-American boys and young adults to build character, to promote citizenship, and to develop personal fitness. The overall mission of the organization was to help instill values and prepare them to make ethical choices. The Boy Scout Law noted that "trustworthy, loyal, helpful, friendly, courteous, kind obedient, cheerful, thrifty, brave, clean and reverent" are principal scouting objectives. These altruistic goals, however, hid the true motive behind the Scout movement in America as it did in England. In England, scouting supporters believed its empire was disintegrating from within. In America, followers feared the corrupting influence of ideas from outside American borders. However, in both America, Boy Scout leaders hoped to use the organization as a way to inculcate the male youth with a doctrine that would preserve America's middle class status quo. [79]

Within a year, scouting chapters sprang up throughout the United States. In Norfolk, the first Boy Scout troop in Virginia was organized in August 1910 under the leadership of the Rev. Dr. Charles Merrill Watson, pastor of First Christian Church. In keeping with racial etiquette, however, Boy Scout Troop No. 1 was limited to white male youth. Nowhere was this truer than in the South, whose intransigence in enrolling blacks as members was partially based on the fear that an integrated system would dissuade whites from joining. Although there was no official policy, segregation in the scouts was de facto. This prevailing unofficial policy, however, did not discourage blacks from aspiring to set up troops for their boys. The ideals of strong moral character, useful practical skills and patriotism appealed to blacks as much as it did to whites. Bolton Smith, Vice President of the Committee on Relationships, Operations, Program, Education, and Interracial Relations with the BSA between 1918 and 1935, spearheaded the development of scouting in the South. Bolton quietly assisted blacks in Louisville in establishing the first southern black Scout Troop. He then moved on to Memphis and other areas in the South, helping other communities to establish similar black troops. Because of Bolton's efforts, black leaders of Tidewater realized that instead of beginning their own separate organization they could appeal to the BSA for an officially recognized program.[80]

Creating a black Scout troop was not an easy accomplishment, especially for southern blacks. Northern blacks were often integrated into the pre-existing troops, although white northerners feared situations in which black Scouts outnumbered whites. Unlike the North, prior to 1926 there were virtually no black Scout Troops in the South. A group of determined black civic leaders would address this omission. In a February 1928 meeting, the Interracial Committee of the Norfolk Council, Boy Scouts of America, agreed to extend the scout program to blacks. This decision resulted in Norfolk becoming the first city in the Tidewater area to permit blacks to become scouts. This would be among the first in the South spurring others to duplicate their efforts so much so that by 1939 over 50,000 blacks were members of the BSA out of a total membership of 1,449,103. Mr. Abner Lee was president of the local Boy Scout Council and called a meeting of the black leaders. Several men, including P.B. Young, Atty. James (Piggy) Harrison, the Reverend Valentine of the Methodist Church, Dr. Samuel F. Coppage, and the Reverend Henderson of Metropolitan AME Church, met and organized their petition to the Norfolk BSA. The Norfolk BSA agreed that the group would be granted a Charter and the Boy Scout Program, but they did not want to grant use of the uniform for at least a year. This upset the committee, which was opposed to such an agreement, and stated in no uncertain terms they would not accept anything shorter than the full program, uniforms included. Finally, the matter was decided and the restriction on the uniform was dropped and the full program was granted. The permanent committee was composed of Abner E. Lee, president, Walter Fulford, secretary, Dr. S.F. Coppage, Prof. Winston Douglas, C.A. Palmer, Reverend Watkins, Bank Street Baptist Church, Reverend Henderson, Metropolitan AME Church, Reverend Harris, Grace Episcopal, Rev. Harvey N. Johnson, Mt. Olive, and Reverend Evans of United Presbyterian. It was agreed that only three troops would be set up and the committee accepted this. Those troops were #70 at Grace Episcopal, #71 at Bank Street, and #72 at Mt. Olive Baptist Church. However, the first troop to actually receive its charter with a formal dedication on February 28,1928 was Troop 72 at Mount Olive during the pastorate of Rev. Harvey N. Johnson.[81]

Despite these successes, the white BSA council in Virginia resisted registering these newly formed black troops for fear they would become part of a county council or district council, thereby having some influence in the decision-making process. They also resisted black Boy Scouts wearing uniforms, threatening to publicly burn a scout uniform in effigy. Undaunted, supporters of the black scout program persevered. In time, white southern councils relented under the pressure from the black leadership, accepting black scout troops and removing the uniform ban. This event was later remembered when a plaque was dedicated by Professor Winston Douglas, principal of Booker T. Washington High School in Norfolk, and placed on the side of the Metropolitan Bank building, commemorating that as the birthplace of boy scouting for African American youth in Hampton Roads.[82]

Prior to 1933, several leaders in the African-American community thought about and wanted to help the youths stay safe and have purpose. They were disheartened to see so many of the children playing in the unpaved, water-filled, and unsanitary streets of Portsmouth. Several of the men in the community, especially the Lincolnsville community, wanted to establish a social program to help raise the dignity of the children. Boy Scouting for the white youths in America had started in 1910 and met with considerable success. So Portsmouth's black community leaders thought that a scouting program would fill the need for organized activities and male mentoring that would help develop the young boys in the community into productive, socially minded leaders. It was this need to build up the character and morale of the black male youths of the city that motivated the creation of scouting for blacks in Portsmouth.

Portsmouth's leaders were encouraged to apply for scout charters a few years after the success of the Norfolk group. The first chartered Boy Scout Troops in Portsmouth began as a boy's club, similar to the one in Norfolk. Organized by Jesse Briggs, who offered his home as the meeting venue, and Moses F. Gibson, this unofficial group, whose members did not wear uniforms, soon grew and began meeting at Emanuel AME Church. Briggs and Gibson approached Rev. Harvey Johnson, who had recently accepted the pastorship at Ebenezer in Portsmouth, about the possibility of getting a troop started for the local youth. Because Harvey had been integral in the formation of the African–American Troop No. 72 in Norfolk, Briggs and Gibson thought he would be their best hope for success. Portsmouth's First Scout Troop, organized by Rev. H.N. Johnson, became the first official African American Boy Scout troop (Troop 82) formally installed at Ebenezer Baptist Church by Troop 72 from Norfolk. Many senior-ranking officials in the Boy Scout program attended this program on December 11, 1933. The local troop committee was composed of the Reverend Johnson, J. H. Green, and E. W. Davidson. Col. M.H. McArdle, the white senior scout commissioner of Norfolk, handled formal installation of the Portsmouth Troop, presenting the troop with its proper credentials, membership cards, and tenderfoot pins.[83]

The program, of which James Fulford, black Scout commissioner of Tidewater was master of ceremonies, included the address, "The Character Building Aspect of Scouting," by Scout Master Leon Alston of Norfolk; H.C. Derby (White) of the local scout council. L.R. Lester, Norfolk Scout Executive presented the Portsmouth troop with its charter and commended the untiring efforts of Reverend Johnson during the past few years to make scouting available to the African-American boys of Portsmouth.[84]

On December 11, 1933, the first black Portsmouth Boy Scout Troop, chartered at Ebenezer Baptist Church, became Troop 82.[85] And Rev. Harvey N. Johnson, pastor of Ebenezer, was again instrumental in establishing another black Boy Scout troop with six young boys as the founding members. F. Farrie Porter was the Scoutmaster, and J.W. Miller served as the assistant scoutmaster of that troop.[86]

Other Boy Scout troops would be founded throughout Portsmouth's black community churches such as Emanuel AME, Third Baptist, Zion Baptist, and Mt. Hermon Baptist Temple. A total of 15 would proliferate with hundreds of young boys participating in the many scouting activities including jamborees, father and son banquets, troop and district meetings, merit badge activities, and parades.

BOY SCOUT TROOPS AND THE CHURCHES THAT SPONSORED THEM. GOSPORT DISTRICT, PORTSMOUTH.

Troop 83	Emanuel AME
Troop 84	First Baptist Church South
Troop 85	Third Baptist Church
Troop 86	First Baptist Church- Pinner's Point (now New Bethel Baptist)
Troop 87	Zion Baptist
Troop 88	Mt. Carmel Baptist Church
Troop 90	Noble Street
Troop 92	Mt. Hermon Baptist Temple
Troop 98	OLV- Our Lady of Victory
Troop 119	Celestel Baptist Church
Troop 128	St. John Baptist Church
Troop 136	Mt. Calvary Baptist Church (Rev. A. S. Hoard)
Troop 138	First Baptist Church Taylorsville
Troop 229	House of Prayer

By 1940, the Boy Scout Troop committee at Ebenezer Baptist Church included John E. Fagan, William Campbell, Albert Holladay, and Madison Spratley. Jesse Briggs and Moses F. Gibson, scoutmaster and field commissioner, respectively, especially worked successfully to further the scout movement. Twenty-nine boys in Troop 82 participated actively in events such as the church-sponsored "Father and Son" Banquet. These kinds of activities were designed to build stronger family relationships, develop solid connections with the church, and cultivate useful citizens.[87]

From the beginning, scouting for African-American youths presented challenges and obstacles not faced by white Scouts. Attendance at the jamborees, general district meetings, and use of general facilities necessary for scouting activities was restricted or barred to blacks. When a boy scout became proficient in certain categories, he earned a merit badge. These badges included the following areas: camping, leatherwork, home repair, first-aid, bird study, safety, reading, and zoology as well as other areas. Former scout member Joseph Ellis recalled a particularly poignant example of how these obstacles had detrimental results. Ellis, who earned 27 merit badges as a Portsmouth boy scout, bemoaned how many of the black scouts did not get to qualify for the life saving and swimming merit badges because they were not allowed to use the swimming pool at the Portsmouth YMCA for training. One scout almost drowned attempting to get the swimming badge after swimming in the local river, far from the safety of a controlled pool environment and a lifeguard. Despite these hindrances, many like Ellis managed to gain numerous badges. Also, it is interesting to note that many of the merit badge counselors were not only dedicated adult volunteers, but professionals—educators, teachers, principals, and doctors. The development of the boy who went into scouting involved many people of the community who gave of their time to help the young boys grow physically, mentally, and morally.[88]

Scout leaders were also rewarded for their hard work and dedication. The Silver Beaver Award was a prestigious award given to an adult Scout Leader who has done outstanding work for the Boy Scout Program. "Upon nomination by the Tidewater Council of the Boy Scouts of America, and with the approval of the National Court of Honor, Scouters receive the highest award for distinguished service to youth." This award is the recognition for vast and devoted work in boy scouting. This award is generated by experience and fueled with new ideas. It is an award worn with pride, knowing that the recipient with a labor of love has earned it. Tidewater Council, Boy Scouts of America.

TIDEWATER COUNCIL BSA, SILVER BEAVER RECIPIENTS 1931-1969, DISTRICT SEVEN

1944	(James E. Fulford)	1956	(John T. White)
1947	(Winston Douglas)	1957	(Hamiel White)
1948	(Moses F. Gibson, Frank Harris)	1961	(James A. Overton)
1949	(Purvis J. Chesson)	1964	(Cessar M. Liggons)
1950	(Rev. Alonzo S. Hoard)	1967	(James W. Holley, III)
1952	(Paul Burton)	1968	(Charles M. Pittman, Sr.)
1953	(Harvey M. Johnson, Otis D. Vick)		

Scouting through the years has been a life-long experience for boys who participated in Boy Scout activities. A tidbit of the origin of black scouting was posted on the Afrigeneas website in March 2002 by Hasker Nelson. "I spent several years as a District Executive for the Boy Scouts (Dan Beard Council, Cincinnati Ohio—late 1960s). In 1971, I was part of a small group of men who successfully pushed to name our newly expanded district after a legendary black Scoutmaster who led his troop from 1928 to 1963. . . . BSA Scout officials, that the Hopkins District is the only BSA district named after an African American. We celebrated the 30th anniversary of that occasion, last September. As part of that celebration, I wrote and published a small book, "SCOUTMASTER: Leo J. Hopkins" on his life and wrote the last page or so on the African origins of Scouting. The irony of the "race" concern is that Scouting was founded in Africa (South Africa to be exact) by a career British military man, Robert Baden-Powell. In a nutshell, he was there to conquer and occupy certain African territories on behalf of the British government. He had been assigned to a number of campaigns in various countries on that continent. So, over the years, Baden-Powell's activities put him in close contact with indigenous cultures such as the Ashanti and the Zulu. Much of what was to become "Scouting" was learned by Officer Baden-Powell in his interactions with black African allies and enemies."[89]

February was a celebratory time for the black Portsmouth troops who observed the founding of the Boy Scouts as well as black history week (and by the late 1970s Black History Month). So popular was this celebration that the *Journal and Guide* publicized the Scouts' celebration schedule. According to the *Guide*, in 1935, the Scouts kicked off the week with a troop celebration day on Friday, followed by the Anniversary Observance on Saturday. On Sunday, they observed Church Celebration Day during which all the troop members would attend their respective churches in full uniform. By Monday, the Scouts would observe School Celebration Day by sponsoring programs that demonstrated important features of scouting at all school assemblies. These activities not only served as a recruiting tool for potential young boys, but it provided organized public activities for its members, acquainting them with skills that would make them good civic leaders who were comfortable in the public eye. Winston Douglas, Chair of District Seven, published an article on scouting in the *Journal and Guide* which sought to recruit members and scout leaders, and garner support from parents. Douglas noted that the purpose of their celebration was not just to observe the anniversary of scouting. Instead they hoped to retell the story of the extraordinary sacrifices and contributions made by a handful of committed men who gave their time to train and mentor boys who would become the leaders of the future. Moreover, the celebration was to publicly recognize and thank those men whose free time had generally gone unrecognized and unappreciated. Douglas concluded with a reminder that parents had entrusted these scout leaders with the lives and futures of their children who devoted their spare time because of the extant needs of many who were underprivileged and poor. He posed the question, "And what is it that holds these faithful leaders to these self-imposed tasks? The silent cry of the underprivileged boy about the streets . . . pleading for a chance to develop into something worthwhile. The gleam of gratitude on the boys' countenance when their leader announces the coming hike; a night outdoors, free from the stifling dust. . . . These are a few of the magnets, which hold the loyal scoutmasters to what sometimes appears to be a thankless task. Their reward is that greatest of joys which comes to the workman as he views a job well-done." What was most emphasized by Douglas's article and struck at the heart of what differentiated the black from the white scouts was remuneration. Douglas noted that among the many men who made the greatest contribution was James Fulford who volunteered his time tirelessly working as field commissioner, a position for which others were handsomely paid.[90]

Despite these commitments by scout leaders, Douglas bemoaned the lack of support from parents who seldom showed up in force to watch the programs of their children. Nevertheless, the countless men who sacrificed their time and energy to be mentors and leaders for these young boys outweighed the failure of many parents to provide support for their children's endeavors.[91]

The story of scouting was an example of the uniquely black American tradition of love of country regardless of circumstances. Even in the face of slights, disenfranchisement, segregation and oppression, those that participated in scouting came through with a greater love of country, a love and appreciation of American ideals, American values, their future and America's future. This history illustrated a patriotism that marched in parades and that supported the war efforts of World War II, Korea, and Vietnam. Moreover, the pride in the accomplishments of the young boys in scouting was seen in the gleam in the eyes of those marching, the straight posture of those receiving merit badges and awards, and the smiling pride of parents, leaders, neighbors, and friends captured in countless photographs.[92]

Thus the story of local Boy Scouts was truly a Portsmouth story and a celebration of blacks in Portsmouth in the 1930s and 1940s. The founders of black Scouting called themselves "God's port" division after the original name of the Norfolk Naval Shipyard. By doing this, they linked themselves to one of the oldest and largest institution in the city and all that that industry represented. Moreover, this was also a story of the black church because most, if not all the scouting troops, were located in churches. Monthly scout meetings and activities provided another layer to the Sunday school lesson and the sermon preached. The black church and church leaders became the bridge and cornerstone that made scouting possible and provided yet another indelible reinforcement of those timeless values. In so many ways the history of African-American Boy Scouts in Portsmouth was a history of created possibilities, broadened imaginations, lessons learned, and minds shaped by the experience. It was a history that we proudly recorded and valued. Lest we forget its inspirational lessons, we remember, acknowledge, and record the dedication and service of those men and women of Portsmouth who provided the community with this rich legacy of determination and love.[93]

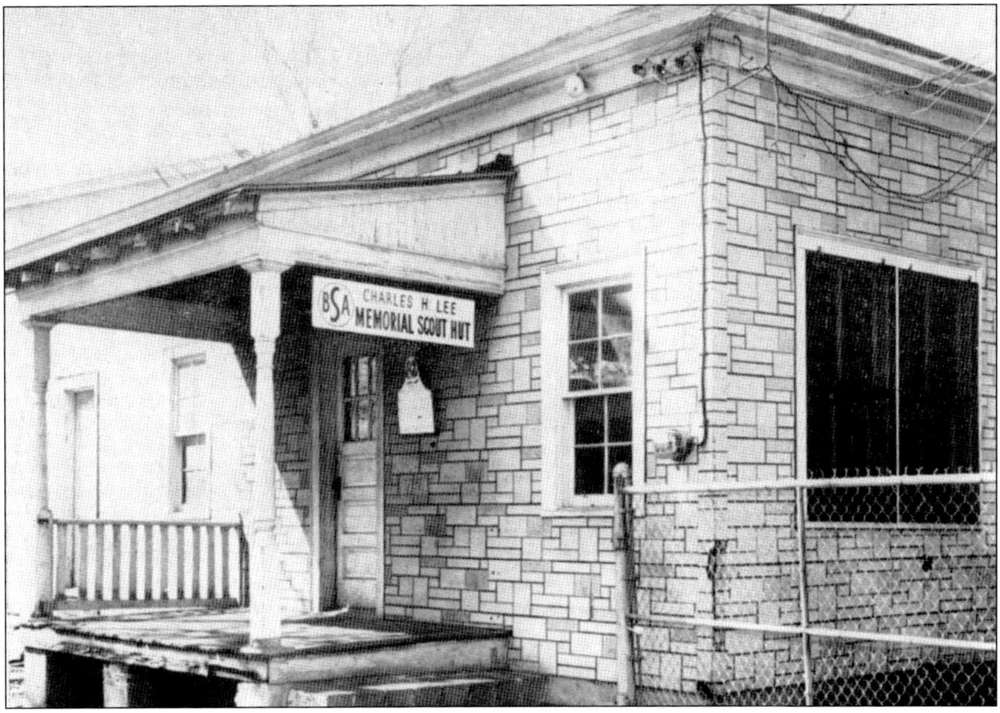

This was the Charles H. Lee Memorial Scout Hut located at Ebenezer Baptist Church, site of the first Portsmouth African American Boy Scout Troop. (Courtesy African American Historical Society of Portsmouth.)

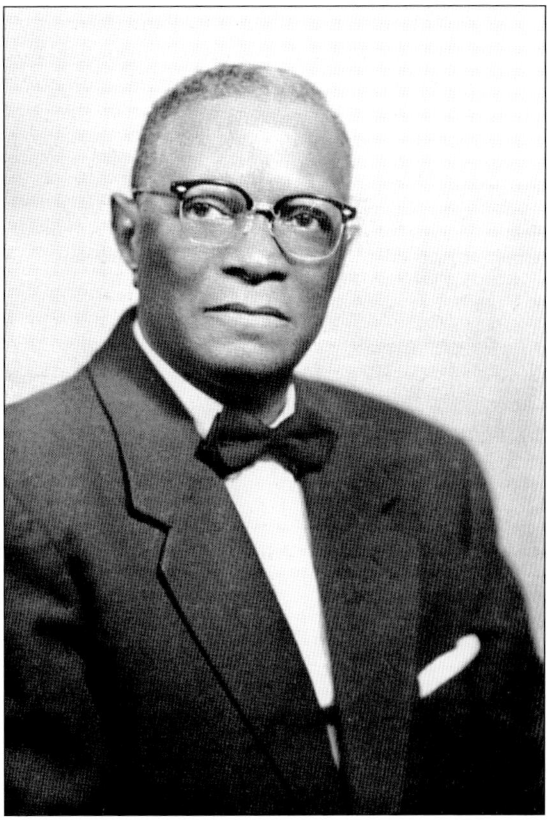

Dr. Harvey N. Johnson Sr. was the architect, builder, and founder of Boy Scouting in Norfolk (February 1928) and in Portsmouth (December 1933). (Courtesy African American Historical Society of Portsmouth.)

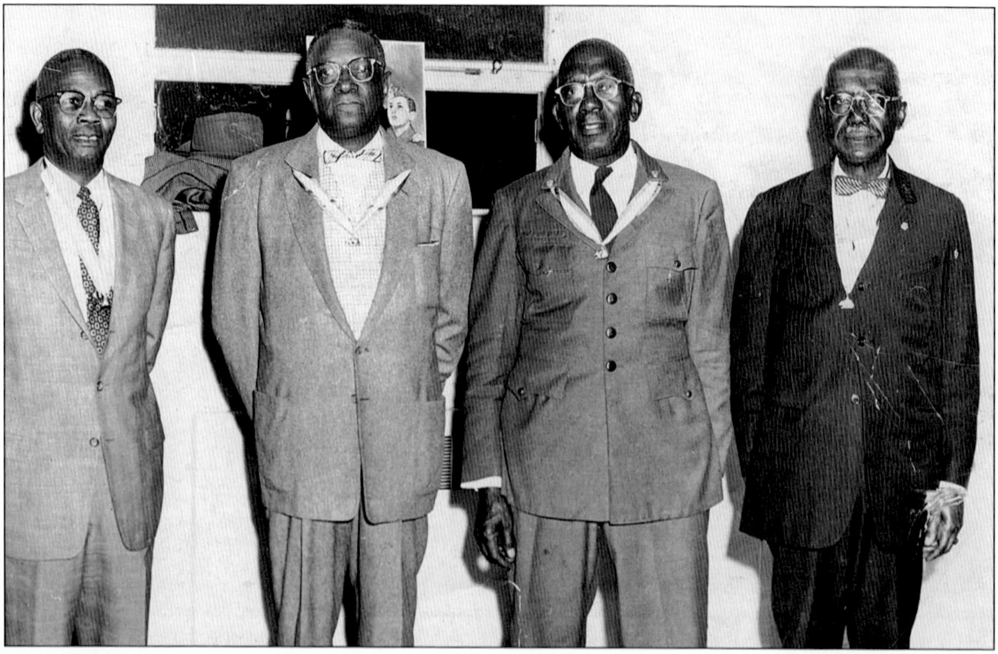

Four of the most influential men in scouting for African Americans in Portsmouth were these top leaders in the 1930s. From left to right are Moses F. Gibson, the Reverend Harvey N. Johnson Sr., Frank Harris, and the Reverend A. S. Hoard. (Courtesy African American Historical Society of Portsmouth.)

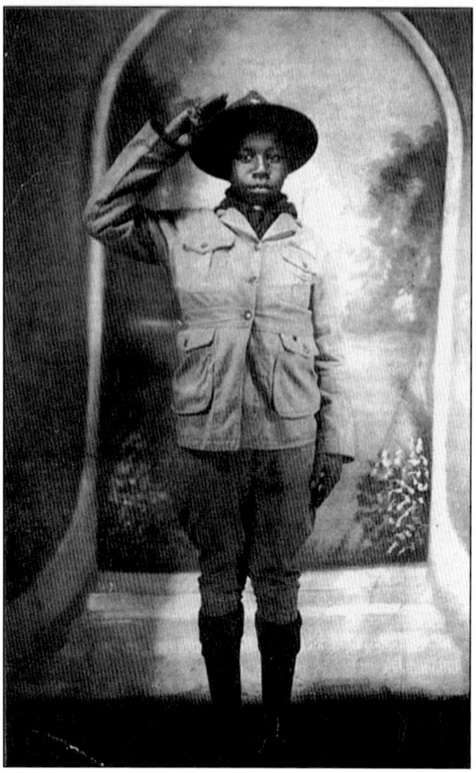

This picture is of Walter "Duke" Freeman saluting with his "Smokey the Bear" hat and wearing his brother's uniform. Uniform sharing was not uncommon at that time, because some parents could not afford more than one uniform. Duke Freeman was in Troop 92 at Mount Hermon Temple. Like his brother, "Ice Cream" Freeman, Duke began in Troop 86 at First Baptist Church Pinners Point, but moved to Troop 119. According to former Scout member Joe Ellis, "That was a big troop and all the boys wanted to go to that troop. Mr. Frank Harris was the Scout Master. Ulysses "Ice Cream" Freeman, Duke's brother, was first in Troop 86 with Mr. Harris, then later went to join Troop 119 that was at Celestial Baptist Church (1943) (Mount Hermon) in the same area of Portsmouth." According to Joe Ellis, Duke finally did get his own uniform the next year by working odd jobs. (Courtesy Joseph Ellis.)

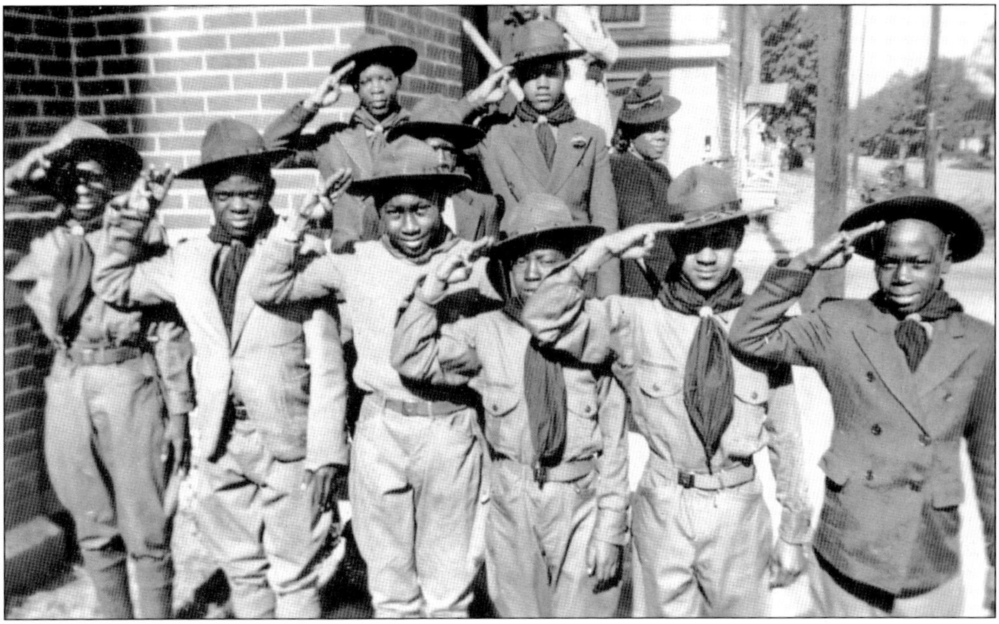

This is a *c*. 1940s photograph of Boy Scout Troop 92 at Mount Hermon Temple. (Courtesy African American Historical Society of Portsmouth.)

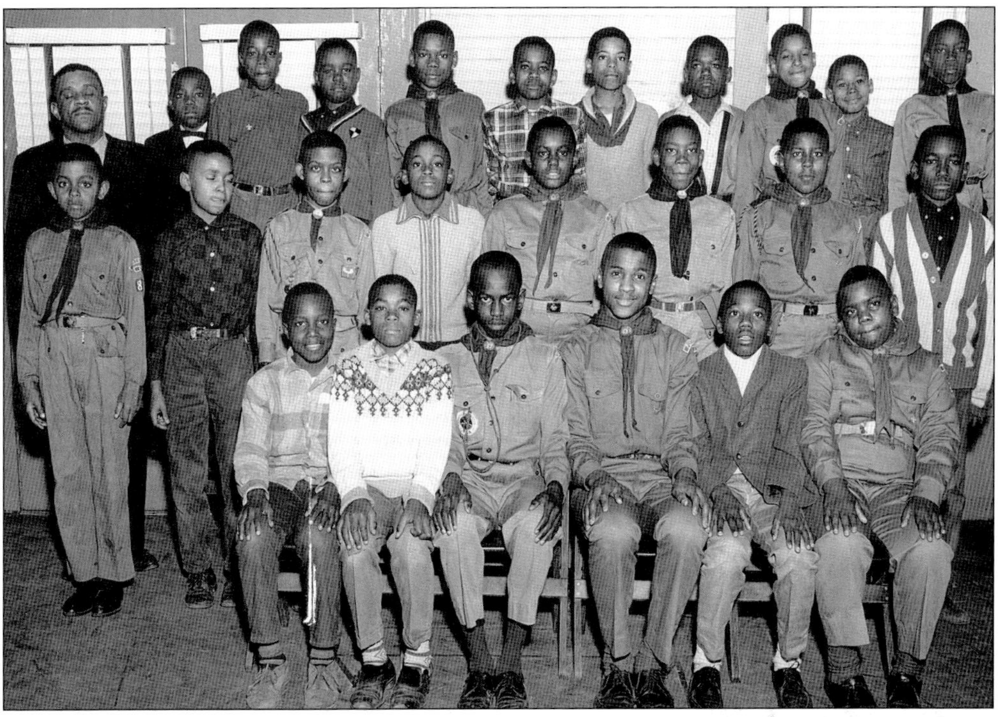

This is the Boy Scout troop at Third Baptist Church in an undated photograph. The scout leader, pictured at the top far left was R. Corbett Jr. (Courtesy Lee Rodgers Collection, Portsmouth Public Library.)

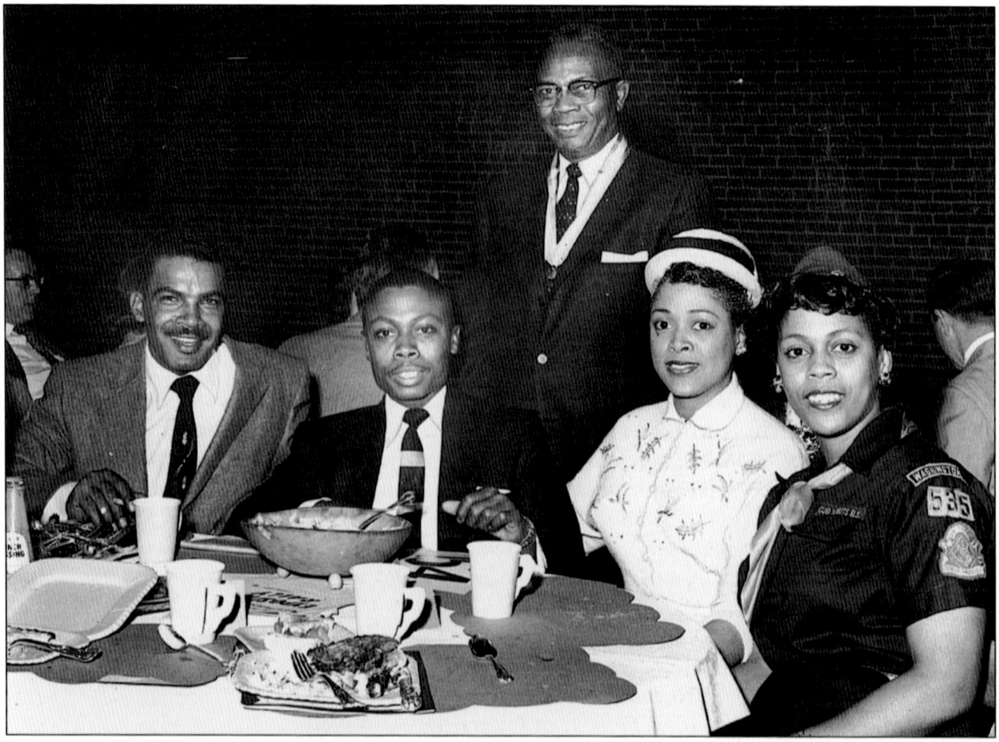

Moses F. Gibson Sr. (standing) poses proudly, wearing his Silver Beaver award ribbon around his neck, in this *c.* 1950s picture taken in Washington, D.C. during the Silver Beaver Awards banquet. From left to right are George W. Parrish, Moses F. Gibson Jr., Rachel Gibson, and Mary Christmas Parrish. (Courtesy African American Historical Society of Portsmouth.)

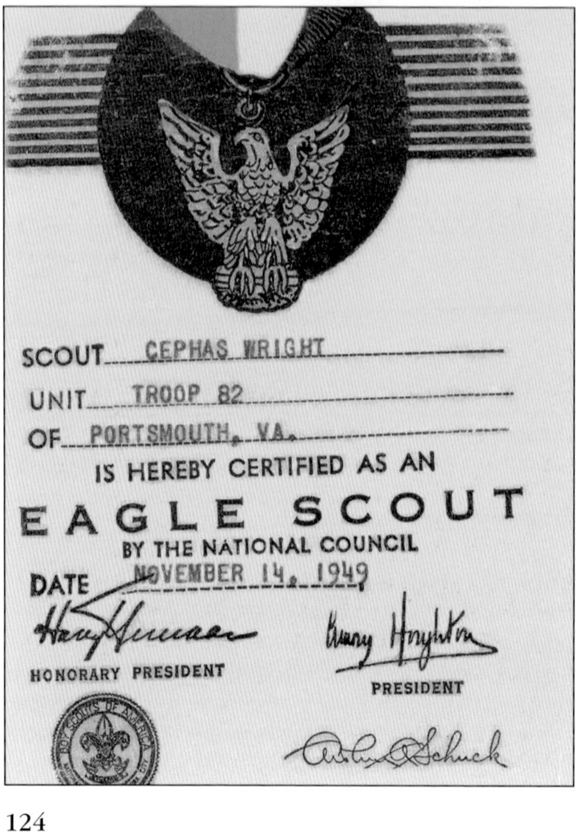

Here is the Eagle Scout badge typically given to local Boy Scouts in the Tidewater area. This one was awarded to Cephas Wright, an African–American boy scout from Portsmouth. (Courtesy Cephas Wright.)

ENDNOTES

1 Marshall Butt, *Portsmouth Under Four Flags* (Portsmouth, VA: Portsmouth Historical Association, 1961), 15; "Portsmouth Blacks," unpublished scrapbook compiled by Bertha Edwards, Portsmouth Public Library, Book 2: James Choate's history written in 1938, 3. Hereafter cited as Bertha Edwards Collection.

2 Lewis G. Jordan, *Negro Baptist History U.S.A.* (Nashville, TN: Sunday School Publishing Board, 1930), 214; Garnett Ryland, *The Baptists of Virginia, 1699-1929* (Richmond: Baptist Board of Missions and Education, 1955), 155, 281. Ryland also addresses the developing policies of the Baptist Church with regard to slavery and to the post-war freedmen.

3 Rev. George Bain's sketch was reproduced in Richard Wright's *Centennial Encyclopaedia of the African Methodist Episcopal Church. Containing Principally the Biographies of the Men and Women, both Ministers and Laymen, Whose Labors During a Hundred Years, Helped Make the A. M. E. Church What It Is; Also Short Historical Sketches of Annual Conferences, Educational Institutions, General Departments, Missionary Societies of the A. M. E. Church, and General Information about African Methodism and the Christian Church in General; Being a Literary Contribution to the Celebration of the One Hundredth Anniversary of the Formation of the African Methodist Episcopal Church Denomination by Richard Allen and others, at Philadelphia, PA. in 1816* (Philadelphia: [Book Concern of the A.M.E. Church], 1916), 353.

4 Richard Wright, 353–354; William Lumpkin, *History of Court Street Baptist Church* (Lawrenceville, VA: Edmonds Printing Company, 1989), 49.

5 *Norfolk Journal*, April 19, 1870, *Emmerson Papers, 18.*

6 *Norfolk Journal*, October 8, 1867, *Emmerson Papers*, 45.

7 Cassandra L. Newby, "'The World Was All Before Them': A Study of the Black Community in Norfolk, Virginia, 1861–1884," (Ph.D., diss., College of William and Mary, 1992), 194–195, 234, 240–241.

8 Tommy Bogger, *The Darker Side of Freedom: Free Blacks in Norfolk, Virginia, 1790–1860* (Charlottesville: University Press of Virginia, 1997), 138.

9 Sing-Nan Fen, "Notes on the Education of Negroes at Norfolk and Portsmouth, Virginia, during the Civil War," *Phylon* 28 (Spring 1967), 199, 203, 206.

10 Charles Smith, Sr., "An Historical Look at the Roots of Black Education in Portsmouth," (Portsmouth, Virginia: I.C. Norcom High School Library, 1973), 4; Cassandra Newby, 235.

11 Charles Smith, Sr., 4–5; Edward Pollock, *Sketch Book of Portsmouth, Virginia: Its People and Its Trade* (Portsmouth, VA: Published by Author, 1886), 218; Bertha Edwards Collection, James Choate's history, 3.

12 Charles Smith Sr., 5.

13 Edward Pollock, 218; Charles Smith Sr., 8–9.

14 Bertha Edwards Collection, Book 2: 3, 11.

15 Charles Smith Sr., 10.

16 *The Currents* in the *Virginian Pilot*, December 26, 1999, 10.

17 Marshall Butt, 4; Bertha Edwards Collection, James Choate's history, Book 2: 3-4; *Norfolk Journal*, May 7, 1868, *Emmerson Papers*, 17.

18 Marshall Butt, 15, 18.

19 Marshall Butt, 17.

20 Nancy Martin-Perdue and Charles Perdue, Jr. *Talk About Trouble: A New Deal Portrait of Virginians in the Great Depression* (Chapel Hill: University of North Carolina Press, 1996), 258–259.

21 Marshall Butt, 26.

22 Marshall Butt, 25-26.

23 Bertha Edwards Collection, Book 2: 1.

24 Marshall Butt, 16; Bertha Edwards Collection, Book 2.

25 Marshall Butt, 16.

26 Bertha Edwards Collection, Book 2: 2, 3.

27 There were three white and one black hospital listed in the 1925 Portsmouth City Directory: Home for Aged (822 Emmet Street), King Daughters' Hospital (910 Leckie Street), Old Folks Home and Orphanage (126 N Green Street (African American)), and the Parish Memorial Hospital (8 Court Street), and the United State Naval Hospital (North and N. Green Street). Interview with Rebecca Williams by Cassandra Newby-Alexander and Mae Breckenridge-Haywood, July 18, 2003, Chesapeake, VA; Bertha Edwards Collection, Book 2: 1, 9; Book 2: James Choate's history, 3.

28 *Talk About Trouble,* 207–208.

29 Robert Semple, *A History of the Rise and Progress of the Baptists in Virginia*, revised and extended by G.W. Beale (Richmond: Pitt and Dickinson, 1810; 1894), 457–458; Ryland, 156; Edward Pollock, 215; Thelma Dunston, "The History of the Negro in Portsmouth, Virginia, Works Progress Administration/ Virginia Works Project life histories, computer file (Richmond, VA: Library of Virginia, 1997). Hereafter cited as (WPA/VWP) life histories.

30 Christopher Silver, *Twentieth-Century Richmond: Planning, Politics, and Race* (Knoxville: The University of Tennessee Press, 1984), 31–33.

31 *Norfolk Journal*, October 8, 1869, December 1, 1869, *Emmerson Papers*, 40, 45.

32 Nina Mjagkij, ed., *Organizing Black America: An Encyclopedia of African American Associations* (New York: Garland Publishing, 2001), 527; Workers of the Writers' Program of the Work Progress Administration in the State of Virginia, compiler, *The Negro in Virginia* (New York: Hastings House, 1940), 293; Philip Morgan, ed., *"Don't Grieve After Me": The Black Experience in Virginia, 1619–1986* (Hampton: Published by Hampton University, 1986), 53; Sarah Hughes, "Social Organization in the Black Community," in *Readings in Black and White: Lower Tidewater Virginia*, edited by Jane Kobelski (Portsmouth, VA: Portsmouth Public Library, 1982), 39–40.

33 Bertha Edwards Collection, Book 2: 1, 7, 10.

34 Bertha Edwards Collection, Book 2: James Choate's history, 1-2; *The Currents* in the *Virginian Pilot*, August 29/30, 1989, 3.

35 Bertha Edwards Collection, Book 2: James Choate's history, 3.

36 Philip Morgan, 71–72.

37 Jerry and Rosa Hinton, interviewed on September 23, 1981, *Lower Tidewater in Black and White* (Portsmouth, VA: Portsmouth Public Library, 1981), Transcript.

38 Video interview transcript with Mrs. Ora Overton on October 27, 1981 in "Lower Tidewater in Black and White, 1776–1976" (Portsmouth, VA: Portsmouth Public Library, 1981), 1-4.

39 Bertha Edwards Collection, Book 2.

40 Ida Barbour was born around 1878 in Portsmouth, Virginia, living with her family in "Lincolnsville." After attending the Institute for Colored Youth in Philadelphia, she returned home and worked as a teacher in the Portsmouth Public School system from 1898–1923. Bertha Edwards Collection, Book 1.

41 Bertha Edwards Collection, Book 2.

42 Bertha Edwards Collection, Book 2.

43 Bertha Edwards Collection, Book 2.

44 Charles Perdue, Thomas Barden, and Robert Phillips, eds., *Weevils in the Wheat: Interviews with Virginia Ex-Slaves* (Charlottesville: University Press of Virginia, 1976), 330.

45 Nina Mjagkij, 527.

46 Winthrop Jordan, *White Over Black: American Attitudes Toward the Negro, 1550–1812* (New York: W.W. Norton and Company, 1968), 73, 75, 82. For a more thorough discussion of Norfolk's Black community, see Tommy Lee Bogger's doctoral dissertation, "The Slave and Free Black Community in Norfolk, 1775–1865" (Ph.D. Dissertation, University of Virginia, 1976). Bogger discussed Norfolk's Black community, and by extension the Portsmouth community, during the colonial and antebellum periods in great depth and scope, focusing on the increasing restrictions placed on free Blacks up to 1865. For a more detailed focus on Norfolk's free Black community, with some discussion of Portsmouth, see his book, *The Darker Side of Freedom: Free Blacks in Norfolk, Virginia, 1790–1860* (1997).

[47] Lerone Bennett, Jr., *Before the Mayflower: A History of the Negro in America, 1619–1966*, 3rd Edition (Chicago: Johnson Publishing Company, 1966), 36; Marshall Butt, 4-5.
[48] 15,000 of Virginia's slaves were manumitted between 1782 and 1810. Of these, 35% were freed through the purchase by other blacks of friends and relatives, Tommy Bogger, 1, 48, 51; Thomas Wertenbaker, *Norfolk: Historic Southern Port*, 2nd ed., edited by Marvin Schlegel (Durham: Duke University Press, 1931, 1962), 73; William Hening, ed., *The Statues At Large Being a Collection of all the Laws of Virginia*, (13 vols., Richmond, VA, 1810-1832), Vol. 11, 39–40; Luther P. Jackson, "The Virginia Free Negro Farmer and Property Owner, 1830–1860," *Journal of Negro History* 24 (October 1939), 390.
[49] In 1850 there were 6,321 Whites, 554 free Blacks, and 1,751 enslaved African Americans. Marshall Butt, 18–19; *Southern Argus*, October 8, 1860, 12.
[50]Marshal Butt, 19–20; Workers of the Writers' Program of the Work Progress Administration in the State of Virginia, compiler, *The Negro in Virginia* (New York: Hastings House, 1940), 148; *Weevils in the Wheat,* 234.
[51] A total of 1400 White males enlisted in the Confederate armed forces from Portsmouth suffering more than a 16% mortality rate. Marshall Butt, 20–21, 23.
[52] Cassandra Newby, 53–57.
[53] Christopher Silver, 11, 19–21.
[54] Bertha Edwards Collection, Book 2: 1; *Norfolk Journal*, June 22, 1867, June 24, 1867, August 14, 1867. *Emmerson Papers*, 21, 32.
[55] The slate of nominees included Euclid B. Holloman (mayor), Albert L. Woodworth (sheriff), William H. Lyons, Barney McManus, George R. Boush, Paul Luke, Thomas Haines, and Samuel Hand (common council for Jackson Ward), George W. Fauth, Severn E. Wilkins, William Lawrence, Jonathan E. Boush, Nicholas Shakelock, and Richard Wright (common council for Jefferson Ward). *Norfolk Journal*, April 9, 1868, *Emmerson Papers*, 16;Virginius Dabney, *Richmond: The Story of a City* (Garden City, NY: Doubleday & Company, 1976), 254; Michael A. Plater, *African American Entrepreneurship in Richmond, 1890-1940: The Story of R.C. Scott* (New York: Garland Publishing, 1996), 5; Howard Rabinowitz, *Race Relations in the Urban South, 1865-1890* (New York: Oxford University Press, 1978), xi; Morgan, 63; Mrs. Jane Pyatt. Interviewed on January 15, 1937 by Thelma Dunston. WPA/VWP Virginia Negro Studies Project. Computer file. Richmond, Virginia: Library of Virginia, 1997.
[56] Marshall Butt, John Hope Franklin and Alfred Moss, Jr., *From Slavery to Freedom: A History of African Americans*, 8th Edition (Boston: McGraw-Hill, 2000), 27.359.
[57] Marshall Butt, 27–28.
[58] John Hope Franklin, 483–487.
[59] Ibid., 482.
[60] Ibid.,506–507.
[61] *Norfolk Journal*, July 31, 1867, *Emmerson Papers*, 39; Sarah Hughes, "Portsmouth Musicians," in *Readings in Black and White: Lower Tidewater Virginia* 49; Vaughn Webb, "Why Don't You Rock My Soul: The African-American Quartet Tradition in Hampton Roads, *Virginia Cavalcade* (Summer 2002), 105.
[62] "Portsmouth Musicians," 50–51.
[63] Ibid., 51-52; Bertha Edwards Collection, Book 2: 3.
[64] "A Portsmouth Son, Graham Washington Jackson," program brochure for "A Night of "Fingers": Presented by the African American Historical Society of Portsmouth's "Remembering Graham Washington Jackson and a Salute to Musical Giants," September 13, 1997, I.C. Norcom High School Auditorium.
[65] Ibid.
[66] Darlene Clark Hine, ed., *Black Women in America: An Historical Encyclopedia Notable Black Women*, Vol. 1, (Brooklyn, NY: Carlson Publishing), 1993; Sarah Hughes, 49–50.
[67] Sarah Hughes, 50–51.
[68] A column long synopsis was reprinted in the *Journal* on July 13, 1867. *Norfolk Journal*, July 6, 1867, *Emmerson Papers*, 40.

69 Bertha Edwards Collection, Book 2: James Choate's History, 1, 3; Norfolk *Journal and Guide*, October 21, 1916. Hereafter cited as *Journal and Guide*.
70 Robert Wentz, *Portsmouth: A Pictorial History* (Virginia Beach: The Donning Company, 1975), 18; Bertha Edwards Collection, Book 2: 1.
71 Bertha Edwards Collection, "History of Capitol Theater," Book 2: 2 ; *Journal and Guide*, September 10, 1939, 5; *Virginia Sanborn Fire Insurance Maps*, October 1943 (New York: Sanborn Map Company, 1920), 38; *Journal and Guide*, December 29, 1925, 12.
72 Bertha Edwards Collection, Book 2: "A History of Capitol Theater;" *Journal and Guide*, October 28, 1939, 18.
73 Bertha Edwards Collection, Book 2: "A History of Capitol Theater;" *Journal and Guide*, June 17, 1939, 16.
74 Earl Lewis, *In Their Own Interests: Race, Class, and Power in Twentieth-Century Norfolk, Virginia* (Berkeley: University of California Press, 1991), 5–6.
75 Earl Lewis, 84.
76 Harold Levy, *Building a Popular Movement: A Case Study of the Public Relations of the Boy Scouts of America* (New York: Russell Sage Foundation, 1944), 16; Michael Rosenthal, *The Character Factory: Baden-Powell and the Origins of the Boy Scout Movement* (New York: Pantheon Books, 1984, 1986), 3, 6; William D. Murray, *The History of the Boy Scouts of America* (New York: Boy Scouts of America, 1937), 6.
77 Michael Rosenthal, 7.
78 Ibid., 254–255.
79 William Murray, 8-9; Michael Rosenthal, 133.
80 "Tidewater Council, Boy Scouts of America" memorandum, 1; David Macleod, *Building Character in the American Boy: The Boy Scouts, YMCA, and Their Forerunners, 1870–1920* (Madison: University of Wisconsin Press, 1983), 212–214; Murray, 161, 293.
81 David Macleod, 213; *Virginian-Pilot: Compass*, March 25/26, 1992.
82 David Macleod, 213–214.
83 *Journal and Guide*, January 13, 1934.
84 *Journal and Guide*, January 16, 1934.
85 The six boys in the new chapter included Joseph Wynn, Carey Winborne Jr., Theodore Chambliss, Jones Lassiter, Leslie Hicks, and Reuben Burrell. Later scout leaders were Charles H. Lee, Thomas Winborne, and Cephas Wright. The scout leaders and commissioners were Moses F. Gibson, commissioner; Charles Harris, Frank Harris, Cessar Liggins, Jesse Briggs, R. L. Corbett, Charles Butts, and George Edwards.
86 Recipients of the highest award . . . "The Silver Beaver Award" were Moses F. Gibson, J. Thomas White, Frank Harris, Cessar Liggins. In 1954, two local boy scouts attended the Scout Jamboree in 1954 with their leader. The two scouts were Carey J. Winborne III and Russell Choate. The scout leader who attended the jamboree with the scouts was John White. The jamboree was held in Fullington, California, in 1954 for a week.
87 This was from an unpublished article written by Charles and Elise M. Woodard, February 1940. Courtesy of the African American Historical Society of Portsmouth.
88 Interview with Joseph Ellis by Mae Breckinridge-Haywood.
89 Reprinted from the Afrigeneas website, March 2002. Courtesy of the African American Historical Society of Portsmouth.
90 *Journal and Guide*, 1934.
91 Ibid., 1934.
92 Taken from the unpublished paper, "Timeless Values," written by Ernest Marshall.
93 Ibid.